Pockets of Air

Finding Breathing Room
in an Upside-Down World

Faith Lynella

Copyright

Faith Lynella (1944)
Also published as Dr. Lynella Grant and Lynella Faith Grant

Copyright © Radiant Library, 2014

Radiant Library is an imprint of Off the Page Press

Paperback Version: ISBN-13: 978-1-888739-19-0

All rights reserved. Produced and/or printed in the United States of America. No part of this publication may be reproduced, stored in a retrieval system or transmitted in any form or by any means, electronic, mechanical, photocopied, recorded or otherwise without the written permission of the publisher. Reviewers may quote brief passages to be printed in a magazine, newspaper, or on the World Wide Web.

Portions of this book are taken directly from *Naked Visionary* and *How to Survive a Spiritual Hangover* by Faith Lynella without attribution. © Off the Page Press, 2007 and 2012

"Binkle" is a registered trademark and copyright belong to The Binkle Foundation, Faith Lynella, and Off the Page Press. All rights reserved.

Websites for Readers

http://FaithLynella.com

http://PocketsofAir.com

http://TheOfficialSeal.com

Contents

BonBons in Chapters		4
Introduction	Drilling for Air	6
Chapter 1	Pockets of Air are Vital for Feeling Great	7
Chapter 2	Notice All the Air Available	23
Chapter 3	Create Genuine Pockets of Air for Yourself	39
Chapter 4	Identify Your Recharge Places	53
Chapter 5	Make Air-rich Choices	67
Chapter 6	Protect Your Breathing Space	85
Chapter 7	Maintain Access to All the Air You Need	99
Chapter 8	Find Ample Air Throughout Your Day	115
Chapter 9	Stress Is Suffercating	131
Chapter 10	Engage in Healthy Air Practices	147
Chapter 11	Enjoy Passion, Joy, and Flying High	165
Chapter 12	Find Air in Your Inner World and Emotions	183
Chapter 13	Discover Air in Simple Pleasures	197
Chapter 14	But What About Me? Taking Stock of Your Air Resources	213
Chapter 15	Treat People and Relationships as Pockets of Air	225
Chapter 16	Treat Your Stuff as Pockets of Air	243
Chapter 17	Making a Difference Creates More Air	259
Chapter 18	Let Fresh Breezes Blow	271
Back		287
Notes		289
Glossary		295
Index		299

BonBons in Chapters

Chapter 2	Smash the Mid-range	24
	Designated Driver	35
Chapter 3	Busy, Busy, Busy	39
	A Good Attitude Stinks	48
Chapter 4	Fat Head	65
Chapter 5	Wake-up Call	68
	Bring Down the Drawbridge	71
	Phony Choices	75
Chapter 6	Ligatures of Devotion	86
	Courage	90
	Getting All You Pay For	92
Chapter 7	To Arise Is the Prize	104
Chapter 8	Democracy Through Action	117
	Hark…Who Speaks There?	126
	Lurking, Lurking, Lurking	129
Chapter 9	Watch out for DIS	132
Chapter 10	Alligator Watch	148
	My Life Matters	153
	Haven't Got the Tim*ing*	162
Chapter 11	I Wanna Have That Wanna-Happen Energy	165
	Ask Not for Whom the Bus Comes…	172

Chapter 12	In Praise of Blubbering and Yammering	188
	Jailbreak	196
Chapter 13	Do Not *Smell* the Roses	198
	Make a Space for Grace	202
	Glorify the Small Stuff	205
Chapter 15	Be the Kind Kind	225
	What Does a Kind Word Cost?	233
	Do Not Judge Is a Place, Not a Verb	238
	Upholding a View	240
Chapter 17	Your Impact	259
	Art, Beauty and Music	265
Chapter 18	Into the Fray	274
	Treat Your Life Like a Garden	282
	Fresh Truth	285

Introduction
Drilling for Air

We drill for oil and mine for minerals, but who would have thought that air would be in short supply?! Yet these days it's the chance to catch your breath that is by far the most scarce.

We're starved for a quiet, unfilled moment, a little kindness, a place that's stress-free and lets the day's pressures fall away, and a chance to recharge and regroup. Places where you can do that are your pockets of air.

Who doesn't want that? All the more so because the high-pressure demands of modern life make you dance faster and faster. Never quite catching up, never quite catching your breath.

This book is about emotional and psychological air rather than the air in the atmosphere. Air is a metaphor for what you need the most to breathe freely and with peace of mind.

In the chapters ahead you'll be drilling for air, claiming a vital resource. Despite the fact that air is all about us, we don't notice it until there's not enough. But much of it is toxic so it's not fit to breath, energy-wise. As you become air-aware, you'll be able to find plenty for your needs. When drilling for air, you won't hit any dry holes.

NOTICE: This book does not provide medical or psychological advice.

No animals have been harmed in bringing it to publication. When in doubt, trust your Wee Small Voice.

Chapter 1
Pockets of Air Are Vital to Feeling Great

Not again! But I was so careful this time. I took my time, chose my words carefully, and took pains not to offend. But even so, what I was trying so hard to avoid occurred anyway! What happened to me has me walking on eggs, gasping for air, and totally unsure about what to say or do next. This whole mess has me by the throat and I can't stop thinking about it.

Sound familiar? If you've had experiences like that, you know that gasping-for-air feeling. They gnaw at you, keeping you anxious and on guard—barely able to breathe. You walk around tensed up and braced for something even worse to come.

Occurrences that keep you on edge and holding your breath are much too frequent in our helter-skelter lives. Most of us find ourselves air-deprived too often—unable to fully relax or to get recharged. Once depleted, we frantically look for any possible way to regain our breathing room and equilibrium again. But the overall effect leaves us feeling tense, drained, and out of balance.

As you read, you'll learn why pockets of air are essential for your happiness, health, and doing your best. You deserve nothing less. This seems like a simple concept but it touches your life frequently throughout each day.

Your energy level is no more visible to you than the air you breathe. Yet both are often compromised by the intense pressures we all live with—which you feel powerless to protect yourself from.

This book shows how to avoid such draining experiences. You can bulletproof yourself from what robs your energy and peace of mind. At the same time, you'll feel happier and charged-up more often.

As you tap into never-before-spotted pockets of vitalizing air, you'll enjoy new freedom and confidence—from finding more air when you need it, to protecting your most supportive air resources, to enriching your close relationships.

Coming Up for Air

Seals eat fish, so they must go underwater to catch their food. They are also warm-blooded, air-breathing mammals so they must come to the surface regularly in order to breathe. This can be a problem in the winter when ice covers the water's surface. When that happens, the seal must find pockets of air or breathing holes in the ice.

Humans are air-breathing animals too. We need air; without it we die. Under normal conditions, there's plenty of breathable, life-sustaining air—so much that we take it for granted. But whenever there isn't enough, alarm bells go off and getting oxygen becomes an imperative.

The average human will die in three to five minutes after their oxygen supply is cut off. Short of that, it doesn't take long without oxygen to suffer irreversible brain damage.

Every breath you take is a matter of life and death. "To stop breathing" is one way to describe death. As long as you can get all the air needed, breath by breath, you don't think about it. But when you can't catch your breath—for any reason—it's impossible to think about anything else.

- Birth = Drawing one's first breath
- Death = Stop breathing at all

A very large number of breaths happen in between (by some estimates, 672,768,000 breaths in an 80-year lifetime). Most of them go unnoticed. Yet the oxygen they bring sustains us every minute of every day. But as George Carlin reminds us, "Life is not measured by the number of breaths we take, but by the moments that take our breath away."

Air Is the Stuff of Life

Struggling to catch your breath needn't be considered normal or acceptable. To the extent you can breathe fully and deeply, you can also live fully and deeply. It's lovely how they go together.

Air is needed for you to breathe, to fill your lungs, to oxygenate your blood, and to supply life-sustaining oxygen to every cell of the body. It is only a small stretch further to see how much you need to find pockets of emotional and psychological air that can sustain your mind and spirit. "Pockets of air" is used as a metaphor for having those energizing psychological needs met.

The chapters ahead are not explicitly about the steady inhale and exhale of breathing. Whole books are written about how to breathe better. Health and spiritual benefits can be derived from learning to breathe a particular way. Breathing techniques are at the heart of certain religious and spiritual traditions—as well as being used for athletic training.

While such a degree of refinement can be beneficial, those skills are not a concern here. Normal, unconstricted, non-stressed breathing is all that's needed for a happy life. This book explores how you can get plenty of rejuvenating air and energy to sustain your peace of mind. It also shows how to avoid common pitfalls which get in the way of doing that.

"Oxygen" and "air" are used interchangeably in this book. But they both are metaphors for having sufficient life-enhancing energy as well. That is not merely survival-level, getting-by energy, but the higher-octane kind that energizes you psychologically and emotionally too.

At its best, that quality of energy is uplifting and vivifying—making you glow with wellbeing. It can power up all your systems—mentally, physically, and emotionally—so they're functioning at their best.

Because your air and energy level are so interconnected, this book refers to them interchangeably as: "air/energy," air, oxygen, or energy. When there's not enough you suffer—even if it's not on a conscious level (or you can't identify precisely what's wrong).

Having adequate air/energy to enjoy a vibrant and fulfilling life can't be treated as a carrot to be reached *eventually*. It has an immediacy. You need it now—every moment! Not having adequate upbeat air/energy leads to a whole range of difficulties—both short-term and long-term; both physical and psychological; both on you individually and on those around you. Insufficient air makes you feel like your soul is dying by degrees.

Struggling to Breathe

The steady rhythm of inhaling and exhaling is among the most fundamental processes keeping you alive. You do not simply breathe with your lungs. The whole upper body is involved in the regular rising and falling of each breath. Muscles in the head, neck, thorax, and abdomen participate. You don't think about your breathing very often because under most conditions it performs flawlessly.

Equally true, the entire body (including mind and spirit) feels the effects of emotional air/energy deprivation. As its quality and availability improve, your overall health and quality of life get better too (just as a long-term decline harms them).

This book is not concerned with respiratory or lung diseases. Nor is it related to breathing exercises, meditation, or air pollution. The EPA doesn't measure this kind of toxic air, even though too much of it makes people sick.

This book speaks to the person who is fundamentally healthy and reasonably happy, but who struggles to find enough energy to handle daily demands. The only "symptom" of concern here is feeling "down" or "drained" on a regular basis. If you're frustrated by feeling short of energy, instead of looking for a medical or psychological explanation, treat your over-stressed and run-down state as a demand for more air/energy.

Some of what's described here as air/energy deprivation is referred to by health practitioners as: stressed, mildly depressed, burned out, fatigued, or lacking affect (appropriate emotions). But those are not simply matters of personal concern since insufficient air harms families and relationships as well.

Many of the side effects of insufficient air are treated more as mental or psychological issues than as medical ones. While the person suffering from them isn't severely impaired, neither can they operate anywhere near their potential.

Living with inadequate air/energy very often strains your coping capacity and immune system. It makes you function sub-par in various ways, and it feels awful!

Even though it's not a specific disorder, living with insufficient air/energy exacerbates any medical or psychological problems you have. A broad array of health benefits and risk reduction is also involved. So reducing your stress level, while increasing your air reserves, will reinforce any other health-promoting measures undertaken.

You'll find easy steps any fundamentally healthy person can take to quickly gain relief from the sense of being overwhelmed by the too-much, too-fast pressures that keep you off balance. Becoming air/energy aware helps you find the breathing room you so badly need.

Just to be clear, nothing in this book rises to the level of providing medical diagnoses or treatments. Nor does it give medical or psychological advice. Nor does it tell you to stop doing or using any treatments you may be employing already. If you think you are in need of such services, please consult trained professionals.

That said, *everything* written here is about gaining immediate relief from struggling to get enough air and energy so you can function at your best. Everything here points to easy-to-do practices that can improve your mental, physical, and emotional wellbeing. They work together, and when any of them brings you relief, you sense a bump up in your energy level overall.

Saga of the Attentive Seal

Visualize a seal swimming deep underwater in the far north. It is wintertime, with a thick crust of ice and snow on the surface. But the seal (that's me) is not worried because I have several breathing holes close enough to reach before running out of breath.

But then, I hear an ominous sound, since sound travels well in cold water. Crunch... pause, crunch ... pause, crunch ... pause.

That's a very scary sound to me. That's the sound of a polar bear walking on the snowy surface of the ice. The ice crystals crunch underfoot with each step. What is even more alarming for me is when the sounds stop walking. That means the bear has found an air hole. It is waiting there for me—waiting for me to come up for air. It is waiting for me to be his next meal.

The polar bear knows if a seal is down here it must come up for air before long. He's gambling he's chosen the right hole for when that happens. When I do come up, I'm gambling it will be at a different hole than the one where the polar bear awaits. The more air holes I use, the better my odds of surviving for another day.

Watch for more of the Seal Saga in chapters to come.

The Body's Reaction to Danger Is Reflexive

There are other, equally basic, physical processes related to your safety. If the brain considers something a threat, a series of physiological changes occur, almost instantly:

- Adrenaline is released, along with other hormones
- Breathing speeds up since more oxygen might be needed; but breathing also gets shallower
- The heart rate increases
- Other, less critical, physical processes slow down or stop
- All the senses and attention become sharply focused on responding to the potential threat

These are reflexes, which means they are "triggered," rather than being governed by logic. That also means the mind cannot turn them off once they begin. Threats (whether actual or imagined) prepare you either to flee the peril, or to stand and fight against it. The resulting physical changes happen fast.

Hormones, like adrenaline, initiate complex reactions throughout the body. The mind goes into overdrive as it assesses the nature of the risks, along with alternative ways to counter them. In addition, an array of emotional reactions kick in.

The combination of reflexive responses suppresses normal breathing. That might not be a problem if the danger soon passes, so customary breathing (and related processes) can resume. But with psychological and emotional threats, there might not be a clear sign the dangers have passed. So constricted breathing could continue repeatedly or indefinitely.

As used here, functioning without enough air/energy leaves you feeling tense and drained. It means "walking on eggs," unsure about the extent of your vulnerability. It means struggling to do even the simplest tasks without emotional strain or defensiveness. Insufficient air is felt by the body, the intellect, and the emotions—each in its own way.

But it also diminishes your perception of what is possible. As such, air/energy deprivation has a dampening effect on the spirit. Having ample air allows you to look up with self-assurance, rather than down with impending dread or defeat. "Too many of us are not living our dreams because we are living our fears," as Les Brown said.

While taking quick and decisive action is appropriate for truly dangerous situations, reflexive behavior overreacts to the kind of threats prominent in modern life. There aren't any bloodthirsty predators around, and it does little to protect you from the con-man variety.

Yet modern life makes you feel vulnerable in new ways. You can see something to be afraid of around every corner: physical dangers, health risks, what the future could bring... Living in a state of high alert wears you out, leaving you little energy for more important concerns.

The analytical mind is able to conjure up endless dangerous scenarios about what could hurt you. Who can function with confidence when constantly barraged with more reasons to be frightened?

As the humorist Will Rogers said: "I've suffered a great many catastrophes in my life. Most of them never happened."

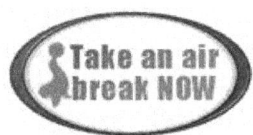

Take an Air Break Now

I interrupt this chapter to say STOP READING! Stop thinking. Take an air break RIGHT NOW. As much as I want you to see what's coming, I also want you to feel charged up during the experience. Take the next moment to breathe slowly, move your body, and step back from the focus reading demands.

It is my sincere hope you don't simply read this book with your intellect, as most books are read. Everything written here is to add more air to your life, so getting more air/energy is for the body and emotions as well. Reading is largely mental, so you need to break the rational loop intentionally and often.

Check in with your physical self and your emotional self now and then, so you stay relaxed. Then use the break to supply something that gives you added air, intentionally acquired air. Bring a quick-fix of air to yourself this very moment.

Try noticing:
- Something beautiful or awe-inspiring
- Moving and stretching your body
- A joke or something funny
- Reflecting on something that brings you joy

The possibilities are endless. The trick is in remembering to seek them out, then to enjoy the surge of air/energy you receive. You can supply something from your bag of tricks. And I've got a few stashed at

http://pocketsofair.com/quick-air-fix (with more being added)

Avoid Bad Air

Shallow breathing due to stress or fear constrict your perception and judgment. Numerous scientific studies confirm they lead to diminished abilities on a wide range of measures. In addition, such distress stifles a person's positive outlook and leads to passivity: Why bother?

When someone lacks enough air/energy for an extended period, they start to function at a lower capacity level. That, in itself, can be disquieting.

Shallow or distressed breathing is rather inhibiting to the flesh, emotions, intellect, and spirit. That's why a person tries to minimize their exposure to risks and uncertainties when they are depleted. But as you pull in, pulls back, and get defensive, your range of possibilities shrinks too. The effect is the opposite of feeling happy and fully engaged with life.

When air is polluted with noxious odors and contaminants, the air quality is compromised. It cannot provide the oxygen needed to sustain life when it's inhaled. In the same way, negative and distressing experiences poison your air/energy supply. It has you "by the throat"— leaving you squeezed in and tense.

Added to that, the conditions of modern life can be so nerve-wracking you don't use much of your air/energy to best advantage. As a consequence, your life tends to become more shallow (superficial) than full in a variety of ways. You feel constricted and depleted (one quart low), even in the midst of plenty.

Of course, you're not at the point of suffocation, even though you sometimes feel like it. But you've probably accustomed yourself to living without enough life-enhancing energy. I call such a condition, **suffercation.**

The cure for suffercation involves finding more sources of air/energy in your everyday life. Then take the time to recharge from them often. Simple distractions won't resolve this impasse. Dealing with suffercation is the topic of Chapter 9.

Building an Air-rich Life

Pockets of air are those places where you can breathe free, relax, and recharge. They are uplifting—quite literally. You function best when recharged and ready for whatever happens. You're *up*—as in charged up. You function best when firing on all cylinders—mentally, emotionally, and physically.

That involves actually sensing the energy of being alive—fully engaged with life. It adds a twinkle to your eye and a spring to your step, along with a sense of being on top of the world. Contrast such a feeling with muddling along on a ho-hum day. It seems rather flat, doesn't it? Having plenty of air/energy makes all the difference.

With ample air, your insights stand out as bright signals against a sea of foggy noise. The added clarity acts as honing beacons, to help you keep your bearings, much as lighthouses used to serve mariners at sea.

> We need a lighthouse to steer ourselves across the choppy waters, to manage the uncertainty and changes of this potential-filled time and steer our world into a good harbor. Our lighthouse is made of our core values, our fiercest hopes and gentlest visions. Let's hold on to this lighthouse and use it to steer through decisions small or large when challenge or opportunities shifts the ground underneath.[1]

Being fully charged makes you feel happy and fulfilled (as in filled full). To maintain your air supply, you need to expand the variety of ways you acquire it. Chapters 3 and 4 show easy-to-accomplish methods to recharge yourself.

It's also necessary to protect your air sources from negative individuals and influences which compromise them. Use your air/energy carefully, so it doesn't leak away too quickly. Those concerns are explored in depth in Chapters 6 and 7. You want to get as much mileage as possible from what you get.

Your degree of happiness depends on your air/energy level. The biggest pockets of air of all can be found through joy and passion, the subject of Chapter 11. But a surprising amount of air can also to found in small pleasures (Chapter 13) and by going within yourself for peaceful moments (Chapter 12).

---

[1] Robbins, Heather Roan, http://www.roanrobbins.com

How you're treated by the people in your life greatly influences your air supply and emotional state. Of course, people are crucial to your ability to find the air and energy you need. Sometimes they're a boost, but at other times they're a drain.

Being able to understand how those close to you influence your air/energy level protects you from the rug being pulled out from under you energy-wise. Chapter 15 describes how to sustain happy, air-rich relationships.

Your possessions act as reservoirs of air/energy for you. So getting the best return from having things is explored in Chapter 16. It also considers the role of money, which exerts such a widespread influence on how you feel.

It's not enough to just talk about how important high-octane air is for a happy life—this is about *your* life, *your* happiness. And getting all you need involves you looking at certain things differently than you're accustomed to.

Greater air awareness alters what you're looking for and notice. (Is there air there?) But greater attention to what energizes you is very rewarding right from the start.

Chapter 14 contains a variety of self-surveys to assess your own situation. As you become more air-aware, you'll see many more air-rich opportunities around you than you ever bothered to see. Each chapter sharpens your ability to read the signals so you can draw on air/energy resources in any situation.

Become More Air and Energy Aware

We can't see or smell air, but staying alive depends on having a constant supply of it. That's why the body has built-in sensors that *usually* let you know if there's not enough. And when necessary it takes corrective action.

Not so with psychological air. When you're deprived of life-enhancing air/energy, you feel the effects but are unlikely to make the connection as to what is wrong. You feel "starved," but are not quite sure why.

However, being "starved" implies knowing what you're *starved for*. Insufficient and toxic air lead to varying degrees of disquiet, but the specific causes are unlikely to be recognized at a conscious level. Even when the lack is recognized, it's often not apparent what is needed to "fix what ails you." That's why developing your air/energy awareness is so important.

Increased air awareness:
- Being alert to air-deprived situations or people *at the time they're encountered*, rather than afterward, once you've become drained
- Noticing when you are *starting to lose energy extra fast*, so you can take protective steps to curb the loss immediately
- Recognizing high-energy pockets of air *early on*, so you fully engage and recharge from them

The critical first step to becoming air aware is to begin noticing all the sensory information about it which you've been *tuning out*. You're about to learn how to read the signals that unerringly point you toward more air/energy in your daily existence. Once you recognize what really energizes you (or drains you), your life will improve across the board.

Also, knowing what is life-enhancing makes it much easier to tell what is important for you, from what is unimportant for you. And as Goethe said, "Things which matter most must never be at the mercy of things which matter least."

Is There Air There?

All of us get lots of advice from a zillion sources over a lifetime—most of it is inconsistent. We've developed a slew of "shoulds" we think we ought to be doing. (That is in contrast to the shoulds that we *actually do*, which have moved off the "shoulds" list and we no longer feel guilty about not getting around to them.)

Your mind tries to direct your behavior as best it can based on those conflicting directives. But it pushes you in too many directions, so they cancel each other out. You get overwhelmed by your own good intentions. Even if the specific notions are sound, it's impossible to follow through with most of them. That alone makes you feel inadequate or "behind."

Paying attention to your air/energy level by-passes the convoluted, and contradictory mental processes, the justifications and "or else's" that try to drive your choices. The awareness of air (whether it's present or absent) is instantaneous. That's because it draws on the instinctive ways the body, mind, and emotions are all monitoring your environment for safety.

Each of them independently reaches an answer which it can relate to. Once the heart, mind, and body have all weighed in on the air question, taking appropriate action if they sense a problem can be rather straight-forward.

Notice:
>**There *is* air there**, or
>**There is *no air* there**.

Once you're paying attention to the presence or absence of air, you've taken the first step toward assuring ample air supplies. When such information is known, you're able to intelligently assess your options and proceed.

Sucking the Air Out of You

Getting along with insufficient air or energy is one thing, but some situations are so intolerable or soul-deadening they squeeze the air out of you. They leave you drained, while killing the spirit, little by little. That's what I call **toxic air**.

Toxic air, like polluted air, is unbreathable. It is stifling—the opposite of fresh air— and unable to deliver the restorative benefits of expansive breathing. We all encounter certain experiences, or people, that prevent us from drawing upon the air/energy we need. They make you tense up so much you barely breathe at all.

You cringe. You hold your breath—waiting for it to be over. You shrink with dread. You can't find any breathing room. *There's no air there*.

Afterward, you feel so drained you collapse into a pile of mush. Those experiences hurt at the time and they can leave you so emptied out that you're slow to bounce back. It's bad enough once in a while. But what happens when you get a daily dose of it?

To the extent you suffer from air/energy-deprivation, you are less able to cope with life's pressures. Nor are you inclined to fully enjoy what you're doing the rest of the time. You must become vigilant enough to steer clear of such draining events.

Make the kinds of life changes so draining experiences are less toxic when they are encountered. Take evasive action at the first sign of being in a toxic-air situation.

Toxic air can show up in:
- Your various environments and activities
- Your relationships
- Your scope of behavior—whether or not you're paying attention to it
- Your ideas and beliefs
- Your habitual routines

Air as Your Carrot

As with the poor donkey, you can be motived to go *toward* something you want (carrots) or whacked to get started in order to avoid something you dislike (sticks). Consider uplifting air/energy states as "carrots" and low-energy states as "sticks." The combination of both drives your choices and behavior.

Of course, what serves as a carrot or stick is a matter of individual preferences. But the desire for breathing room and happiness are universals we all want. It could be argued the twin desires to be safe and happy lead people *toward* what they value most—their carrots. But those desires also lead them *away from* the discomfort from inherently low-energy interests and activities.

You can enjoy your life more—and more often. Take a moment to notice whether the time spent doing something leaves you feeling more alive and energized—or not. Does it make you appreciate how your day is going? How your life is going?

Feeling upbeat and happy is laden with benefits. It's too important to be treated as an optional extra.

> The source of the happy moments does in fact matter, for it influences the ability of the experience to be self-sustaining. Although the bliss of a sinful pleasure can trigger the same kinds of intellectual, social, and physical benefits as the bliss of hard-earned effort, the sinful pleasure is over quickly and, what's more, can leave guilt or other negative feelings in its wake.... One of the chief reasons for the durability of happiness activities is that unlike the guilty pleasures, they are hard won. You have devoted time and effort to meditating or avoiding overthinking or committing acts of kindness. You have made these practices happen, and you have the ability to make them happen again. This sense of capability and responsibility is a wonderful boost in and of itself. When the source of positive emotion is yourself ... it can continue to yield pleasure and make you happy. When the source of positive emotion is yourself, it is renewable.[2]

Observe Your Energetic Ebb and Flow

Feeling energized is not a steady state—it flashes bright, then gradually fades away. It is up and down. Sometimes the swings are small; sometimes they're very wide. By paying attention to your air/energy level, you notice *where* your supply goes, and *how quickly* it goes.

Staying attentive could, at the very least, soften the effects of life's natural cycles of ups and downs. In that way, you're able to be even more productive during the lower-energy times. You'll be capable of spotting bright spots even then.

Recognizing your need for both physical and psychic air/energy requires keeping a watchful eye on what you always took for granted. Getting enough means breaking some never-before-noticed energy-wasting habits. You sense the need to dole out your energy on things that matter to you, frittering away less of it.

---

[2] Lyubombirsky, Sonja, *The How of Happiness: A scientific approach to getting the life you want* (New York: Penguin Group, 2007), 265-6.

Becoming aware of how your consumption also shows you how to make what you have last longer. You're more alert for additional ways to replenish your supply—and to avoid wasting what you have needlessly. Chapters 8 and 10 give you the key to establishing energy-wise habits that will change your life forever.

The biggest boosts to gaining and feeling ample air/energy are: love, wonder and joy, as well as being in situations where you feel creative, grateful, or inspired. Besides, happy people are a lot more pleasant to be with. So be one yourself and hang around with those who make you feel good.

Which came first?

Chicken *or* Egg = Air *or* Happy

In the spirit of "which comes first?" does being happy lead to your having more air? Or does having more air make you happier? The answer is yes and yes. They magnify each other. They rise and fall with each other. They both attract psychological boosts that make you feel more vibrant and fulfilled.

When we think about being happy, we want to be happy *all the time*. Then we're disappointed when we aren't. In truth, we don't have to be happy all the time in order to be *happy right now*. If you're O.K. this very minute you're O.K. Right? With regard to air, you only feel the need to have it breath by breath. If you have enough air to breathe this moment, you don't fret about needing more later.

So when you can feel happy breath by breath, you don't need to fret either. Just keep taking the next breath, without fretting about all the future breaths. Don't jump ahead, and your ability to feel happy goes up too. All you have to do to be a happy person is to be happy one breath at a time.

It's Not Just You

Widespread air and energy depletion is not simply a matter of poor time management or of your failing to smell the roses. It is a malady of our times which infects us all to some degree. We feel compelled to dance faster and faster, never quite catching up, never quite catching our breath.

While you cannot turn back the clock, you can become more sensitive to the negative impact of anything in your life that "sucks the air out of you." You can be more selective and non-compliant about what calls your tune. To the extent you can find ways to staunch your energetic drains and supply your needs better, you improve your life. And that in turn could become a trend of its own.

> There are two extreme trends occurring now that are massively impacting our society and causing tectonic changes in our culture.
>
> Trend 1: Technology is exploding exponentially.
> Trend 2: We are becoming less happy.
>
> Technology has begun to distract and overwhelm us while many of us find ourselves suffering from a strange malnutrition, a malnourished emotional state. This is because technology has expanded at such a rate that nearly every aspect of our world has been affected—our economy, medical industry, manufacturing, military, and education, and especially how we interrelate with each other—and technological growth is now happening so fast that we live in an ever-changing environment, which allows us to become masters of nothing. Yet with the exponential growth of information technology, there has been no corresponding expansion of personal happiness. Instead we find our society depressed, anxious, sleep deprived, and overmedicated.[3]

We often struggle because it's so tough to match our needs and expectations with the arduous pressures we live with day in and day out. Certainly, it doesn't need to be so hard! Certainly, we can find a sane way out. And so we hope.

---

[3]Strom, Max, *There Is No App for Happiness: How to avoid a near-life experience* (New York: Skyhorse Publishing, 2013) 5.

Chapter 2
Notice All the Air Available

Treat Your Life as a "Find the Air" Treasure Hunt

A pocket of air is like an oasis in a desert. It's a great place for rest and relaxation—letting you soak up what your emptied-out, dried-up psyche needs. Recharge. Regroup. Recuperate. Once your battery is charged, you can return to your routines restored and ready.

Hang out at whatever places serve as your favorite oases. Bask in them. But if it feels like there's too much time or distance between your pockets-of-air moments, you need more quick fixes too. Rearrange your priorities and habit patterns so the time to do it isn't lost in the shuffle.
.

The oasis concept needs to be supplemented with a broad assortment of restorative places. Be alert for a wider range of activities and social situations where an energetic recharge could be available. Treat the best of them as exceedingly valuable, for the places, people, and experiences able to restore you without fail are your true and boundless treasure.

Part of increasing your supply includes being attuned to sources which you overlooked or rejected before. Try new things. Explore what's unfamiliar to you and take note of what moves you (or zizzes you). Seek out involvement with groups and activities which support air-rich goals for participants.

There's no limit to what you can find by the simple effort of really paying attention to what lifts your spirits. Paying attention to something always comes with a cost, however. It requires you to *pay less attention* elsewhere because it fills your perceptual field. So when paying attention, spend it on things that are worth it and matter to you.

Becoming air-savvy shows you what's adding vital energy, or wasting it. With greater sensitivity to those factors, you'll gravitate toward more energy-wise choices. Cut back on obligations that suck too much air/energy from you, without giving much back.

Of course, there are some must-dos you can't neglect each day, but fewer than you'd think. And even those can be accomplished in a more air-aware way.

Smash the Mid-Range
A BonBon

Awareness doesn't work like an off-on switch—it's a continuum. One end is dead or close to it, like sleep. The other end is heightened perception, filled with inexpressible joy. Between them we live—with our awareness fluctuating: notice, distracted, drifting, daydreaming, attentive, vague, focused. We shift; we drift.

Many days awareness comes, flits in and out, turned down like a pilot light ready to ignite when interest summons it. Attention is "On Call," waiting to be roused from its daydreams, so close to the sleep end of the scale. Habit runs the show, leaving little room for innovation or flexibility. We get through the day, sort of, without noticing all that happens to us. Aware, yes—but just barely.

Could that possibly be enough? Awareness is such a powerful tool it can deliver much much more, into our lives, into our days, into every minute. Crank it up— push it to reveal the rich texture available in each event, each person, each idea you encounter. Engage every one of your senses and your mind at the same time. Penetrate beyond superficial impressions. See, hear, feel, sense, notice what else is present also—sensations more subtle, yet very real.

Pause to register and enjoy. Experience intently and intensely, basking in whatever you discover. All that you feel now can be even more enhanced. As awareness is sharpened, held, and focused on the details, it shifts. Then a bigger, more complete and complex picture forms. You can get better at it simply by practicing it and enjoying it. Your capacity to live fully is much greater than routinely used.

Mostly, we stay in the middle of the scale—aware, alert, but filtering out details we don't think we need.

But the wonder and the fullness are not there. They are up the scale of awareness, where we become fully involved. Why not live there, since it takes no longer, but provides so much more?

© 2014, Faith Lynella, from *BonBons to Sweeten Your Daily Life* or *More BonBons and Treats*   http://faithlynella.com

Make a Reality Check

Modern adults are conditioned to stay in our heads most of the time. Even though you're breathing, your eyes are seeing, and your ears are hearing, most of what happens to you goes by without your being fully present.

Instead, you're attending to the thoughts running through the brain. You find yourself drift along in your habitual patterns, without noticing the extent of the exquisite reality that's all around you.

Checking in with yourself throughout the day breaks you out of the tendency to sleepwalk. SNAP OUT OF IT! Pay attention, relax, breathe, re-engage.

Look around and breathe it all in:
- Where you are—along with who else is present?
- What's the general mood of your surroundings—as well as your emotional level right now?
- What am I tuning out? This is tricky because to find it out you have to disengage, step back, and take a broader view. What is then perceptible matters less than the disengagement

Now, give this moment another chance, this time with your eyes and ears alert, your heart open, and your sense of wonder or curiosity engaged. Don't waste what's going on because you failed to notice it. This is where the air is. This is *always available*—if you are.

Now resume what you're doing, but with your fogginess gone. Hint—air is not available during sleepwalking, so tapping into air is both the solution and the reward for staying fully engaged with life.

Going within and enjoying the simple pleasures (Chapters 12 and 13) connect to air and energy reservoirs that can nourish you in every possible way. Without their positive influence, the day's distractions pull on you until you're feeling down and discouraged. That's when a fresh injection of air and focus can work wonders.

BonBons Feed the Spirit

Throughout this book, I insert BonBons where they're appropriate. Each of them carries a timeless message that comes to me like a postcard from my higher self. I don't exactly write them and barely edit them. The first arrived in 1994 and about 80 of them were published as *BonBons to Sweeten Your Daily Life* in 1996. Another volume of those written since is soon to be published as *More BonBons and Treats*.

BonBons are verbal illustrations of abiding truths. In that sense, they speak to what is enduring within each of us. When I collected them for publication, I visualized them like a box of candy. They're called BonBons (French for a sweet goodie) because they are wisdom in bite-sized pieces. But they are far from sweet and cloying fluff.

In the spirit of this book, every BonBon is a pocket of air/energy sprinkled through the chapters. I hope sharing mine will encourage you to seek out those poems, books, music, or stories which have served such a role in your life. They deserve to be revisited and shared.

Also, frivel punctuates my writing. Frivel is inspired wordplay. That's another word I made up. It's playful and fun. Sometimes frivel points out unexpected meanings and connections residing in the words and phrases we use.

Slow Down—Catch Your Breath

When a person is stressed or off balance, the urge to breathe faster and shallower kicks in. Such a reaction is instinctive and reflexive. The only way to counteract it is *intentionally* and *gradually*. The response which needs to be made at such times is to *relax, slow down,* and *breathe deeper*.

Take that frenetic breathing off auto-pilot as you make each successive breathe-in and breathe-out an intentional endeavor. Hold back the galloping thoughts and emotions colored by panic and confusion.

To slow down the run-away train, you must slow the intellect, emotions, and body so all three can get in synch with each other—at a more measured pace. Avoid making decisions or taking action until they're all aboard, if possible. In the meantime, give a full measure of attention to breathing at a slower-than-usual rhythm.

Pause. Don't rush. Don't panic. Empty your thoughts and expectations. Just breathe—think about the breath, nothing else. Sink into exaggerated slowness. Whatever follows the stepping-back disconnection will feel more relaxed.

How can you tell something unpleasant is resolved or a danger is over? You sense, "I can breathe again." A weight which has been getting heavier by degrees falls from the shoulders. There's a fundamental desire for a relaxed letting go—as you sink into a peaceful moment. Whatever philosophy or name it goes by, such an urge to breathe free is a universal desire.

After the high-pressure situation or crisis has passed, reflect on how you got there. Was it foreseeable? Preventable? A *déjà vu* you've seen before? What can you learn for next time? Is that kind of problem avoidable so it won't recur.

What would be required? Are you willing to do that? How much of what set the event in motion "pulled your strings" without your conscious awareness?

After that, re-assess what just happened based on what you know about your air/energy needs. That's exactly the kind of information which makes you air-savvy. Also, consider your answers with regard to Chapter 7 on ways to maximize your energy supplies.

Saga of the Worn-down Seal

I just don't get it. I'm a good seal. I do all the things responsible seals do, and I don't hurt anybody. Except fish, of course. I get along with the other seals when we get together, and I live a simple life.

So why is it so darned hard?! I don't remember it ever being this tough just to swim around and do my thing. But I'm tired and draggy all the time. I just don't seem to have the sense of wild abandon I had as a pup? Am I getting old? Is this what old feels like?

It beats me. All I know is that, doing what I've been doing all along doesn't seem to satisfy me like it used to. But what choice do I have? It's not like I could go anywhere else, or do anything different. I am a seal, after all!

I wouldn't call myself ambitious, but I'd be willing to make a few changes if it would just bring my energy back. Is eating more fish the answer? Is more (or less) time basking in the sun what I need? I'm about at my wit's end...

Stay Alert for Signs of Energy Depletion

Many routine difficulties of life can be traced to insufficient or constricted air/energy. It's sensed as an all-over feeling of being "off." The heart, mind, and body each have its own ways to signal that it is out of kilter. They vigorously object and demand your attention whenever there's not enough to function effectively.

Each of their protests is a cry for something to change right away. But mostly their cautionary cries go unheeded. Any of those warning conditions can lead to feeling irritated or out of focus. Unless adjustments are made, your health and wellbeing could be compromised. At a minimum, you feel out of balance.

Signs of air/energy deprivation:
- Mental—stuck, negative, forgetful, bored, distracted, fuzzy-headed
- Emotional—dissatisfied, over-dramatic, wide mood swings of highs and lows in short order, frustrated, depressed, discouraged, sad, empty
- Physical body—stressed, exhausted, tense, irritable, inefficient, tentative, defensive

Although these are listed as though they're separate reactions to when you're wrung dry, more than likely it's their combination that sets your overall mood. Unfortunately, if the run-down condition continues too long, it almost starts to feel "normal."

When reflecting on your energy state, take particular note of those experiences (or assumptions) which make you feel drained and trapped, over and over again.

Feeling Overwhelmed

Feeling cowed and tense make for a walking-on-eggs frame of mind. And nobody is able to operate confidently from there. Breathing room allows you to relax and let those pressures fall away.

You feel the need for more:
- Time to do what you need to
- Space to maneuver—so you don't feel so closed in
- Money or other wherewithal to function
- A change of pace that's not so frantic
- Flexibility to change directions or priorities as needed
- Autonomy and freedom from relentless demands

- Fewer competing claims on your time, money, and energy

What happens if you're air deficient during many of your waking hours? Those times you do get an energy boost just barely keep your head above water. The "up" experiences only offset the deprivation felt the rest of the time. When those patterns become entrenched, it seems like just marching in place.

The free-floating sense of oxygen-deprivation is being driven (in part) by the pervasive anxieties of modern life. Added to that, we've been lulled into accepting too many things which are toxic to a healthy outlook. We assume we must grin and bear them as though they can't be fixed. Not so. We can and must do more to counter toxic air—in both our personal lives and in the public space.

What may start as a sense of disquiet can grow and become more pervasive if it's not solved. It could lead to feeling vulnerable and overwhelmed. Nobody does their best thinking from there. It saps your power and snuffs out self-confidence.

For things to turn around requires two things: 1. reducing the air/energy leaks keeping you drained; and 2. an influx of additional air on a regular basis. Becoming more air-savvy resolves them both.

A person requires extra air/energy after a shocking experience or severe crises. But sad to say, it is not as easily found under pressure. That's when a stash is needed most. But not much air/energy can be saved for a rainy day. It doesn't hold. Ascertain your never-fail places and activities so they can act as a pilot light to spur your bouncing back.

Insufficient Air Often Goes Unnoticed

Most of us go through periods when we're not getting all we need to thrive. We disregard the signs of air-deprivation and are as blithely unaware of our peril as the boiled frog in the oft-cited tale.

They say that if you put a frog into a pot of boiling water, it will leap out right away to escape the danger. But, if you put a frog in a pan filled with water that is cool and pleasant, and then you gradually heat the pan until it starts boiling, the frog will not become aware of the threat until it is too late.

It seemed like a good idea at the time

The frog's survival instincts are geared toward detecting sudden changes. This story illustrates how humans have to be careful to watch slowly-changing conditions in our environment, as well as reacting to the sudden or dramatic events. Feeling air/energy depleted sounds a warning for us to pay attention—not just to obvious threats, but also to those which are less visible. They jeopardize our peace of mind.

Like the frog in a pot, the perils we all face must puncture our complacency regarding our air/energy state. Once a person notices all the signs of air-depletion they endure on a regular basis, it's common sense to start looking for what is missing—psychological air.

How bad do things have to get for you to pay attention and to take steps to fix what's wrong? Slightly hot or a house on fire?! What makes you move? Becoming attentive means you don't need to burn your house down to make you take a walk.

Fill your lungs, expand your point of view, and stop tolerating situations and relationships which don't provide enough air/energy for your overall wellbeing. That also includes standing up for the air/energy needs of others. We all gain when there is more air available for everybody.

Each of us must discover additional ways to gain the air and breathing room we so badly need in our lives. Respect your warning signals of toxic air when they arise. Such discomfort calls attention to problems that are too easy to miss—and too risky to be ignored. More than likely, the uncomfortable warnings you've already been getting (and ignoring) will start to make sense.

How can you tell you're running on empty? For one thing, you feel desperate to find *any* pocket of air or some way to numb yourself. You're starved for a recharge and feel sorely out of balance. Some might call numbing activities an "escape," but I see them as frantic efforts to restore depleted energy at times you've run dry (Chapter 9).

The physical and emotional after-effects of depleted and toxic air are almost as draining as running a race. For they leave you without any reserves to draw on. Parts of yourself which were hit the hardest won't be able to fully function until your air/energy equilibrium is restored.

Bouncing back could take days… or weeks… or years. At its worst, the effects of depletion could affect your mental or physical health enough to become a chronic illness.

Don't Run Out of Air

Where did my air go?

Germans are known for having very precise expressions. They use two terms for air to appreciate the value of getting sufficient air to function throughout the day:
- *Luft holen* means "getting air"
- *Die luft is raus* means "out of air" or a loss of power (the opposite)

Both phrases point to different ways which having enough air can greatly influence what you're able to accomplish. *Luft holen* refers to taking a short break from your activities in order to relax and take a deep breath (find a pocket of air). It means to stop and wait or to "Hold on a moment!"

By contrast, *Die luft is raus* refers to having no energy or momentum—whether it's with a person, an experience, or a relationship. As a visual metaphor, hot air balloons which have air rise in the sky, but being deflated is a sign of tiredness and lack of drive (air depleted).

Die luft is raus also indicates that "the excitement is gone," "someone is exhausted," or "the wind went out of his sails." As you become more air-aware, nuances like these will become more clear and informative as they're happening. You'll read the signals and recognize the extent to which your air/energy needs are being met.

Your Favorite Air/Energy Sources Are an Individual Matter

It isn't so much what you like to do as whether the doing of it enlivens you. A particular activity could be boring for one person and a delightful pocket of air for the next. So your mindset and preferences determine how likely you are to even recognize an air/energy source when it's available.

Additionally, we might reject even what we badly want when we get it—unless it comes in the "right glass."

In the middle of the night, a toddler calls from her crib, "Water... water...water..." The bleary-eyed father drags himself out of bed, goes down the hall to the bathroom, fills a glass with water, then presents it to the screaming child. The child vigorously shakes her head and refuses what her father brought. He tries repeatedly to get her to take the water, but she protests: "It's in the wrong glass."

Rather than being a fussy-child issue, it speaks to context. The surrounding circumstances (the glass) are part of any pocket of air/energy. The source and context of what you experience determine how desirable certain air might be to you. If it's too weird, unfamiliar, or tinged with sad memories, you can't relate to it.

Therefore, part of broadening your air supplies is by noticing the air that's already available to you in unfamiliar or previously-rejected glasses. Developing a larger repertoire of glasses leads to enjoying much more air, with almost no added effort. Similarly, it's easy to get so excited about a particular glass (person or situation) you fail to notice there's no air there (or it no longer works).

What Makes You Happy?

Each of us will have a different answer which reflects so many ways we're unique. But some of the things that make for being happy are universals. They're part of what makes us feel human, and they have the power to bring out the best in us.

"Happiness cannot be traveled to, owned, earned, worn or consumed. Happiness is the spiritual experience of living every minute with love, grace and gratitude," according to Dennis Waitley.

While pockets of air/energy can make you happy, there's more to them than being pleasant moments. They can recharge your inner fire, put a twinkle in your eye, improve your health and performance, and expand your sphere of possibilities. Energizing moments remind you about being connected to something larger than yourself and of those concerns we all have in common.

Air/energy exerts a positive pull that's beyond mere satisfaction. As you tap into pockets of air, you are invigorated since they nourish your deepest awareness and fire up your sense of purpose.

You experience life on parallel tracks:
- What you want to happen (your desires)
- What you think is happening (your perceptions)
- What really is happening (the context)
- What could be happening, here and now (the possibilities)

When these views all converge and match you are most satisfied and effective. The more sharply they diverge, the more they pull in different directions from each other, the more off balance you become. As you come to know and accept yourself in even more ways, these differences diminish. That adds a level of harmony and contentment to your existence.

Getting to know yourself in more ways leads to a broader frame of reference. That in turn gives you more "glasses" to drink from. There really is more to you, more wonderful aspects of yourself, than you have yet discovered. Many of the pockets of air you want the most depend on additional sides of your nature being involved.

It permits more three-centered experiences, in which body, heart, and mind are all fully-engaged participants in your daily reality. That leads to living ever-more effectively, joyously, and energetically. Your life feels full.

Make It Fun

The search for air pockets doesn't have to be all earnestness and drudgery. Good humor and silly stuff also water the roots of novelty and wellbeing. Increasing your air/energy capacity does not need to be tough going. And sometimes it can be done playfully. Being lighthearted can be energizing in itself.

Don't pooh-pooh pleasure. You can find pleasure in a silly TV show or in being wholly absorbed in a lecture on astrophysics. Both types of pleasure contribute to a happy life, and both types of pleasure can give rise to the multiple benefits of positive emotions, like feeling more sociable, more energetic, and more resourceful. An avalanche of studies has shown that happy moods, no matter the source, lead people to be more productive, more likable, more active, more healthy, more friendly, more helpful, more resilient, and more creative. This means that positive emotions actually help us achieve our goals (reinforcing the feeling that we are working toward something important) as well as help us strive for meaning and purpose in life.... Happy moods lead people to perceive their lives as more meaningful; for example, the more positive emotion people experience during a particular day, the more meaningful they judge that day. That seriousness and greatness must be accompanied by grumpiness is a myth.[4]

With increased intensity of desire and awareness, it's possible to find ways to bring the various ways of experiencing life closer together. Start by noting when they are at odds with each other. As you gain a sharper focus you both discover and reveal your true identity through every action you make.

Notice the Direction the Air Flows

Some experiences consume far more of your air/energy than they give back. That could pull you out of balance. Assess each demand, situation, or responsibility you're already living with for whether you gain energy from doing it. Is it positive, negative or neutral air-wise? (Work through the questions in Chapter 14.)

Minimize the time you spend doing activities bereft of air. Downgrade your sense of obligation to air-deficient concerns. How else can the same result be achieved—if it's needed at all? Such activities are costing you more energy than you can afford to spend fruitlessly day-in and day-out.

The direction the air flows matters more than the amount that's gained or lost. Notice if a particular activity is recharging or draining you.

---

[4] Lyubombirsky, Sonja, *The How of Happiness: A scientific approach to getting the life you want* (New York: Penguin Group, 2007), 265.

> **Is air coming in?**
> **Is air going out?**

Increase the inflow of air, while reducing the nonproductive outflow. Little steps and choices in the direction of more air add up. As Tolstoy said, "True life is lived when tiny changes occur." The changes needn't be large to pay off because getting even a tiny puff of air proves something you're doing is working. And they reinforce each other.

Low Hanging Air Is Easy

Each of us is trying to find out how we can belong in life. One way of telling what works for you is by noticing which of the areas of your life are functioning best. They bring a satisfaction and a warm glow. That's not where you're frazzled.

Not having enough air diminishes your scope of activities. Air-depletion is a not-so-subtle clue something is amiss in your hectic world. Attending to your air/energy intake and usage improves your odds of getting enough to keep you going. Doing that involves having plenty of whatever energizes and restores you.

On the other hand, those concerns causing severe air/energy loss need to be fixed without delay. Seal the leaks where so much of your precious energy is wasted. They prevent you from reaching the life you desire. Gather more of the low-hanging air whenever and wherever you can.

Where do you place your confidence in tough times? Who (or what) always comes through for you? Where you turn most consistently provides your low-hanging air—that's within your grasp. Stretching farther widens your scope of resources.

Part of broadening your air supply is by *getting more of it from yourself than you currently do.* Although you will expand your number of air pockets in the world around you, you're sitting on the Fort Knox of air already. Greater self-knowledge provides the "open sesame" to take all you want (Chapter 12).

Designated Driver
A BonBon

> Each of us is either NEED driven or VISION driven. The difference between them appears small, but like a fork in the road, will lead to radically different life views and dramatically different outcomes. Whatever drives you

influences your every choice and determines where you eventually arrive.

If you have ever been fired by a personal vision or a burning desire, you treat it as more important than anything else in your life. Its primacy makes all other choices secondary to it. Each event is interpreted as whether it will further the accomplishment of that goal. Even trivial choices thereby become charged with direction and relevance.

Often, the achievement of the vision or desire is less important than the way it animates and makes purposeful all the other parts of your life. You feel a positive pull toward the distant, but discernible, realm where your vision can flower.

Your vision need not be about major long-term life goals. It may be expressed in as simple a manner as the way you live and function. For example, if you choose to be careful and attentive to the emotional needs of those around you, it will influence all your social interactions. Any heartfelt resolve can be the way you express and demonstrate that personal vision.

Lacking a vision leaves you to be need driven. Steady physical and psychological demands can control you, for they are not subordinated to an overriding purpose. When the hungers and fears arise, you feel compelled to satisfy them to reduce their discomfort.

That is, you act to cancel the negative urges, to avoid the unpleasant rather than to achieve a desired benefit. Such needs keep you busy, but provide slight satisfaction, leaving you enslaved and driven.

Which drives you? How much control of your choices does it leave you?

© 2014, Faith Lynella, from *BonBons to Sweeten Your Daily Life* or *More BonBons and Treats*   http://faithlynella.com

Stop Criticizing Yourself

Don't misinterpret what's causing the problem. When you're running on empty, there's simply no gas in the tank. Running dry is not a moral failing. You're not lazy, inefficient, unmotivated, or procrastinating. Feeling wrung out is not a sign you lack determination or moral fiber. That's when you should be especially gentle with yourself.

Nothing is going to happen until there's a chance to refill your tapped-out reserves. Snappy motivational slogans won't change anything when there's no energy to turn over the starter. And neither will beating yourself up—especially since it is damaging and done for the wrong reasons.

Your need for recharge and renewal when depleted is real and should be recognized as such. That is not the same as accepted, however. Getting recharged needs to be treated as a high priority. Put it ahead of anything else. Feeling deprived is a pressing demand for you to find more air ASAP. Also, think twice about continuing to do whatever led to such a sorry state.

Don't automatically jump to the conclusion your lack of oomph means you're sick—not to start with, anyway. Begin by seeking out small air/energy moments throughout your day. Avoid ambitious, do-or-die challenges for now. Build up to them when you've got a full charge.

Give yourself some credit for managing to hang on. That's big! Not yielding to the barrage of pressures you're facing which could take you down is worthy of applause.

As you remedy your air/energy imbalance, expect to see those gains build on each other—and extend to unrelated areas of your life. In truth, all of you is connected, so air/energy gains can't help but flow through your whole system and the way you live.

It's hard to illustrate air. I can point to its presence, but there's nothing to see. I liked the ideas of a balloon since it can show "full of air" or being popped.

Air   No Air

Introducing The Official Seal

Here is The Official Seal. His job is to announce: There's Air There. And since he's "official" his presence signifies the Seal of Air Approval.

The Official Seal will swim beyond the pages of this book, to scout out where there's ample air available. If we can get people to stand up for air, we'll all be better off. The seal will bestow the Official Seal where warranted. Follow his blog. Both websites will serve as ongoing air/energy resources.

   http://TheOfficialSeal.com
   http://PocketsOfAir.com

Chapter 3
Create Genuine Pockets of Air for Yourself
Air Shortages Are a Reality of Modern Life

It seems that our fast-paced world is complicit in chronic air/energy depletion. The news provides a steady barrage of reasons the sky is falling. Alarming signs of chaos and social disintegration appear wherever we look, whether it be the latest health risk visited on us, incompetent government policies, the coarsening of social discourse, impending climate change, or the failure of our schools to prepare young people to support themselves. The list of perils only gets longer and more disturbing.

The sense of collective disquiet clutches at us because we sense that no matter how many problems we hear about, many more are about to be revealed. Everyone is looking for relief and sanity to be restored.

At the same time, our ability to trust has taken a beating. It seems harder and harder to find something—anything—that's trustworthy. It's not what actually happens that ties us in knots as much as having to bear all the things that *could* happen as well. And that's on top of the individual pressures each of us faces in our own lives.

~~~~~
## Busy, Busy, Busy
### A BonBon

We get swept up in the demands of our constantly-busy lives, that leak into each minute and demand we respond. Not enough time, not enough energy, not enough attention—so we feel pushed, pulled, driven and pressured. Nothing we could do would be sufficient.

Say, ENOUGH!

You cannot do it all. So do as much as you can, knowing you can get more out of whatever you're already doing. You can silence the voices that drive you—for a moment.

Find a few seconds of breathing space in each little activity. Hold yourself apart long enough to pause and remember yourself. You neutralize the mounting frenzy each busy moment that you pause to enjoy or reflect.

It needn't take long. Reclaim the crumbs of time that feed your heart, that reconnect you with timeless eternity. You'll still be busy and your days will be full. But you'll also experience reminders of what's really important, after all.

© 2014, Faith Lynella, from BonBons to Sweeten Your Daily Life or More BonBons and Treats   http://faithlynella.com

~~~~~

Let it go. Emerson advises "Finish each day and be done with it. You have done what you could. Some blunders and absurdities no doubt crept in; forget them as soon as you can. Tomorrow is a new day. You shall begin it serenely and with too high a spirit to be encumbered with your old nonsense."

Enjoy an Air Break Often

Be still for a moment. Take a deep breath. Slowly… Let it out… Slowly… Take another deep breath. Sink into it and relax. Defocus your thoughts and disengage from your spinning emotions. Lean into the quiet space, as you allow restorative energy to flow through you. Savor it. Let that buoyant energy replace your doubts and fears.

Sense the expansive ripple flowing through you. Feel it open your heart and restore your frazzled body. By contrast, doubts and fears shrink your outlook to fit their diminished view. Whenever you discover anxiety has you in its grip, open yourself to an influx of fresh air. Sense the all-over lift and associated feelings of wellbeing as you are recharged.

Thích Nhất Hạnh said, "Breath is the bridge which connects life to consciousness, which unites your body to your thoughts. Whenever your mind becomes scattered, use your breath as the means to take hold of your mind again."

Your breathing patterns change along with your emotional states. It becomes shallow when you're frightened or anxious. But it deepens when you're relaxed, happy, or asleep. Breathing easily and fully can be pleasurable in itself, for the motion is experienced by the whole body as fluid, soft, and light.

Humans are as surrounded by air as fish in the ocean live in water. It is by our breathing that each of us is constantly attuned to the atmosphere which sustains us.

It's as Simple as Breathing

The choice to seek more air-rich experiences is not a difficult one. But it must be made repeatedly—then again, and again. Staying engaged with noticing your ebb and flow of energy takes resolve and focused attention. For the instant you forget, habitual, unthinking behavior patterns return and you start to drift. Of course, it's easily remedied on the next breath, or the next…

> **Mindfulness Conserves Energy**
> It is fortunate that we can learn to do tasks skillfully. It is unfortunate that this skill enables us to go unconscious as we do them. It is unfortunate because when we go unconscious, we are missing out on large parts of our life. When we 'check out,' our mind tends to go to one of three places: the past, the future, or the fantasy realm. These three places have no reality outside our imagination. Right here where we are is the only place, and right now is the only time where we are actually alive.[5]

Your attention to your breathing or pockets of air breaks the sleepwalking that creeps in as the mind drifts. It pulls you back into this moment—this breath. That's the point, isn't it?

Being a Walking Pocket of Air/Energy

In an air-deprived world, each of us encounters air-starved people all day long. Some of them you see in passing and don't even know their names. Some are your regulars, whose paths you cross often. While others are your nearest and dearest, with whom you spend most of your time.

But what quality of energy is passes between you? If those in your life are more often "off" than "on," they're air/energy deficient and needy. How does that effect you when you're up? When you're down? Do you have more low-energy relationships than high-energy ones?

In the larger scheme of things, you want energy to be a two-way street—sometimes you get more; sometimes you give more. But if it only flows in one direction, the relationship is unable to lift your spirits over the long run. Watch out for certain individuals who receive much more from you than you get back on a regular basis.

---

[5] Bays, Jan Chozen, *How to Train a Wild Elephant: And other adventures in mindfulness* (Boston, Shambhala, 2011), 6.

As you find easier and more consistently ways to supply your air/energy needs, all those around you gain as well. Ralph Waldo Emerson said, "Happiness is a perfume you cannot pour on others without getting some on yourself." It changes how you "smell" to everyone. It effectively effects the very air you breathe.

When you care about getting enough air/energy for yourself, that also benefits those around you. Plus, you gain immeasurably from being around those who have an abundance of goodwill and air/energy. That's the crowd I want to hang out with.

When you're charged up yourself, you're able to bring an extra measure of air/energy for other people. As you spread those good feelings around, you act as a bright spot in their day.

Make a direct and engaged connection:
- Smile—the shortest distance between two people
- Look the person in the eye—an unwavering eye to eye; hold it
- Listen to them without judgment or preconceptions; don't rush it
- Pause—hold the moment; slow the timing
- Disconnect from everything else as you do so

Doing that sincerely helps you relax toward each other, and toward the world at large. It's a form of communication which says through your body language, I want you and me to trust each other. The words exchanged matter less than their tone. Anything less than mutual respect is a missed opportunity.

Much more than social niceties are being observed. Of course, a smile speaks a universal language, but it also speaks to us on many levels which are hard-wired in our brains. Signs of caring "speak" to you most intimately and sincerely, making you glow. All of which supplies air that can enrich any encounter.

Leo Buscaglia said, "Too often we underestimate the power of a touch, a smile, a kind word, a listening ear, an honest compliment, or the smallest act of caring, all of which have the potential to turn a life around."

We all have fond memories of celebrations overflowing with pleasant energy. How supportive are your friendships and close family ties? Do you derive much air/energy from them? Are they marked by caring and warm-heartedness so you glow with acceptance?

Consider the phrase, "You had to have been there," which someone says to describe a previous gathering. Even when they try hard to explain what happened, the essence of what made the event worth commenting on doesn't seem to get through. It is not simply that words can't describe what happened or what went on was too complicated to sum up.

The participants felt an energy, a melding which made it all hang together in a memorable way. What the person is trying to describe is the mood and energy beyond the tangible specifics of who said what. All those present were tapping into air there. And that's the impossible-to-convey element to those who weren't present.

Here's to you having many more "you have to have been there" moments because with the right spirit, most gatherings can be like that.

Creating Fresh Air

When people really connect in a sincere way, they actually *create more air and energy*. You're not merely tapping into existing supplies, but creating more. That's one of the main reasons healthy relationships matter so much. They essentially create an abundance of fresh, unpolluted, satisfying, high-octane air and energy for all involved.

We need other people, and how we relate to each other has a major influence on whether we have plenty of air. Your social life influences you in countless ways—ways which determine your satisfaction with life. As Jane Howard said: "Call it a clan, call it a network, call it a tribe, call it a family. Whatever you call it, whoever you are, you need one."

No one lives alone. Many of your greatest challenges and frustrations come from the people closest to you. They also can bring you your greatest joys. Each of us feels a constant tug-of-war between being true to yourself and your own needs, and being accommodating to those you care about.

If you want strong relationships, you must find ways to achieve both goals at the same time. It's a form of tightrope walking. The need to serve both yourself and others needn't be in conflict. You can't afford to take either one for granted, or to allow one of them to languish in the background. But the price of strong ties is mutual respect, engagement, and constant readjustments.

Making air-supportive choices doesn't just benefit yourself. Your increased vibrancy imparts positive energy and warmth to those you connect with directly. By contrast, low-energy, mean-spirited, and toxic relationships are costly to your energetic wellbeing. Negative contacts are not only missed opportunities to create fresh air, but they pollute what you've got already.

Notice the Kinds of Happiness

As you start to recognize the full cost of insufficient air, you become sensitized to finding even more ways to acquire enough for your needs. Failing in that, your discomfort serves as a warning you're running low. Pay attention to any struggling to breathe as soon as it starts.

> There are three distinct kinds of happiness, and though they are not related, they are not usually in harmony with each other.
>
> - *A Good Day* A good day can be filled with many mild pleasures, repeatable and forgettable, and some rewarding efforts.
> - *Euphoria* Euphoria is intense, lasts powerfully in memory, and often involves some risk or vulnerability.
> - *A Happy Life* A happy life requires a lot of difficult work (studying, striving, nurturing, maintaining, negotiation, mourning, and birthing), sometimes seriously cutting into time for a good day or for euphoria.
>
> Anything we do may facilitate one kind of happiness and inhibit another.... A lot of what looks like a lack of willpower is a series of positive choices in favor of one of the other kinds of happiness.[6]

---

[6] Hecht, Jennifer Michael, *The Happiness Myth: Why what we think is right is wrong* (New York, HarperCollins, 2007), 10-1.

While any of them can provide you air, each of them serves a different purpose in your life. You need some of each kind and a balance of them all. After all, a life devoted only to pleasure seeking is unable to sustain a sense of energized wellbeing. But short-term satisfactions are needed as well.

Being fully recharged reflects the harmonious interplay of the various kinds of happiness. So don't "settle" for only one, or think one kind precludes the others. Hold out for the combo-pack.

Mark Twain said, "The two most important days in your life are the day you are born and the day you find out why." That second day is when you discover your sense of purpose. The rest of your life thereafter demonstrates what you do with that knowledge.

Saga of the Worried Seal

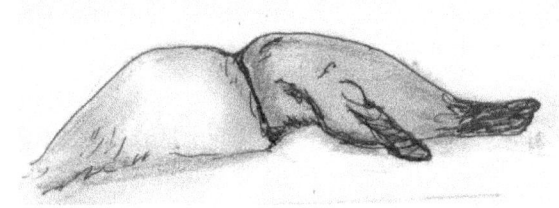

If I don't notice, maybe it will go away

So I'm minding my own business. Swimming, diving, eating fish – the usual stuff. I was feeling rather satisfied with my life. When out of nowhere, I started to feel bad. Real bad. Real, real bad.

What if there aren't enough fish? What if the polar bears come back? What if the hunters kill my pups? I saw all the terrible things which could happen. And I couldn't think of a single thing I could do to prevent them.

So even though I'm not able to stop them I keep on fretting about them. Now I'm worried. Isn't there anything I can do to feel safe again?

I'm not the carefree seal I used to be. That makes me sad, too.

Dealing with Air Depletion

Signs of air-depletion:
- Feeling driven by duty or obligation but without many rewards (too many sticks, but not enough carrots)
- Plugging away, without feeling good about it
- Forcing yourself to do routines because your heart's not in it
- Always searching for your diversions

- Constantly wishing to be somewhere else—or with someone else
- Feeling burned out
- Feeling resigned instead of eager or prepared to proceed

Prolonged air deprivation starts to feel normal after a while. It colors your personality and constricts your point of view. Two familiar forms of adjustment I dub the glums and numbs. Both are coping strategies for feeling down. But they do nothing about making things better for yourself.

The glums and numbs distort reality and perpetuate more of the same. If they persist too long, you could start thinking that's all that's possible.

Glums are giving yourself permission to feel bad—as though there is no other choice. It can be anything from mildly grumpy to severely depressed. You feel justified for being in such a mood, and to some degree inflict it on others. The flavor of negativity varies, but until it passes you're under a dark cloud.

Numbs are whatever you do to avoid your feelings. That includes denial and world-weariness. It could be reinforced by drugs, alcohol, or anything taken to make you forget or to keep you distracted. Numbs are the emotional band aid you apply to small hurts and disappointments. One form of them is called blinders.

Numbs are crutches which should only be used short term and transitionally. Any time you attempt to dull or deaden your pain, the effect will be temporary. They might make you feel better for a moment, but they don't solve the problem or make it go away for good. Since distraction is not a cure, what you're avoiding can return at any point—probably stronger than before.

Also, people too easily become reliant on their distractions and numbs to the point of over-dependence (even if the activities re not negative in themselves). If either glums or numbs hang around too long, they stifle your feelings and rob you of essential get-up-and-go.

It's an error to expect one big holy grail pocket of air to do it all for you. But by expecting that, you might fail to appreciate the kinds of air coming to you in all sorts of ways. What makes something in particular act as air for you? You find yourself breathing free and something inside relaxes.

You can sense the full, deep intake of air/energy as it happens—"I can breathe again!" That's one way you recognize you weren't getting enough air before. Breathing free leads you away from air-deprived circumstances, breath by breath.

Air as Manna

In the Old Testament story of Moses (Exodus), when the Israelites wandered in the desert after escaping from Egypt and the parting of Red Sea, God provided manna to sustain them. Fresh manna to eat was given each morning, and every person was required to gather as much as they needed for that day. Manna could not be stored or held over to consume on subsequent days (except the Sabbath). Old manna was "wormy" and unhealthy.

To my way of thinking, air/energy works the same way, but with a much shorter time frame (one breath versus one day). Humans (and all air-breathing organisms) must be constantly gathering fresh oxygen, using it as soon as it's taken in. While it is possible to get by on limited rations for a while, a person cannot function as well when they do.

By a quirk in the way people think, no matter how consistently your needs have been supplied, day in and day out, you still don't fully trust it will keep happening. That's because like air, trust and confidence won't hold. So it, too, must be gathered up again each day.

What I call the Paradox of Manna is not a lapse of logic or faith, but the way the mind and either-or thinking file information. (Negative events are more likely to be remembered than positive ones.) So the challenge to be met is to renew your confidence in a benevolent world frequently—despite all the evidence to the contrary. Both what sustains you, and your trust in it, must keep being rediscovered anew.

Fresh Lemons, Please

If someone hands you a lemon... Make lemonade

As the saying goes, lemonade is something good you make out of something bad that happens. It's time to ask, is it a fresh lemon or an old shriveled-up squeezed-out, lemon? What kind of lemonade would crappy lemons make? The saying ignores the quality of the lemonade—let alone your feelings in the matter. Such things count.

The lemonade message is about having a good attitude. But in my opinion, there's very little air/energy to be derived from such lemonade. Lemonade is an example of counterfeit air. Having a good attitude is actually a sign of air deprivation.

Most people would object: "Really? I thought a good attitude was a good thing.

No—it's a fake! It's an indication you didn't get air when or how you wanted to get it. So you're going to *pretend* you got something better. And worse yet, you never even get to reveal that it doesn't feel O.K. That's denial heaped on top.

That's not to say that you can't *transcend the lemons* that life hands you. But a good attitude is not the way to do it. A good attitude glorifies fake air.

A Good Attitude Stinks
A BonBon

You CANNOT get through life on a good attitude.
What you need is instead an attitude that is good—one that brings you joy.

A good attitude is better than a bad attitude, but that's about all. Although we are often urged to have a good attitude, it is not a good thing. It is a counterfeit of something good. It's what you have settled for *instead* of getting what you really wanted.

A good attitude is based on "I don't like this, but I'll be good about it, or "I'm having a terrible time, but I'll pretend it's O.K." When did you have to have a good attitude about something you really enjoyed doing? It's unthinkable!

Enjoyment and a good attitude are opposites. Who would be sincerely pleased about a counterfeit reward? The more things you have a good attitude about, the more things you really don't get to enjoy. So, don't be so proud of having a good attitude—it's not the right answer. It is partly right (bad attitude is also not the right answer), but it's simply not enough.

Whenever you find that you are having a good attitude, recognize it as a clue that "there is something amiss here." Like a determined detective, you must take a closer look; search for other clues. Look with candor and see what it is you don't like. Often it is something that others have imposed on you, like rigid rules or a power play. Sometimes, it can't be changed, like the weather or a personal tragedy.

Whatever it is, say to yourself, "Instead of having a good attitude about his, I'm going to find a way to enjoy myself anyway. I'm going to find some way, however small, where this situation cannot dictate how I must react. And I'm going to turn it into something positive for myself."

That effort shifts you from feeling powerless to gearing up to discover an outcome that would be even better. You have also avoided the smelly trap of a good attitude. Instead, you've demonstrated "an attitude that is good." Notice how totally terrific you feel!

Such detective work is very powerful and satisfying. Once such clues start coming to your attention, there's no telling what else you'll solve—and how good you'll feel, again and again and again.

© 2014, Faith Lynella, from *BonBons to Sweeten Your Daily Life* or *More BonBons and Treats*   http://faithlynella.com

~~~~~

Maybe the saying should be:
When life hands you a lemon…
Go find a pocket of air. Real air, not fake air.

Hitting Your Limits

As any athlete knows, going the distance means learning how to pace yourself. A lifetime can be likened to a marathon. It is not a sprint, but requires long-distance endurance. And being able to get enough air is a large component of training for the long haul.

My husband was a marathon runner and world-class Nordic skier (U.S. Biathlon Team). During his years of competition, he was forever training and fine-tuning his technique. He thrived on the challenges of racing—much of it being devoted to strength and endurance building. But such a competitive climate demands steely self-control and an ability to rise above the body's insistence that it can go no farther.

I've waited anxiously at the finish line for runners (or skiers) to arrive. So I could see up close how much brutal determination was required for racers to cross the line. Once across, some competitors collapsed in agony, some threw up, some pumped their fist in pride. But they all succumbed to a deep, agonizingly prolonged gasping for air.

But they were also exultant! They made it!

Their success trumped their exhaustion. Winning is nice, certainly, but that prize only goes to a single winner. Surpassing one's limitations is a triumph available to anyone who's determined to push past the body screaming: No more! No more! No more! Victories over our limitations are much more available and widespread than one per race—and probably more meaningful.

While I can't imagine pushing myself so hard for a race, I am well acquainted with the exultant feelings that come from transcending what seemed impossible, of surmounting formidable physical and mental limitations.

So many times I exhausted all my reserves when working around the clock to meet a deadline, or to keep going when I was dog-tired but not at a stopping point. I learned how to hold out for the second wind—then to ride its surge of potency.

The Second Wind Kicker

When nothing is left, when you're bone weary and down to your last particle of energy, something out of your control can happen. It couldn't occur until there's absolutely nothing held back. You tap into another pocket of strength, air, and resourcefulness. However, it is not simply more of the same as what you were using before. The second wind is not merely more physical strength that comes on-line.

There is a disagreement among the experts about whether the second wind results from a surge of endorphins in the system, or the person reaches an optimal balance between oxygen and lactic acid in the muscles (or of other physical processes), or that it reflects a psychological shift which breaks through customary mental limits. All those may be factors, but they do not account for the added potency of a second wind.

It has a *different quality of energy* because your actions seem effortless. It imbues you with clarity and certainty, a feeling of being in your prime. That, more than their standing in the race is the racer's-high moment. But of course, such a second-wind kicker can occur in any situation when you put it all on the line and push beyond what you thought you could do. For artistic activities, this is when the Muses speak the loudest

A second wind also gives a sense of being outside of time. Time stretches out, totally unable to hold you back. Routine barriers can't block you. A second wind is one of the forms of high-octane energy (Chapter 7). Each time it happens provides a clear reminder of why breaking through perceptual barriers is so exhilarating.

Broadening Your Air Sources

Each of us has a dominant personality style which we lead from:
- Mental (M)
- Emotional (E)
- Physical (P)

What's your dominant style? Your primary approach (first) is not going to change, and probably is where you find most of your low-hanging air. It comes most naturally for you. It's your default state—the one you fall back on without thinking. Over the years, your dominant mode has worked closely with one of the others—its sidekick (second). Which is your customary sidekick?

That leaves the other one as your least-used style (third). Line them up; that's your style formula. For example, mental, physical, and emotional would be: (M) (P) (E). If you're not sure, work through the questions in Chapter 14 to find your style.

We like to spend all our time operating from the first or second style. The third, the least chosen by us, remains awkward and mysterious. But if you're not using all three approaches, you're leaving too much air on the table. Consistently using a mix of all three styles greatly increases your flexibility and range of possibilities.

Using the third approach feels "wrong" and unnatural. So it has been left on the shelf all along. However, certain advantages come with using your third choice more often and *intentionally*. You're ignorant about how it "thinks" or makes decisions—even though it's part of yourself.

You're tone-deaf to the specific input it relies on, so you're most likely to ignore or misread what it understands. You're definitely *not identified* with its approach. That makes its arena largely unexplored territory, packed with untapped air.

Such additional input has been in your face all along, but was totally missed. As you read the coming chapters, don't just think about what's being said from your customary mindset. Also consider how the least-favorite mode of yours would interpret this information. Once you're past the initial reluctance to exploring the third mode, its unaccustomed perspective provides you a rather fresh way to understand more of what you experience.

What you start to notice can deliver those "fresh eyes" so essential for innovative thinking. The third mode uses parts of yourself which never got relied on before. Turn it loose and see what it shows you—*there's air there*.

There's another reason to consider your style formula when making decisions. The most-favorite mode is where the bulk of your habits and assumptions are well established. You're blind to them, letting them operate on auto-pilot (Chapter 6). They're riddled with old thinking and some long-standing uncorrected errors.

Not so with the two modes you only employ if you have to. By setting your dominant mode of operating aside temporarily, you really are liberated from influences which you didn't realize to be running your show. When you begin to discover how many ways the unrecognized tail has been wagging the dog in your behavior, there's no telling what doors it will open.

Chapter 4
Identify Your Recharge Places

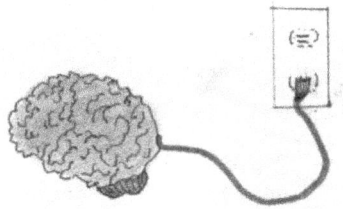

Locate Your Safe Havens

When it feels like you're running on empty you need an ollie ollie in free.* It's a protected place to retreat to which is sheltered from anything that doesn't feel safe.

> * A phrase used in such children's games as hide and seek to indicate that players who are hiding can come out into the open without losing the game.

If you are fortunate to have such a space, and individuals around you who afford you that security, consider yourself most fortunate. Look after it and them. Heap praise upon them, and do whatever you can to keep it or them inviolate. That's a safe haven.

Whatever is treated as a safe haven for you will have a familiar "my cup of tea" quality. Some safe havens take the form of a special place, a comfort zone where you feel protected from the world. But it could also be a special time—a time kept isolated from life's cares to nourish your spirit. Some resemble an escape, when you step off the treadmill for a bit.

Safe havens can be physical places or mental places (like favorite memories or daydreams). Some safe havens are tied to time, as in: time for myself, a time-out, or a holiday. At least one of them should serve as your "home base," where you hunker down. Many ways to recharge involve doing something which brings you comfort, like food-related activities, social gatherings, listening to music, or while immersed in a favorite hobby.

Your home base should be a place of peace and quiet, where the pummeling of outside pressures is stilled. In that sense, it is not quiet to the ears so much as quiet to the mind and spirit. But pockets of air and peace can be found almost anywhere.

There is a saying: "Peace does not mean to be in a place where there is no noise, trouble or hard work. It means to be in the midst of those things and still be calm in your heart."

Of course, family life which includes children is never all that quiet. I find that as a retired person, who has a quiet and relatively well-ordered home life, it's the hustle, bustle, and noises of children I miss the most. Give me the congenial chaos of family life any day to make my heart beat faster.

What safe havens have in common is they're where you go for shelter and revitalization. But they also *feel good* to you while you're there, and you're in no hurry to leave. For some people, it's important to be alone much of the time as they decompress and recharge. So their safe haven could be geared to solitary and alone time. That is not to say other people aren't important to them, but not all the time.

Your safe havens:
- At home
- At work, school, or away from home
- At special places or times which are set apart because you highly value them
- In your imagination, vision, or treasured memories
- Going within yourself
- Certain people who nourish your heart; healthy relationships
- Activities you enjoy the most
- Supportive groups, organizations, and churches

Pockets of air have an element of freedom to them. You breathe free—without having to do a song-and-dance to anybody, without apology or justification. You sink into it—a brief or long time-out, where the pressures of living are temporarily pushed back a notch.

Over the next few days, make a mental tally of where your most reliable recharge places are. Then pause in gratitude for the role which each of them plays in your life. Maybe let the people involved with it being there for you know they make a difference to you. Acknowledgment makes air pockets even larger and more available.

> Meaningful and pleasurable activities can function like a candle in a dark room—and just as it takes a small flame or two to light up an entire physical space, one or two happy experiences during an otherwise uninspiring period can transform our general state.

I call these brief but transforming experiences *happiness boosters*—activities, lasting anywhere from a few minutes to a few hours that provide us with both meaning and pleasure, both future and present benefit. Happiness boosters can inspire and invigorate us, acting as both a motivational *pull* and a motivational *push*.[7]

Saga of the Hunkered-down Seal

People who live in houses and have lots of stuff think that's what's necessary to hunker down and feeling cozy. But I care about feeling homey, too. I care about having a place that fits my needs and suits me just fine.

I care about my offspring having a safe place to live and grow up. Without that, even a seal won't sleep peacefully.

I need:
- *Water that has enough fish to feed me*
- *A shore or rocks or frozen ice where I can get out of the water*
- *Air and water that aren't polluted*
- *A chance to get around other seals when I feel like it*

And nothing on this list is about getting or having stuff. Notice I don't carry anything with me—and I don't miss it. That would all be a distraction from just enjoying my life. And I'm pleased to report that having a comfy and hunkered-down existence suits me fine.

Gather Air from Renewal and Resting Up

Opportunities for recharge can be scattered throughout the day, as well as in a full retreat from the world. Their duration is less important than their frequency and easy availability. Don't pass up chances to renew yourself, assuming you'll catch-up later.

---

[7] Ben-Shahar, Tal, *Happier, Learn the secrets to daily joy and lasting fulfillment* (New York, McGraw Hill, 2007), 130.

Many small recharges add up as they offset what is being used or lost. The objective is to stay charged up—as close to full as possible.

Emotional renewal is as important as eating and sleeping for dealing with life, so don't stint on it. Look for occasions to pursue whatever energizes and inspires you. Spend more of your day engaged in energy-rich concerns. Include others who want more air too. Shift your involvement away from so-so interests to more air-rich and energy-rich ones.

Make small improvements in the way you conduct all your affairs so they work as smoothly as possible together. Changes like that reduce energy leakage, frustration, and lost momentum. Better yet, you maintain a steady equilibrium, rather than enduring frequent starts and stops. You *flow along* through the day with less drag and energy costs.

Minimize your interest in polluted air and things which bring you down. Avoid negative thinking, whether it's your own or done by those around you. Make choices in favor of those situations where jarring events are less likely to happen. When that's your aim, it's possible to find ways to turn almost anything into a pocket of air for yourself.

Best places or activities for recharge:
- Close to nature: growing plants and animals, running water, awesome vistas
- Enjoying the arts, whether as a performer or audience; learning an artistic skill (beginner's mind)
- Making something just for the fun of it (from mud pies to real pies, to pie in the sky)
- Genial social activities and warm close personal relationships
- Recreation and sports for the sheer enjoyment of doing it (but be cautious about too many rules or breaking records that bring out the competitive spirit, which can trigger lower-grade energies or aggression)
- Peaceful and meditative activities; quiet time; disengaged from "doing"
- Light-hearted playfulness and fun
- Your own favorite time, place, or activity which never fail to uplift you

Make a Break in the Action

Even at places where you might have little control, such as at work or school, it's up to you to find air supplies *within them* which can be visited during the time you're there. Supportive co-workers can make all the difference.

For instance, do you make the most of lunch breaks and coffee breaks—so they serve as pockets of air? It can also be spelled b-r-a-k-e, which means to stop or disconnect. Use that time to totally disconnect in order to obtain a quick charge. Such breathing room also operates as a break (as in torn away from) that's out of your just-preceding events or mindset. Use them as an intentional unplugging for the purpose of catching your breath.

A friend of mine would ask, "Why should only smokers get a cigarette break?" So she invented what she called a Fake Break which non-smokers could use to claim "smoking" time outside several times a day.

Quick charges:
- A cup of coffee or tea; something you savor as you consume it (not a whole meal)
- A telephone call to a loved one with some emotion in it
- A memento (picture) which reminds you of something or somebody special; a souvenir or keepsake
- Take a cat nap
- Stretch and walk about—indoors or out
- Switch out of your mind and into your senses—smell, look at, touch, and listen to something that makes you smile inside

While you are probably doing such things now, add the desire that you be recharged as well. Give the experience your focused attention, listening to your senses one by one. Use such moments for reflection (not the run-away thinking kind but the step-removed, quiet kind) and appreciate how it feels.

Sinking into the experience makes all the difference in the world. "The art of being happy lies in the power of extracting happiness from common things," according to Henry Ward Beecher.

Be Kind to Yourself

What you do to be kind to yourself should actually be good for you—all of you. It should restore your equilibrium as well, so you don't feel one step away from sliding over the edge of self-control.

Grabbing a brownie or a few beers are a quick fix that might counteract the drain, but they won't take the place of something which builds your reserves and makes you glow with a sense of satisfaction. Indulgences don't touch you deeply on an emotional level.

Little indulgences have their place. Enjoy them and don't feel guilty about partaking occasionally. But they are not enough to restore you. You need to find pockets of restorative air as well to make life feel worthwhile.

> I've known many people who have spent years exercising daily, getting massages, doing yoga, faithfully following one food or vitamin regimen after another, pursuing spiritual teachers and different styles of meditation, all in the name of taking care of themselves. Then something bad happens to them and all those years don't seem to have added up to the inner strength and kindness for themselves that they need to relate with what's happening. And they don't add up to being able to help other people or the environment.
>
> When taking care of ourselves is all about me, it never gets at the unshakable tenderness and confidence that we'll need when everything falls apart. When we start to develop maitri [unconditional friendship with yourself] for ourselves, unconditional acceptance of ourselves, then we're really taking care of ourselves in a way that pays off. We feel more at home with our own bodies and minds and more at home in the world. As our kindness for ourselves grows, so does our kindness for other people.

Go Back to Nature

Your human-scale travails lose much of their sting when you step closer to the natural world. It stirs up a sense of grandeur, and awe, and timelessness which bring you a more impersonal perspective. You need that since realignments to something larger help you keep your bearings.

But plugging into nature doesn't need to be done on a large scale, or even outdoors. Plants, animals, and spectacular vistas are emissaries from our primordial home, reminders that we too are part of the natural world. Nature, truly seen, is majestic. But that also can be found even in small things which touch your emotions—like a blossom on your desk or a close-up photograph of a beloved baby.

Find an air fix in:
- Plants and flowers, which pull us into their beautiful perfection
- Pets and the animals we encounter which gladden the heart
- Inanimate natural wonders, like watching the sunset or waves breaking against the rocks

Visit Your Breathing Room

Your inner world is your closest and most reliable sanctuary. Going within yourself is always an option for a quick pick-me-up. You don't need to meditate. Simply disengage and turn your focus inward for as long as time will allow. Turn off your mind and time sense.

According to Hermann Hess, "Within you there is a stillness and a sanctuary to which you can retreat at any time and be yourself." It is even available when you are agitated. But our very striving to relax and reach it is likely to push it away. Relax and sink in.

Your core self knows what is true and abiding for you. But it's easy to forget in the jostling pressures of your daily demands. Fortunately, each genuine connection with something meaningful, or an air/energy recharge, reminds you that you *can* tell the difference. Chapter 13 is devoted to drawing strength from the simple pleasures.

You can go to your place of sanctuary and recharge whenever you align with peace, even if only briefly. At moments when you're in touch with what's most important in your life, your heart opens to the upsurge of tender energy. Such brief reconnections, repeated frequently, are enough to keep you from losing your tether.

Your own air pockets:
- Find them; identify them
- Claim them
- Make them prominent among your priorities
- Mark them, designate them as important and worthwhile
- Revisit them often
- Find more; enlarge them
- Enjoy them

Places where you go for air provide protection, even when you must go out in the world. Now set to work locating a variety of them for yourself. Finding fresh sources needs to be an on-going activity. Some air pockets come as unexpected surprises—never to be revisited.

Some you can share, some you can only visit when conditions are right. But some never fail you when you return to them. Watch for the people and places who nourish you and seek them out. The more of them you can claim and use, the happier you'll be.

Treat every place or experience in your life as an opportunity to tap into more air. They're there, lying in wait for those eager to discover them. They flirt with you and make you feel well-rewarded for "smelling the flowers."

Air is infinitely elastic and it is its nature to expand. It resists being compressed or forced to conform to a fixed, unyielding structure. I like to think of the human spirit in the same way. It does not want to be suppressed or clamped down too severely. In doing things you truly enjoy, your expansive nature is set free. Living with that in mind brings more balance and fresh energy into your life.

Air is plentiful. There's quite enough of it to go around. Air doesn't conform to the fixed-pie model where there's only so much available, so people must compete for it. In a fixed pie reality, here's only so much to go around. So if one person or group gets more it means that others will get less.

However, no one can corner the air in such a way that they can have it all (or even much more) for themselves. Adding air/energy to any situation shatters the fixed-pie model. When one person receives more air and passes it on there is considerably more of it for everyone else too. And everybody's world expands a tad.

Stir Up Stale Air

There is a human tendency to stop noticing or appreciating something that's always available. We place greater value on what's scarce or hard to attain. When even a greatly-valued object, person, or event gets too familiar, it ceases to gratify us as it once did. That's like stale air.

But living with scarce air is not like giving up chocolate for Lent. It's not a symbolic sacrifice in favor of something else. And there's no advantage from doing without. More fresh air feels better; having less of it feels "off." But even your safe havens can't work well for you unless they're kept as fresh as the air you're trying to find.

Even wonderful things you worked hard to acquire (like a caring spouse or lovely home) can become habitual if you fail to notice their desirable qualities anymore. As familiarity takes hold, you might no longer pause in their enjoyment—the quick intake of air at your good fortune. In that case, they might stop serving as well for your rejuvenation.

So a necessary component of guarding your recharge space is to keep it fresh and vibrant in your awareness. Watch out for stale air and your own indifference creeping in. The things you stopped appreciating didn't change—*you did.* Find ways to pay more attention to them. Or else.

Your Home or Room as Your Sanctuary

The saying, your home is your castle refers to you being in control of your space. It's where you spend the most time, eat, unwind, and sleep. All of those are forms of renewal. But some people live in a place controlled by others—a place where they don't feel safe and cozy at all.

How big it is (a room or a house) or how long you spend there at a time (an hour or a weekend) matters less than how well your hunker-down space is protected from stress and outside pressures. In that sense, shared space needs to be carefully configured so each party has some safe haven in it. It's a matter of them all acting from mutual respect as they establish their boundaries.

Be careful about who or what you invite into your personal space. This is where you're most "naked" and relaxed—where you drop your guard and let your hair hang down. Does yours feel snug and wholesome? Is the energy level and mood you've established there for yourself supportive and harmonious?

Your home sets the tone, as stated in this Chinese proverb:

> If there is beauty in character, there will be harmony in the home.
> If there is harmony in the home, there will be order in the nation.
> If there is order in the nation, there will be peace in the world.

This is your nest. How you decorate your space is not just a matter of being functional or attractive. It should also include things which make you feel good and lift your spirits. That's why your pictures and souvenirs of heart-warming events make your place feel homey. Mark your territory with things which bring you joy.

Keep it clean, tidy enough to feel comfortable, but not so "perfect" you can never feel it's good enough. Your space or nest is there to support you. Don't let maintaining it just so become the primary obligation of the time you're there.

Who else shares your space, and/or lives in your home? Those aren't the same question (unless you live alone) because it refers to how much dominion you have over your space. Is it your cozied-up hidey-hole where you hunker down and feel safe? Even little kids fix up comfy nests for themselves to play in. And as adults we long for that feeling as well.

Added Air/energy Strengthens Your Sense of Purpose

Psychologists have long studied the impact of positive emotional states on happiness, health, and attaining important life goals. Repeated studies found the attainment and pursuit of pleasure does not always lead to happiness. And we know of too many rich and successful people who are miserable.

Researchers identified two basic types of happiness: eudaimonic and hedonic. **Hedonic wellbeing** argues that increased pleasure and decreased pain lead to happiness. This is summed up in the term: the "happy or good life." It endorses the doctrine of hedonism: Pleasure, particularly of the senses, is the sole or chief good in life. So all choices should be made to maximize one's pleasure.

By comparison, **eudaimonic wellbeing** demands that choices have meaning in order to bring happiness. It resembles Maslow's concept of self-actualization. Eudaimonic wellbeing states a person feels happy if they experience challenges and growth. So happiness is related to fulfillment. Its approach argues that happiness is not achieved simply from the pursuit of pleasure, but also through developing individual strengths.

Eudaimonic wellbeing—"the meaningful life"
1. Sense of control or autonomy
2. Feeling of meaning and purpose
3. Personal expressiveness

4. Feelings of belongingness
5. Social contribution
6. Competence
7. Personal growth
8. Self-acceptance

Meaning is linked to a person's sense of having a higher purpose, or of feeling a responsibility to a larger community than before. It involves using your particular strengths and personal qualities to contribute to the greater good. Humans need to feel that what we do matters.

Science has found a strong link between living your life with a sense of purpose and having a strong immune system. The predominant form of happiness a person pursues plays a crucial role in their health. Chasing shallow forms of happiness (hedonic happiness) has been shown to weaken the body's health and immune system.

It corresponds with increased inflammation and decreased antiviral responses. Whereas, eudaimonic happiness is associated with lower levels of undesirable factors. However, researchers note that both types of happiness often share common sources and they can reinforce each other.

Such findings seem to suggest that optimal health also requires a genuine sense of meaning and a larger purpose. In addition, your state of mind and overall health will also impact those around you, as well as your larger environment.

While pockets of air can be found with either kind of happiness, you're best served with a mix of those experiences to assure adequate short-term and long-term, long-range supplies. The ways you're fulfilled should not be at odds with each other since each has its place.

> The life committed to nothing larger than itself is a meager life indeed. Human beings require a context of meaning and hope. We used to have ample context, and when we encountered failure, we could pause and take our rest in that setting—our spiritual furniture—and revive our sense of who we were. I call the larger setting the commons. It consists of a belief in the nation, in God, in one's family, or in a purpose that transcends our lives.
>
> In the past quarter-century events occurred that so weakened our commitment to larger entities as to leave us almost naked before the ordinary assaults of life…. High divorce rate, increased mobility, and twenty years of low birthrate are the

culprits in the erosion of family.... So put together the lack of belief that your relationship to God matters, the breakdown of your belief in the benevolent power of your country, and the breakdown of the family. Where can one now turn for identity, for purpose and for hope?[8]

Food and Cooking as Air

The big three daily requirements are getting food, sleep, and air. We barely notice air. We're conked out during sleep, so food and the activities surrounding it can easily become a major preoccupation. Eating is itself a pleasant experience, laden with delicious flavors and delightful emotional associations. It has been the centerpiece of countless mealtimes, celebrations, and happy family gatherings.

As children, we developed a deep love of certain smells, places, tastes, and foods which we forever after associate with feeling safe and being loved. As an adult you have only to re-encounter a particular smell, taste, or sense of place to bring some of those memories and their related feelings back. How many of your air pockets are related to food or eating?

We all find deep satisfaction in the enjoyment of cooking that nourished our spirits along with our bodies. No wonder they're called comfort foods. In a world of too much indifference and disappoint, such heart-warming associations with food and eating together stand out as pockets of air which you long to return to.

Each of us has favorite tastes and smells which conjure up all sorts of pleasant experiences. Certain foods can be counted on to make you feel loved and special. Even the preparation of what you eat provides a large measure of the satisfaction which comes with putting food into the mouth. Nutrition takes a back seat to the flavor sensations and emotional connections which arise while eating.

We've found so much enjoyment and renewal when eating, that when we feel air-depleted some of us turn to food. Food is an easy-to-get, socially-approved fix for feeling down. And it does work to some extent—often to the point of it acting as a drug. That, more than the calorie count of our food choices explains why so many of us are overweight.

---

[8] Seligman, Martin E.P, *Learned Optimism: How to change your mind and your life* (New York, Vantage Books, 1992) 284-5.

When stressed, I head to the kitchen because for me cooking is soothing. I enjoy preparing good food even more than eating it. I enjoy cooking for people I care about most of all. As any mother will tell you, giving food is an expression of love and caring.

For most of us, mealtime is less about getting the nutrition we need than getting to eat something we like. Unless you have no control over what goes into your mouth (as when someone else makes those decisions or because of medical restrictions), food is a small freedom you can look forward to several times a day.

As long as you live with much stress, you're likely to over-use food for the distractions and rewards it provides. On the other hand, when you aren't air-deprived and have ample supplies, food and all those things associated with eating, will recede in importance.

Fat Head
A BonBon

"I'm too fat," "I've got to diet," "My clothes are too tight," "I'm eating too much," or even "I'm too thin." Such recurring mental chatter has a way of creeping in throughout other activities. It colors the enjoyment of many things other than food: our friendships, our job, our leisure activities. It tears at our self-confidence and redefines our self-image.

Yet, the solution is not primarily related to what to eat—or even how much to eat. Changing eating habits, or resolving to change them, would make little real difference. The problem of weight control has less to do with your eating habits than you think. It has less to do with will power than you think.

It has less to do with genetic disposition than you think. Each of those, and all the other areas of our ready excuses, are only secondary. So it's no wonder that placing your attention and resolutions on them has so little effect.

Food and the way you relate to it have become TOO CENTRAL in your life. Eating (or not eating) doesn't deserve to be your primary concern. Figure out what you prefer to have as your central concern. Find a guiding passion, a commitment to something you really feel strongly about. Put more time and energy there. Find ways to make it central to your daily activities. Invest yourself in that pursuit—think and dream about it.

As something more significant fills your attention, your preoccupation with food or your weight recedes. It then takes its proper place in your life. Once food ceases to have an over-riding influence, you can enjoy it and stop treating it as a stick you use to beat yourself.

© 2014, Faith Lynella, from *BonBons to Sweeten Your Daily Life* or *More BonBons and Treats*   http://faithlynella.com

Chapter 5
Make Air-rich Choices

What You Choose to See Determines Your View

Humans have the power to make choices. And we do so all day long—eggs or bagel for breakfast, what clothes to wear, whether or not to swing by the bank on the way to work… Most choices deal with the practical concerns of daily life. But each choice you make includes the possibility of you gaining or losing access to air and energy.

Taken together, the choices you make add up to your way of life—one that reflects your core identity and priorities. Some choices can dramatically improve your air/energy level. And when good-air practices are incorporated into your lifestyle they will continue to provide your high-air experiences.

On the other hand, as Shakti Gawain wrote, "Every time you don't follow your inner guidance, you feel a loss of energy, a loss of power, a sense of spiritual deafness."

The difficulty rests on where you place your attention. Each moment you must choose from the innumerable attractions pulling at you. They come at you from all directions—out of which you can select just a few. Being attentive to *how* you make those decisions makes you mindful.

As Jan Chozen Bays describes it, "Mindfulness is deliberately paying full attention to what is happening around you and within you—in your body, heart, and mind. Mindfulness is awareness without criticism or judgment."

Saga of the Air-savvy Seal

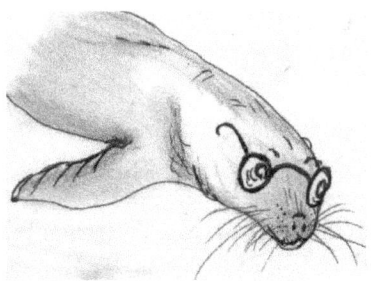

I wear air-colored glasses

Wake-Up Call
A BonBon

Each day when you wake up there is a new world ready for you. Your battery has been recharged, so your mind is clear, the frustrations and bruises of yesterday seem far away. Feel fresh, with a sense of expectancy for what awaits, like a child with boundless energy and enthusiasm, who is unfettered by life's burdens.

The challenge of each day is to see how long you can sustain the fresh new start. How far can its initial momentum go?

Keeping the precious innocent, unlimited sense of fresh beginnings is a deliberate choice. Like any other choice, it helps to prefer it, want it, sacrifice for it, and decline whatever contradicts it. Demands can't be permitted to sap the precious energy. The pristine perspective (a fragile treasure) can be hoarded. As you enjoy it, it does not dwindle. It enlivens you and whatever you pursue.

Sure, it's mighty hard to keep it. Most days that fresh energy is gone in a twinkle. But, just wanting to sustain it, wanting to stay fresh stretches the attention, the alertness. It remains at the level of choice, where you ask: "Do I want this more than anything else?" The repeated attempts to choose it keep it close and energizing.

How long until it is forgotten and it flies away? Probably you won't even notice, not until your energy has dwindled and the day has turned ordinary. Pause to realize you can still choose how you spend the rest of your time and energy.

Be glad—in the morning it all is back again. Keep taking those steps forward. There's a fresh start and a fresh outlook offered every day and a potent way to proceed through the inevitable ups and downs.

Yes, there will be ups and downs, ups and downs, ups and downs. But take that first step, confident that your journey will reward you: new experiences, personal growth, challenging companions, intrigue, detours filled with adventures.

If you're to reach your destination, you will use everything you've brought, and more. But your journey will ceaselessly reward and renew you.

© 2014, Faith Lynella, from *BonBons to Sweeten Your Daily Life* or *More BonBons and Treats*   http://faithlynella.com

Multiply Air Gains for Yourself

Choices which lead to more air are self-rewarding in the short term, as well as gains that build for the long-term. There's the immediate increase of air and energy—which could be extended into a whole day, or the sense of flying high. But two additional factors magnify the benefits of air-rich choices.

First, you're *not sticking with* something which drains you (so you're reducing drag). Further, the more inclined you are to prefer the air-likely choices, the more of them you seem to encounter. Gradually, the not-selected, air-deficient alternatives fall more and more by the wayside.

Such a consistent shift in the direction of added air/energy increases the more often it is made. But the pay-off from having more air starts to be felt right away. Another way of looking at each of your choices is by considering whether you're committing to them just for the moment or for the long run. There's no need to be torn. One breath at a time is all that's needed to build an energy-rich future.

Having ample air/energy exudes a powerful attractive force. As you become more adept at having sufficient buoyant energy and oxygen, you open the door to unexpected possibilities. People want to be near those who are overflowing with positive energy. They're eager to share your air pockets—perhaps even to create some new ones together.

> [For anyone who would like to become] more aware, happy, and at ease within the flow of a busy life... you don't have to go to a month-long meditation retreat or move to a monastery to restore peace and balance to your life. They are already available to you. Bit by bit, daily mindfulness practice will help you uncover satisfaction and fulfillment in the very life you are living now.[9]

---

[9] Bays, Jan Chozen, *How to Train a Wild Elephant: And other adventures in mindfulness* (Boston, Shambhala, 2011), 2.

You're Shaped by a Constant Stream of Choices

Take a step back and consider each of your potential choices according to whether it will sustain you or drain you energy-wise. And to what extent?

When you're unhappy with what's happening to you, it's time to make both large and small adjustments which increase your air supply. And common sense dictates you turn in the direction of where more air/energy could be available to you.

Constant choices being made:
- The people you associate with—or avoid
- The ethics you bring to bear as you interact and make commitments
- The advice and sensory input you choose to give, take, or ignore
- The amount of attention and energy you devote to something
- Who you give priority to—and why
- The value you place on your time and existing priorities
- How much uncertainty, novelty, or inconvenience you're willing to tolerate
- The way you spend your money—and for what
- The way you spend your time—and on what

Helen Keller said, "We betray ourselves into smallness when we think the little choices of each day are trivial."

Keep Tabs on Your Attention

Where you put your attention has significance. You are constantly choosing what to notice. The more you focus on a particular thing, the more important it become in your reality. On the other hand, what you ignore, suppress, or overlook becomes less and less important to you. It doesn't go away, but your attention is elsewhere.

Never forget, you are responsible for the presence, or absence, of air in your own life. Seeing the need for it will guide you to look for more circumstances which renew you. Air-bereft interests, let alone chasing fame or playthings non-stop, are poor substitutes for enjoying what you desire most.

Out of all the situations and people you encounter—which includes your memories of the past and your hopes for what is yet to come—you choose the focus of your attention at this very moment. It's always possible to make choices which maximize your air, while you remain calm and unruffled. There's more about the mental drawbridge in Chapter 15.

Bring Down the Drawbridge
A BonBon

Our attention is courted by thousands of suitors every day. Every person, every product, every activity we encounter stakes a claim on our attention, on our time. Yet, at each moment, whenever we notice one thing we fail to respond to the rest. The demands on our attention are so great, we have to be selective—to respond only to those things which capture our interest.

Our minds are like a well-fortified castle. When we are threatened or uninterested we pull up the drawbridge. We withdraw. Only something of interest can make us bring the drawbridge back down. Much of what passes for communication occurs while one or both people are locked within their closed-up mental castles. No information can be transferred when the drawbridge is up. It is not the information that is sent, but what is received that determines communication. We get both drawbridges down only when both parties are open to each other.

Each of us needs to invest the time and trust to get the other person's drawbridge down *before* we send our message. It is important that we continue to speak in ways that do not make the other person withdraw their open bridge. To sustain real communication, we must continue to re-establish trust and shared areas of interest. It is worth the trouble. Otherwise, we end up only speaking to ourselves.

© 2014, Faith Lynella, from *BonBons to Sweeten Your Daily Life* or *More BonBons and Treats*   http://faithlynella.com

Note: This image was my Problem D'Solver logo when I was a speaker and trainer. My slogan: Every problem is an invitation to open your mind and heart.

It's ideal if both parties have their respective drawbridges down before starting to talk. That's what real conversation requires. Doing so permits a two-way exchange, not just of information, but also of air. Harriet Lerner said in *The Dance of Connection:*

> The goal is not to put a patina of false brightness over problems. Rather, you can aim to speak in a balanced way to both the good and the bad. You can use words and actions to create an emotional climate in which people can be open and thoughtful, feel respected, appreciate, and heard, be more of their best selves, and give the relationship the best chance of succeeding. Constructive criticism and loving warmth each prepare the way for the other.[10]

Being "Sort of Happy" Isn't Good Enough

Surveys by the Pew Research Center ask the following question: "Generally, how would you say things are these days in your life—would you say that you are very happy, pretty happy, or not too happy?" Poll results have remained rather stable across the years.

Americans report:
- 34% say they're very happy
- 50% say they're pretty happy (not unhappy)
- 15% say they're not too happy
  Fully half of respondents consider themselves *not unhappy* most of the time. How sad! That's what I call **happy-ish**. That's not

---

[10] Lerner, Harriet, *The Dance of Connection: How to talk to someone when you're mad, hurt, scared, frustrated, insulted, betrayed, or desperate* (New York, Harper Collins, 2001), 156.

really happy—nor is it really unhappy. In my opinion, that's drifty, which lacks the energetic lift which can raise experiences out of the humdrum.

While a happy-ish person isn't miserable most of the time, neither does anything make them jump up and down.

There isn't enough intensity for them to chase after carrots, and the sticks aren't painful enough to force needed changes. Happy-ish is "handling it" well enough to keep going, but it is a very low air/energy way of living. *There's not enough air there.*

The opposite of happy is not depressed or any of the emotions. It is the flattened, dull, colorless, low-energy place we call "unhappy." Unhappiness is evident not by what it is, but by *what it is lacking*. And we all certainly can tell the difference by how it feels. Blah!

Neither happy-ish nor unhappy provide enough air/energy to get yourself fully engaged or your blood pumping. Don't settle for being happy-ish because it's just another flavor of a good attitude. It stinks.

Max Strom describes the heartbreaking situation of settling for a near-life experience.

> A near-life experience is to know that you had the opportunity for a rich and meaningful life but missed it because you instead chose, or resigned yourself to, something far less. A near-life experience could be the saddest tragedy of all because it is an avoidable one, because it is a result of our own choices.[11]

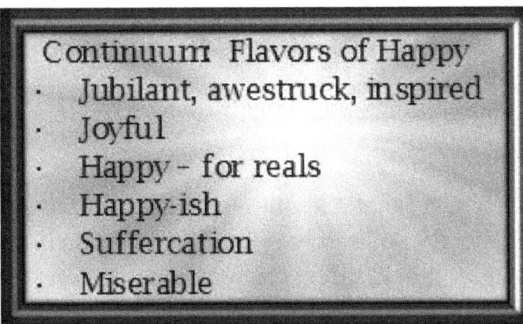

Continuum Flavors of Happy
- Jubilant, awestruck, inspired
- Joyful
- Happy - for reals
- Happy-ish
- Suffercation
- Miserable

---

[11]Strom, Max, *There Is No App for Happiness: How to avoid a near-life experience* (New York: Skyhorse Publishing, 2013), p 4.

Make Healthy Choices for Your Body's Sake

If you drive a car, you know how important it is to keep it tuned up, with gas in the tank and all parts in good repair. Yet how casually we treat our physical selves. Most of us give less thought to our body's needs than we do of our car's. Yet we expect it to keep going uphill and down.

Making healthy choices permits your physical self to perform at its best. It's impossible to stay fully charged up without your body's participation. Doing so includes breaking harmful habits and changing routines which waste massive amounts of energy. According to Todd Henry in *The Accidental Creative,*

> Few of us think much about how our energy level affects our ability to create. Energy consumption is more difficult to measure than time management and other markers of productivity. Also, our energy is a renewable resource, so many of us believe that it is perfectly acceptable to race through our week until we crash, spend the weekend recovering, then start the cycle all over again.[12]

Your body requires:
- Enough sleep, plus rest breaks when needed
- Good food—high in fresh fruits and vegetables, vitamins and omega-3 fats; low in processed grains, sugars, saturated fat, additives
- A respect for your physical limits, without undue stress or pushing too hard
- Staying physically and mentally active—stretching your body and mind
- Avoidance of excessive alcohol, tobacco, or drugs (prescription or illegal)

You don't need to be a fanatic about them. But you should recognize feeling good physically is directly related to how much air/energy you can get or hold onto. It also effects how much you can accomplish before you poop out.

---

[12]Henry, Todd, *The Accidental Creative: How to be brilliant at a moment's notice* (New York, Penguin, 2011), 116.

Rest and relaxation are on the road to peace and contentment. Visit them along the way. It is not lazy to disengage from the constant stream of obligations and "do nothing." It's really not nothing.

Being contented is fundamentally different from being lazy. Laziness applies to those who are not engaged with life, whereas contentment requires a person to be *fully engaged* with life. But they've learned to pace themselves and smell the roses.

To be content is anything but idle or passive for it takes considerable effort to attain it. In such a state, there's an awareness of wanting for nothing—for all is well. While true, it's so easy to forget or put off relaxing into that embracing place. And feeling contented, or any other way, always comes back to where your attention is.

Phony Choices
A BonBon

You have just found yourself in a very unpleasant situation, painted into a corner, without any palatable choices. You've made your best efforts to work it out—and failed. It feels awful; you feel defeated, lonely, scared, but even worse, you feel foolish. "How can a halfway intelligent person make such a mess of things?"

From time to time, each of us has found ourselves in such a fix. The significant issue is not how you got into the soup, but rather what you choose to do next. Are you focusing on the failure or on the unanticipated opportunity that is always lurking in its shadow?

There is a temptation at such times to look back and puzzle over how we got there, to examine the choices we "should have made." We are inclined to conclude, in retrospect, that we're wrong to be in this fix because there are right choices we "should have made." Beware! That is a trap of the rational (and rationalizing) mind.

Despite what we like to think, few of our decisions are ever made for logical or rational reasons. More often, we decide on the basis of emotion, self-image or other people's expectations. Later, if things don't turn out well, we so badly want to make sense of our pain that we look for something or someone to blame, often ourselves. We want to be able to say: "If I had made another choice this wouldn't have happened." Nonsense!

Each of us always makes the best choice considering WHO WE ARE and the facts as they exist for us AT THE TIME. (It is also true that there are always more available choices than there appear to be. There are NEVER only two choices, even though that's the way it often seems.)

But when we look back, we are inclined to wonder, for example: "Why did I marry Pete instead of (going to college, marrying Steve, becoming a nurse, etc.)" or "Why didn't I choose a career that pays more money?"

We mis-remember. Given the choices we actually got we always picked the one we thought would be the better one. There were reasons we didn't select the other alternatives, but those reasons are seldom filed in memory.

Choices are easy in hindsight. But choices are actually made without hindsight, based on the information as we know it AT THE TIME.

Another mental trickery says, "I could have chosen differently, and then I would be [rich or happily married, or respected etc. (a totally fictional alternative outcome)]." The truth is, that option wasn't offered as one of the perceived choices. No ninny will say, "I'll marry George so I can have a miserable life instead of being rich and successful."

The choices we make are those we think will bring us what we want. Whenever you compare real with fiction, the fictional possibility looks like the "right" choice. But you never actually had that choice, so stop regretting that you failed to take it.

Anyone can learn to make better choices, but not in the past. We must make them as they come along. Our sincerity, character and attention to details improve our ability to choose. And these are skills that grow as we do—not in retrospect.

© 2014, Faith Lynella, from *BonBons to Sweeten Your Daily Life* or *More BonBons and Treats*   http://faithlynella.com

Becoming More Choice-savvy

Researchers have shown our brain's ability to make decisions is significantly influenced by factors we're totally blind to. The decision-making part of your brain resembles your physical muscles. It gets tired if it's used too much, and it needs to recover before it can function effectively again.

The more decisions you make, the more tired your brain gets. So you give later choices less thought or merely select the lower-risk alternative without much consideration. And that unwitting avoidance becomes even more of an issue when the really difficult decisions need to be made.

After people have been making choice after choice, the brain needs a break to avoid decision fatigue.

> These experiments demonstrated that there is a finite store of mental energy for exerting self-control. When people fended off temptations … they were then less able to resist other temptations. … Willpower turned out to be more than a folk concept or a metaphor. It really was a form of mental energy that could be exhausted.[13]

Decision fatigue explains why decisions are harder to make at the end of the day, or after a string of other decisions. Your cognitive resources are regularly depleted because you're fighting an uphill battle every day—physically and mentally, both at home and at work. Understanding your vulnerability to decision fatigue allows you to find better ways to combat it and to make better choices.

This is different from ordinary physical fatigue because it comes from being low on *mental energy*. You can't make decision after decision without being more likely to make poor decisions. But also, after a point there's not enough energy left for dealing with the big problems and questions.

---

[13] Tierney, John, "Do You Suffer From Decision Fatigue?," *New York Times Magazine*, August 17, 2011.

Scientists have determined you should make more of your decisions early in the day, when serotonin is at its highest and the brain isn't tired. Serotonin is a hormone in the brain which influences how smoothly you make connections. It plays an important part in the regulation of learning, mood, sleep, and appetite. Since it calms your brain, more serotonin makes you less risk averse. As the day goes along the serotonin level drops, and you're less willing to make decisions. So you opt for indecision or to simply put them off.

As a general rule, people don't want to decide when they're offered too many choices. It leads to a choice overload, whereupon they start to take the *easiest* choice. That's not necessarily the best one, or even what they'd decide under other circumstances. But they choose the one which takes the least effort (at least in the short term).

Being honest and ethical is still another form of choice. Similar research has also found honesty gets harder later in the day. As serotonin declines, the self-control which helps you resist cheating or lying wears down. So people demonstrate less principled behavior when their mental energy is depleted.

Plan your activities in such a way that different kinds are spread throughout the day. Make big decisions (and those with greatest future impact) early in the day. When you have decision fatigue, avoid making choices where a poor decision would have significant negative repercussions.

Whenever possible, make the kind of decisions which free you from needing to make more decisions later. Doing so also leads to greater consistency.

As a side note, the brain requires considerable physical air in order to make good choices. The ventilation in the physical space where decisions are made matters. Studies found as the carbon dioxide level increases, the person's mental ability declines enough to diminish the quality of the choices they make.

Choice as a Chore or a Pleasant Activity

Making lots of decisions might not be considered as hard work, however. Compare making numerous decisions for business purposes with choosing something you're excited about doing, like planning a holiday or redecorating a room.

That's when exploring countless options and combinations before arriving at a decision could be seen as fun. Your imagination is wrapped up in visualizing the alternatives.

Individual differences also apply. For example, consider the stereotyped difference between men and women buying clothes. Women who consider shopping enjoyable spend hours going from store to store and trying on many outfits. Spending the day doing that is a treat. Most men would find so many hours spent trying on clothes torture. Their ideal shopping spree would involving one store, trying on only a few garments, and being done in 15 minutes.

As a nod to childhood, we can all recall when getting to choose was a big deal—more important than what was being chosen. Choosing something we wanted while everybody else had to go along with it, made us feel important, as though we had some control. There were elaborate rules about being fair and whose turn it was to choose this time. So in the interest of it being "my way" or "my turn," not getting to choose can be downright distressing.

Is making the particular choice considered an obligation or something you've anticipated with pleasure? Also take into account how much is riding on the outcome. Who else cares about what you decide? Why do they care, and how much do they care? Such considerations greatly influence whether making certain decisions would be considered a treat or a burden.

Choosing What Matters to You

Be clear about what's most important to you and save your big guns for them. But where enjoyment is involved, anticipation and savoring potential choices to come can often do as much for your energetic state as actually getting what you want.

Although having too many options can lead to paralysis or poor choices, that doesn't apply in matters we're passionate about. More choices and more complex choices are exciting! Aficionados can detect miniscule differences and might pay a premium (in money or effort invested) for certain highly-valued or exotic products (or experiences).

I consider having access to all the choices we want a quality of life matter. We each select what we want with different criteria in mind: price, quality, size, ease of use, social status, availability, familiarity, cuteness, uniqueness, snob appeal, etc.

What you ultimately select is not just a matter of the amount of money or time invested in getting what you want. It's also reveals how central the particular decision is in your life.

As an example, those with discriminating tastes in any area of interest become attuned to very small differences. Anything from music to wine, to paintings, to antiques has a field of experts who've devoted a lifetime to identifying the barely-perceptible nuances which set one item or experience apart from similar ones.

Developing such a degree of refinement requires discernment—noting small clues related to your passion or area of expertise. For example, I'm a foodie who finds my time in the kitchen relaxing. In weaving flavors together, I keep at least eight kinds of mustard and six vinegars on hand. I care about the difference they make in what I cook. By contrast, I only have one choice of shampoo because I barely care about it.

Figure out what really matters to you; then savor making those decisions. So far as the vast number of concerns which don't interest you, don't invest much time or energy in them—just enough to be competent. They don't deserve it; nobody cares. So save your brain energy for bigger fish.

With a wealth of choices, the ability to find contentment from them gets much harder. Further complicating the decision process, the more choices people have, the less likely they are to be content with whatever is chosen. Buyer could feel remorse even if the final decision is clearly correct.

Why having more choices make you less happy:
- More effort is required to weigh alternatives
- Tangible and intangible costs of the other opportunities which were not taken
- Conflicting values related to the alternatives—even imposed from what was not chosen
- Pressures to choose can be stressful and draining
- Possible blame or loss if the decision doesn't turn out the way you want
- Second-guessing yourself

Air Depletion and Being in Balance

A balanced existence involves somewhat more than superficial appearances. It is rooted in values and a belief system. It shows a combination of principles and appearance which work in harmony with each other. Part is tangible; part is not. Part is grounded in everyday reality; part points to something timeless and larger.

It's easy to get so fixated on the trapping of good living that a person never looks beneath the surface to check for things like being happy or fulfilled. Success is likely to focus on the pretty picture and ignore any evidence that all is not as someone wants it to be. To live a life that perpetuates standards you never fully embraced or questioned is risky because it's not grounded in anything real.

Lacking a foundation, when cracks appear, as they will from time to time, the flimsy façade is stripped away. And the person's whole world could collapse. Sad to say, the loss is seldom confined to a single aspect of their daily life. Even if those concerns are kept separate from each other, the lack of balance in any of them has a detrimental effect on the rest.

Zig Ziglar said "I believe that being successful means having a balance of success stories across the many areas of your life. You can't truly be considered successful in your business life if your home life is in shambles."

Poor Choices Waste Air and Energy

Stay alert to the quality of air available. Many things are not what they appear to be on the surface. Not all your choices are harmless to your energetic peace of mind. You need to assess opportunities and unfamiliar situations as to their air-availability potential.

Add the "air potential" of something to the other criteria you factor into your choices. Look at the other participants involved. Do they show signs of having ample air and energy? Or the opposite? *Is there air there*. Choose your course of action and companions accordingly.

It might take a while to recognize a particular situation (or person) is repeatedly pulling you down or sucking the life-force out of you. So be attentive to the shifting energies during each encounter. When you're drained, track back in your mind to see how it happened. It's up to you to learn from such experiences so you develop better evasive strategies.

Be sensitive to words and ideas which are crafted to mislead. Watch out for influences pulling you off course, especially if there's little or no positive energy in the mix. Don't be satisfied with only the promise of getting some air *eventually*.

Even more distasteful than the quantity of serious problems in the world today is the amount of fear being enflamed *on purpose* for economic or political gain. Fear mongering has replaced genuine dialog or intelligent judgment on a dizzying array of concerns.

When people see the world as an unsafe place, they do not make their best choices, let alone operate from an attitude that the difficulties can be resolved. Unfortunately, there are those who gain an advantage by exploiting our fears and indecisiveness. They are the same people who benefit from us making poor choices.

The best protection you can have from being bamboozled or vampired is by being sensitive to what lacks air/energy for you. *There's no air there.* Be suspicious of anything or anyone that's air-bereft because some part of yourself can tell the difference. Listen to it. Trust it. Then whenever possible make the air-rich choice.

Questions to Ruminate On

These are not looking for right-wrong, multiple-choice, or top-of-the-head answers. They are even broader than essay questions. They're posed not to get an answer, but to make you think. They (and others which occur to you) are to draw you away from your superficial or public-face way of thinking.

Questions like these get to the root of what makes you tick, what makes you unique. They are essential to figuring out "who I am." And you should revisit them from time to time for quiet reflection. For how you respond to them will grow and change as you do.

Pondering such questions will help you to see your penumbra. That's an astronomy term which has been adapted to other contexts (this being one). The penumbra cannot be seen except from a different angle of view or with the aid of multiple perspectives.

Penumbra
- A shadowy, indefinite, or marginal area
- The partial or imperfect shadow outside the complete shadow of a solid body, as a planet, where the light from the source of illumination is only partly cut off

When looking directly at a planet the penumbra (the layer surrounding it), cannot be seen. Astronomers must rely on an eclipse or redirected light from other sources to view it.

In a similar way, you cannot see some parts of yourself by looking at them directly. To do so requires resorting to different perspectives than you usually use. You need: 1. more than one point of view (multiple eyes) and/or 2. somebody able to listen (without judging or inserting their own opinions) who can reflect what they see back to you.

Questions like these help you get an oblique view of your ideas and behavior. Considering them can reveal a tuned-out (mostly invisible) area of your identity that's really front and center. To the extent you care about such matters, you start to value the oblique view, seeing things out of the corner of your eye.

Just as having two eyes permit seeing in depth, adding an oblique awareness tunes you into the fuller (deeper) picture of yourself.

Ponder:
- Where you've been—what hardships you've overcome (and who helped you through it). What you learned or gained because of it
- What you like about your life now. Compared to what it used to be, or what you want it to be
- How you define happiness. Do you think about it?
- Would you describe your life as a happy or fulfilled? If not, what stands in the way? Is any interference beyond your ability to fix?
- Name the most joyful adult(s) you know. How do they, or what they do, influence you in a positive way?

- When was the happiest time or experience in your life? How does thinking about it make you feel? Do you revisit that sensation for a lift?
- What do you consider your life purpose or primary mission? What are you passionate about?

Chapter 14 is comprised of a variety of self-surveys and questionnaires, but they don't dig as deep as reflecting upon questions like these.

Chapter 6
Protect Your Breathing Space

Guard Your Air Pockets—You *Need* Them

Protect your air/energy pockets from invaders. That includes saying no to those around you who suck you dry energy-wise. That includes saying no to yourself when you waste too much of it indiscriminately.

Treat air as a part of your value and reward system. And take note of which of your activities and commitments measure up. Maintaining your air/energy supply should be a high priority since so much of what you want out of life depends on you having enough. Make choices which protect your air/energy resources, while stopping whatever messes with it.

Stand up for your right to have sufficient fresh air. That includes how, where, or how often you're able to recharge. Your flexibility require many different kinds of recharge sources. Having a wide variety of sources improves the likelihood of getting all you require.

If you rely almost entirely on one type of renewal, like food or sex, it creates an unhealthy over-dependence. That might even lead to addictive behavior (Chapter 9).

You use different kinds of pockets of air for a variety of situations. Getting recharged shouldn't get squeezed out by the hustle and bustle of life's obligations. Respect your early warning signals if you find yourself in toxic air. Take self-protective action without delay.

Your air/energy has considerable value. Not only do you need it for yourself, but those in your life expect to share what you have as well. That's fine when there's a mutual exchange between you. That's what normal give-and-take is all about.

But some people take much more from you than is being offered. They're willing to keep you drained for their own gain. It can be debated the extent to which it's done on purpose, but such an imbalance points to the need for maintaining healthy boundaries.

Making Desired Changes Is Tricky

While change is an unavoidable fact of life, growth is optional. Once you reach adulthood, physical growth is minimal. But the opportunities for mental, emotional, and spiritual growth do not cease. The choice is yours, however, whether to take them on or to let them pass you by.

You discover a never-ending flow of possibilities the more you fully embrace life. Your capacity for enjoyment and inner development continue for as long as you pursue them. Caring for others and novel answers provide all kinds of energy-bearing rewards.

Once it comes to your attention how little of your energy is supporting what you want the most, you will feel the need to fix things. Can you endure letting situations, or people, which keep you energy-depleted carry on as before? What to do about such imbalances might not seem apparent, but the discomfort will gnaw at you until something improves.

As you consider making changes in your life, move in the direction of more air. However, don't try to make too many changes at once. It takes time for each to settle into your behavior pattern and feel natural. Also, take into account which aspects of your life are working well enough air-wise to support the adjustments which any change will cause.

When trying to change behavior, don't discount the existing (often unconsciousness) rewards for doing things the way they're already being done—or of hanging onto what you've always thought. There are ample benefits besides inertia for the person wedded to the old ways. Even if many of the pay-offs and reasons aren't on a conscious level, those pattern has been reinforced by a zillion repetitions.

First off, changes rock the boat, and they lead to numerous readjustments—many with unintended consequences. And those in turn set off even more shifts. It takes a lot of energy and resolve to stick with it. Never underestimate the amount of effort required to move away from what's familiar.

Ligatures of Devotion
A BonBon

Inspiring!... Powerful!... Life changing!... Motivating!... A moving call to action!...

The speech was a knockout. Everyone in the audience was touched, moved, and challenged. To a man, they got the message and vowed to follow the call. They were persuaded, willing to make the necessary and desired changes.

Then, to a man... nothing happened. Nothing at all!

While it is important to kindle the vision and muster the resolve, that is the easy part. All of that motivation achieves nothing unless you also cut your ligatures of devotion. They bind you and blind you to achieving heartfelt desires, challenging goals, or a greater vision.

These strands may be small, but there are many of them:
- Habits, those things you do routinely without thinking or attention
- Cold slogans and clichés that have long served you, but which have lost their relevance
- Relationships, along with their related expectations, that have ceased to grow and nurture
- Unexamined assumptions
- Dogmatic and slavish devotion to the past and the familiar
- Ways you regularly waste your time, energy, money, and opportunities
- Causes and commitments that no longer suit you or serve you
- Short-sighted values and priorities
- Passivity, indifference, and inertia
- Self-defeating behaviors that repeatedly lead to unintended, yet predictable, consequences
- Irresponsible desires and activities
- Early childhood programming that you've never examined or outgrown

Each of these ties can be changed or broken in a moment's effort—once you pay heed to their restrictive pull. But you must first notice their presence, their negative influences. They are your *status quo*. Each of them asserts a powerful drag that keeps everything (and you) just the same.

Their tendrils hold you, tied like a prisoner of your own past and unexamined habits. Whenever you break those ligatures of faded devotion, you are like Gulliver, severing his puny bonds. After you're freed from those many small ties, you can move forward—toward your beckoning goals.

Your devotion to many of the old and cold connections doesn't serve you. Inquire, "Does this link bind me to strengths or to limitations?" Sever those restrictive ligatures. Each snip acts as a liberation! Finally, your resolves and desires can move you forward decisively! At last, whatever has inspired you is within your grasp

© 2014, Faith Lynella, from *BonBons to Sweeten Your Daily Life* or *More BonBons and Treats*   http://faithlynella.com

~~~~~

Become a Canary in Your Life

A canary in a coal mine acts as an early warning signal of danger. Miners used to carry canaries down into the mine tunnels with them. If dangerous gases such as methane or carbon monoxide leaked into the mine, the gases would kill the canary before killing the miners. When the canary showed distress, the miners knew they should leave the mine immediately.

You need to heed the signs of noxious influences around you too. Greater air/energy-awareness helps you spot them early on, when they're easier to deal with. Finding yourself regularly drained and suffercating should be treated as your own canary in the coal mine. It says, get out of here pronto!

Look for ways to change those interests of yours where energy leaks away to others more likely to restore and excite you. The choice to replace energy-deprived and depleting activities for more life-enhancing ones is not a hard one. But the desire for improvement must recognize that long-standing influences to keep things the same are dug in.

Everybody is at home with what's familiar. So unless you're prepared to stir things up considerably in pursuit of greater air availability, not much is going to be different. Any behavior which persists for a person either has an inherent reward built in for doing it, or a possible penalty for not doing it, or both. That's why unless you face up to those as well, trying to change behavior is so difficult.

An immediate benefit of greater air awareness shows available air you're failing to claim. It's yours for the taking. You can see *there's air there!* On not. On the other hand, such an unawareness makes it abundantly clear why certain things you claim to want—want really, really badly—won't ever happen. *There's not enough air in there for you.*

How many times do you say: I should _____? Now take those intended-to-do items and rate each of them as to their air-generating potential in your life. All of a sudden, it's not such a mystery why so many of your desires never seem to happen, why they're relegated to daydreams without a grounding element.

You aren't getting enough of an air or energy bump from it to seal the deal. Or you failed to "burn your boats" so it was too easy to return to the old ways.

Follow the Breadcrumbs of Air

Getting little gasps of air (relief) when you most need them may actually nudge you in a particular direction—toward larger air pockets. Air-rich experiences can open doors for you (just as a major setback can close them). In that sense, pockets of air may be breadcrumbs which can redirect your path. With practice, you can find supportive pockets of air in almost any situation.

Consider how simple life can get when you follow the air and don't apologize for treating your need for air as a high priority. Ample air helps you to think more clearly and get through the obfuscation of what doesn't make sense. With sufficient air/energy awareness, the fog clears about the puzzling behavior of those around you—and why they treat you as they do.

Fog results from so much water being suspended in the air that it prevents seeing very clearly or very far. Consider foggy thinking or "being in a fog," as evidence of needing fresh air. Increased air/energy clears both your thinking and comprehension.

Air deprivation usually goes unnoticed and unremarked upon. But once you recognize the need to avoid toxic air, you'll be "pointing a finger" at some rather smelly elephants in the room. To clear up your air supply requires stirring up the *status quo*. Doing so requires considerable courage.

As Winston Churchill both said and demonstrated, "Success is not final, failure is not fatal: it is the courage to continue that counts." Stand firm against anything which destroys or compromises your air/energy level. You're going to need all you can get for the long haul.

~~~~~

Courage
A BonBon

Courage is very private and very lonely. Although courage is seen as the stuff of greatness, you do not feel great when confronted with a need for courage. Far from it. The need for greatest courage comes precisely at the time when you are most aware of your limitations, your sense of powerlessness, and your unpalatable options in the face of overpowering difficulty. At that point, it takes enormous courage to go forth boldly and willingly to confront the Hydra (many-headed beast).

Perhaps the monster cannot be defeated. Perhaps you are wise to avoid the unwinnable battle. Yet to yield to the reluctance to stand firm denies the silent strength that arises only in the face of such difficulties.

When you pit yourself against a great challenge, you are forced to take your measure. And you seldom feel that you "measure up" in your own eyes. It takes courage to confront the threat when you "know" yourself to be insufficient to the task. Yet you resolve to do your best, or what little you can do, *anyway*.

Courage exists when your determination triumphs over intelligence in the face of self-doubt. The effort you make in the face of overwhelming odds is your true victory. You may fail, yet you can't be a failure because you tried. You may succeed against all odds and feel triumphant.

The point to remember is, the outcome does not validate or diminish your courage. Your WILLINGNESS to proceed *anyway* is the true hallmark of courage.

Every day each of us encounters situations that call on us to act courageously. To live fully challenges us to frequent acts of courage, but it's up to us to make that choice. The first act of courage is the willingness to act with courage.

© 2014, Faith Lynella, from *BonBons to Sweeten Your Daily Life* or *More BonBons and Treats*   http://faithlynella.com

~~~~~

Habits Rise Again

If you've ever tried to break a long-standing habit (like smoking or biting your nails), you know how difficult it can be. Broken habits have an insidious way of creeping back in when your attention is elsewhere. Your mental and emotional habits have been with you for a long time.

Even though your intentions might have banished them, they're not really eliminated. Unconscious triggers tied to them are still in place.

Even after you "pulled 'um up by the roots," don't think you're done. You're likely to have withdrawal symptoms and regrets. In some ways, you're going to miss those bad habits since they've helped you deal with stress and emotional swings for so long. You've relied on them to make yourself feel better. They are part of your air-restoral strategy.

What will you do *instead* to get through rough patches? Take steps to make falling back on them very inconvenient. If you don't intentionally establish air-providing replacement behaviors, the old habits will creep back without you ever noticing.

Leaving the old and familiar behind is not a sign of being wishy-washy or uncommitted. Instead, these new behavior patterns are a vote for going in another direction. If you're willing to change in fundamental ways, or to embrace new ideas when something better comes along, you'll be miles ahead of those who dither around and miss the chance. Just make sure your heart, mind, and body have all signed on.

Jettison outworn and outmoded ideas or your habitual ways of doing things. Which of them have outlived their usefulness? Which keep you tethered to the past? Remember, small choices often determine the bigger choices. Reconsider those which fail to provide a reasonable air/energy return for what you put into them.

Some changes you attempt won't work out. That doesn't mean it was a wrong choice or a waste of time. Something worthwhile might have been accomplished simply by *moving away from* what was already in place. Many changes require a series of choice points and supporting decisions. Their fruits are slow to develop. Just keep tinkering with yourself as a work in progress.

The Rewards of Letting Go

Equally important to making good choices is learning from mistakes. If you want to expand and grow, expect to take risks and make some mistakes. There will be failures and disappointments. Give yourself permission to fall short.

Failure doesn't come from the mistakes themselves, but from your failing to learn from them. It's even smarter (and less painful) when you can learn from other people's mistakes as well.

Getting All You Pay For
A BonBon

Some of life's most valuable and precious lessons can only be learned by failure. If we then sink too deeply into disappointment or embrace self-pity, we fail to get the message that we have paid such a high price to receive.

Insist not just that the suffering stop, but that a lesson is received for each setback. Most people are satisfied just to have the difficulty go away, even at the risk that it will return.

Unless we insist that we learn the meaningful message that comes through suffering, we haven't gotten the benefit we "paid" so dearly for. It is not possible to prevent some of life's upsets, but we can demand that we get an understanding from them.

Hold on until you can say, with sincerity (you have to really mean it): "Painful as it was, I'm glad it happened, or I wouldn't have learned *_____." Whatever you say to fill in the blank is a trophy you can use forever—you've earned it, and it is valuable beyond price. That is the way that wisdom is achieved.

We have the right to hold the universe accountable for the lessons it sends us, and it will give us a valuable answer—but only when we insist.

* It's for you to decide; fill in your own blank.

© 2014, Faith Lynella, from *BonBons to Sweeten Your Daily Life* or *More BonBons and Treats*   http://faithlynella.com

A Buddhist scholar once explained to me that most Westerners mistakenly think that nirvana is what you arrive at when your suffering is over and only an eternity of happiness stretches ahead. But such bliss would always be shadowed by the sorrow of the past and would therefore be imperfect. Nirvana occurs when you not only look forward to rapture, but also gaze back into the times of anguish and find in them the seeds of your joy. You may not have felt that happiness at the time, but in retrospect it is incontrovertible.[14]

The Power of No

If you wish to live a productive, happy, and healthy life, you have to be willing to say no to things which won't get you there. Henry Todd said,

> We have to make choices so that what's important gets the energy, while things less important to us are left undone. We have a threshold for how many creative problems we can effectively manage at a given time. Taking on any additional obligations or commitments will decrease your overall effectiveness, and removing too many will mean you're settling for less than your full potential. You want to feel stretched but not overextended.[15]

Say no to:
- Unnecessary or low-return commitments so you have the time needed to enjoy life and rejuvenate
- Negative influences which poison your air
- Mindless distractions, so you can focus on what's most important to you
- Temptations which pull you off track, without providing what you require

"Saying yes to happiness means learning to say no to things and people that stress us out," according to Thelma Davis. Give yourself permission to extricate yourself from whatever you know to be detrimental to your mental, emotional, or energetic wellbeing. Doing so sure beats having to put yourself back together afterward because you didn't.

---

[14] Solomon, Andrew, *Far from the Tree: Parents, children, and the search for identity* (New York: Scribner, 2012), 47.
[15] Henry, Todd, *The Accidental Creative: How to be brilliant at a moment's notice* (New York: Penguin, 2011), 128.

A recent study reported in the *Journal of Consumer Research* showed using the right words when saying no makes it easier to stick with one's resolve. Researchers compared saying "I *can't* do X" and "I *don't* do X."

Participants who said "I *don't* do X" when presented with a choice (temptation) were much more likely to stick with what they intended to do than those who replied "I *can't* do X."

Saying "I *can't*" creates a feedback loop in the brain which reminds a person of their limitations. They see it as a restriction, rather than as a choice. On the other hand, saying "I *don't*" leads to a feedback loop reminding them they have control and power over the situation. The study concludes that such a small change in perception can push a person toward making the changes which break bad habits and support good ones.

Recognize that saying no is not permanent. You are really saying, "Not now." You can and should feel free to revisit prior decisions to consider whether you'd make the same decisions today—or whether they still make sense. When prior commitments are viewed from an energy-wise perspective, you might weigh your options differently.

Being able to say no to yourself depends on having the proper kind of self-love. It rejects whatever attempts to draw you into fear and anxiety. It says no to drifting along or resorting to indulgent impulses. Saying no to what's harmful to your peace of mind provides the strength to put what's important for you ahead of what's unimportant.

Along with being strong enough to say no, you must also understand when to say yes to yourself. Standing up for your vision and heart's desire says yes to something you want even more than what's already here.

It says yes to the countless actions to come which will be needed to support that desire. In doing so you vote in a very tangible way for being *who you want to be*. This the way ligatures are cut. This is how you change your future.

Being Selective Requires Cutting

Energy management also requires you to be selective. We all have many more interests and desires than we can ever expect to accomplish—and we keep getting more. Some of them are first rate and deserve a second look—or a full-fledged commitment.

You might consider them worthy opportunities. But at what point does the overabundance of interests become distractions from your primary ones?

Leave some time and space unfilled for reflection, for recharge, for breathing room. That's where peace and insights can land.

You've heard the saying: "You can have *anything* you want, but you can't have *everything* you want." And you certainly can't have it all at the same time. You'd be overwhelmed. Even if you could "have it all" or "do it all," to what end? That's a treadmill that brings little satisfaction. Just the assumption that it's possible or desirable adds to our modern stress.

You are better served to have a few intense, high-priority, front-burner interests that really matter to you, instead of a bland stew that's lukewarm about everything (Chapter 9). According to Todd Henry,

> As you craft your life and make decisions about what to act on versus what to abstain from, you must recognize the importance of negative space in developing creative ideas. The time between your active moments is when ideas are formed, insights are gained, mental connections are forged. If your life is a constant blur of activity, focus, and obligation you are likely to miss critical breakthroughs because you won't have the benefit of pacing and negative space. What's not there will impact your life as much or more than what is.[16]

𝓢aga of the 𝓡edundant 𝓢eal

Watch Out for Too Muchness

As a culture, we applaud pushing our limits and reaching grand goals. We revel in the stories of those who succeeded against enormous odds, those who were rewarded with great fame or wealth for what they achieved.

---

[16] *Ibid.*, 130.

We want to believe we could do it too. We've gotten to think excess is one of the perks of success, of living up to your dreams. But excess is also an indication of being out of balance or out of control.

When you're not well-grounded within yourself, it's easy to get unbalanced. It could show itself as doing too much of what doesn't work or doesn't matter, while failing to do what's critical. Once you are air-depleted, your efforts to make things right can veer between not enough and too much—without you being able to find the right balance.

Until you locate your own comfortable equilibrium (not the passive *status quo* since this is three-centered and engaged), be sensitive to signs of "too muchness." They're counter-productive and seldom work out as you hoped.

Energy-wise, too muchness uses excessive energy, while failing to gain a sufficient return for your efforts. It's one step away from being counterfeit air, and it's certainly not a wise long-term strategy.

The tip-off is in the word "too" as in: exaggerated, excessive, or offensive. There's absolutely nothing wrong with the particular activity itself, but in its heavy-handed, tone deaf overuse. It comes across as insensitive or inappropriate.

Flip-flopping between doing too much and too little is much more draining on you than maintaining an even keel. The first step to regain your footing is to notice too muchness—whether it's your own, or exhibited by those around you. Then consider the energy costs involved. Maybe there's a much simpler, less too-y way to get something done.

Examples of too muchness:
- Spending too much—using money unwisely; ditto for time
- Extreme mood swings between highs and lows
- Running hot and cold—sending conflicting, perplexing, or half-baked signals
- Trying too hard—which is seen as needy or lacking confidence
- Pushy or argumentative—insisting on always being right or in charge

People who are not confident about what they're doing are likely to display a variety of too muchnesses. And being stressed only makes the over-reaction worse. The remedy can be found through greater self-awareness and moderation. Pace yourself—relax. Treat too muchness as a wake-up signal for you to ease up a little. Break the insistent rhythm and catch your breath.

Being too needy is a mindset, not a bank balance. Neediness is rooted in fear—fear of not being good enough in some regard. And nobody can function their best from there; it's an air-depleted place. Take time for a recharge. But in the meantime, stay mentally upbeat if possible. And don't let yourself beg, plead, or grab the short stick.

Chapter 7
Maintain Access to All the Air You Need

Increasing Your Energetic Capacity

Your energetic level tracks with your emotional state. When your energy level rises, your spirits go up too, and *vice versa*. For instance, feeling inspired and grateful coincide with an energetic boost, whereas feeling angry and ashamed reflect a diminished energetic state.

Increasing your capacity to handle more intense and buoyant energy opens the door for all aspects of yourself to feel elevated. Such a sensation leads to your feeling more complete and unified—exactly right.

You need to be more alert to the unintended ways your air/energy leaks away. Losses can be greatly reduced simply by noticing how and where your oomph went. What a waste to use too much energy on things you don't even care about—especially if it's at the expense of what matters more to you. Finding and repairing energy leaks is a key component of building your reserves. It reduces inefficiency.

"Inefficiency" in this sense does not simply mean non-productive effort, but there is little or no energetic lift gained from the activity. Neither does it count as resting-up and renewal time. Time spent in play, daydreaming, and doing nothing are certainly not inefficient. They can be quite productive because of their ability to recharge you.

Anything which makes you function at a much lower energetic level is sensed as drag. Drag wastes energy and prevents you from flowing naturally with the possibilities available in the moment. It drags you down. Drag could also show itself as strong negative emotions like outbursts of anger or fault-finding—whether it is directed at others or yourself.

As your energetic capacity increases, a person is inclined to become more expansive and vocal about what they want to do with it. More opportunities beckon, often with an impossible-to-ignore urge for more spontaneity and fewer constraints. However, acting on those aspirations requires a certain confidence in what is ahead. Doing so includes strengthening your ability to handle whatever comes.

Each individual's energetic fingerprint reflects thousands of choices, coupled with their subsequent energetic adjustments. Building up your capacity for more air/energy happens over time. It involves letting go of non-productive old baggage or habits, coupled with drawing on more air-rich experiences. What's coming into focus is a more comprehensive and delightfully-inclusive worldview.

Adapting to more air is gradual because there are so many low-energy distractions which catch your attention. And the energy leaks they cause each need to be dealt with before the door can be closed on them.

A Lick and a Promise

Being too rushed and busy leads you to make shortcuts, figuring you can make up for insufficient breathing room or energy later. Such shortcuts are not an example of greater efficiency since they're usually superficial efforts made without care or enthusiasm.

You figure you can catch up later—when there's "time to do it right." So you allow the stresses to take their toll because you feel that just hanging on is the best you can do—for now. That's what I call "deferred breathing."

The net effect is that too many of those efforts are both half-hearted and half-assed.

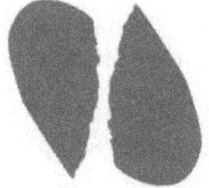

Half-hearted Is Half-assed

The "rob Peter to pay Paul" mentality contributes to feeling "behind the 8 ball"—in a weak or losing position. Catching up acts as the illusive carrot which never seems to be quite within reach. In some sort of mental accounting system, you think you're being clever and squeezed more mileage out of a tank of gas. But it's how you fool yourself, since much of the time you were coasting.

The culture is complicit in holding up role models like Super Mom or hard-driven employee who can keep innumerable balls in the air. The American Dream believes we can, and should, have it all. So our expectation are out of whack with what is humanly possible. It can be done, but at the expense of various humanizing qualities. There's an unacknowledged cost.

The very concept of multi-tasking is based on the notion a person can do two or more things at the same time well. But the brain really can't do them well. In, *Getting Organized in the Google Era* Douglas C. Merrill shows the flaw in that reasoning.

> Multitasking is something we all do these days. The problem is, our brains just aren't cut out for it. When you multitask, you're interfering with your brain's efforts to put information into short-term memory—a process that's fragile enough to begin with. And if the information doesn't make it into short-term memory, you won't be able to recall it later… Multitasking—especially when you're trying to accomplish two dissimilar tasks, each requiring some level of thought and attention—makes it difficult to encode information into long-term memory…*Multitasking usually makes you less efficient.*[17] (italics his)

Repair Your Internal Plumbing and Wiring

Increasing your air/energy level involves two questions:

1. How to get more air/energy?

That requires upgrading your "electrical system."

2. How to keep the air/energy you get from leaking away?

That requires upgrading your "plumbing system."

Unless you resolve both issues, you'll find it difficult to sustain enough to avoid feeling drained. Getting them in equilibrium involves steady tinkering over time. Some adjustments show immediate results. But the end goal is to have ample energy consistently, rather than living with wild fluctuations.

Air/Energy Management is the ability to sustain a consistent and ready supply. Once you start looking at life through "energy glasses" or "air glasses," you can't help but consider the air/energy costs and trade-offs of the decisions you make. Without an adequate high-octane energy supply, you're severely limited in what you can accomplish. It also puts you at greater risk for abrupt crashes because you ran dry.

---

[17] Merrill, Douglas C, *Getting Organized in the Google Era* (New York, Broadway Books, 2010) 9.

Don't get discouraged by minor setbacks—or major ones either. Take to heart Winston Churchill's definition of success. "Success is the ability to go from one failure to another with no loss of enthusiasm."

Failures are not what matter. Holding on to your enthusiasm *despite them* is the true measure of success. His approach supports energy management.

Intangible costs from such choices:
- Squandered opportunities—dropped too casually because they were uncertain
- Forever waiting for things which never happen—whether that's your fears or your dreams—because you *never got fully engaged*
- Avoiding open-hearted relationships because they could make you vulnerable
- Thinking defensively—setting too many rules and limitations which inhibit your choices
- Becoming inhibited and defined by your rigid self-protections

Attend to Your Air/Energy Requirements

Much of your ups and downs of daily life can be traced back to having erratic or insufficient air/energy levels. But rather than attending to your energy level, you instead blame what you did or said—or what others did or said to you. Those matter less to your peace of mind than how much air you have access to on a regular basis.

As long as you don't notice what raises or lowers your energy level, you'll misread the signals about your own behavior—let alone anybody else's. Cause and effect get all mixed up with "shoulds," assumptions, and rules—and who knows what else?! They're barking up the wrong tree.

Simply put, falling below the amount needed to keep going hurts you. It makes you feel boxed-in and constrained. Being depleted also kills any momentum toward what you really, really want—along with your sense of wellbeing.

Running dry requires you to start over and gear up all over again… and again… and again… Preserve your precious air resources by spending them consciously and carefully. As you take the amount available into account when deciding what to do, the easier it becomes for you to stay charged up. Don't squander what you get, and be discriminating about how and where it's spent.

Again, plumbing and wiring are metaphors and do not correspond to the nervous system or any specific body parts. But it is also undeniable they do influence each other. When you run out of gas, there could be a major energetic wipe-out with some physical fall-out.

That's an extreme, but most of your plumbing and wiring repairs are undertaken to prevent such dire outcomes. However, try as you might, into every life a little crash-and-burn will fall.

Energy costs of crash-and-burn:
- Loss of momentum or sense of progress
- Actual costs of repairs, do-overs, and to replace what was lost or broken
- Lost time to get back in place to resume; opportunity costs because of delays
- Psychological wounds: second-guessing oneself, disappointment, self-criticism, defensiveness, timidity
- Slower pace upon resuming
- Healing and rebuilding required on numerous levels

Something valuable may be learned in the process, but it does not come cheap—energy-wise. Over time, you get smarter about when to withdraw and regroup, when to watch "which way the wind is blowing." You develop skills at riding the currents, rather than plowing full speed ahead or slamming into easily-avoided obstacles.

On the other hand, resilience is hard-wired into us. Our ability to bounce back, even after life-threatening setbacks, is remarkable. In *The Happiness Advantage* Shawn Achor wrote:

> Adversity never hits us quite as hard—or for quite as long—as we think it might…. Simply speaking, the human psyche is so much more resilient than we even realize. Which is why, when faced with a terrible prospect—for example, the end of a love affair or of a job—we overestimate how unhappy it will make us and for how long. We fall victim to 'immune neglect,' which means we consistently forget how good our psychological immune system is at helping us get over adversity.[18]

---

[18] Achor, Shawn, *The Happiness Advantage: The seven principles of positive psychology that fuel success and performance at work* (New York, Crown Business, 2010), 126.

However, it is also fair to point out that not everyone is able to fully recover from traumatic events. Research has found some people having significantly lower happiness levels even seven years later. They level off at a new, much lower state than they had before. So although most people do bounce back over time, there are those who cannot regain the level of wellbeing they felt before the ordeal.

To Arise Is the Prize
A BonBon

I am not so smart that I cannot make foolish choices.
I am not so strong that I cannot be broken.
I am not so confident that I cannot despair.
I am not so aware that I cannot be fooled.
I am not so determined that I cannot fail.

SO WHAT!
In every case I am willing to try again!
The valor of the effort is not diminished by the outcome.
To try AGAIN, despite disappointment, IS a triumph.
The VALUE of the effort (in this circumstance alone) exceeds the value of the consequences.

© 2014, Faith Lynella, from *BonBons to Sweeten Your Daily Life* or *More BonBons and Treats*   http://faithlynella.com

Upgrade Your Wiring

I treat the electrical system as the way you acquire air/energy, then use it as you go through the day. I treat the plumbing system as concerned with how that precious resource is wasted. In either case, you want to maximize the amount of air which can be spent on things you want most.

Assess your electrical system:
1. Where and how are you getting your current supply?
2. Is it adequate?
3. How do you use it? Lose it?
4. How can you avoid energy crashes?

Energy flows. But wherever it's blocked, disconnected, or shorted out it stops flowing. Maybe it's being redirected to uses you don't know about and would vehemently disagree with. Paying attention to your wiring will help you discover how much of the air you acquire is actually available for accomplishing what you want it to do. You must also avoid shorting out, along with finding better ways to recover from them.

"Shorting out" your wiring
- Blow up, throw a fit
- Snap, go ballistic—using massive amounts of power with maximum disruption but minimal benefit
- Collapse into a "pile of mush" or tears
- Run amok—irrationality coupled with emotional blasts
- Project your anger and hostility toward some convenient external cause or scapegoat
- Withdraw from responsibilities or from those around you
- Shut down completely; drop the ball
- Deny that anything is amiss—when it's obvious to everyone else it is

Notice each method of shorting out has an emotional component. Such reactions are entirely *out of proportion to whatever triggered them*. They are also rather destructive, both to you and whoever feels the blast.

Your blow-out could be directed outward, toward others, or inward, against yourself. Whichever form it takes is influenced by your history, the amount of risk or safety you feel at the moment, and your coping skills. Either way, it's an electrical "short."

Treat such out-of-control behavior like a blown fuse. That's because it prevents a potential larger-scale blow-up or fire. Shorting out indicates exactly where new wiring (repairs and clear thinking) must be installed. Except for the blown fuse, the festering problem which triggered it wouldn't have come to light. Urgent essential repairs would remain undone.

Notice several things about a "short":
- Touches an already-tender place where there's unresolved pain or fear
- You've been there before (*déjà vu*)—didn't solve it then, and feel anxious about it. But you're no longer blind to the air/energy influences involved, so know what to do about it

- As one energy-draining issue gets resolved your confidence grows; you find yourself able to handle the next problem or repairs easier
- Rather than feeling embarrassed or justifying past failings, try being grateful for what the short shows you

Repair Your Plumbing System

What becomes of all the energy which comes your way? How do you use it? Where does every day's fresh supply go? And are you getting a decent pay-back from the activities where you invest your time?

Leaks result from cracks in the pipes where water (energy) can seep out. Big cracks require immediate action. It's a hemorrhage. When energy leaks away faster than you can restore it (even occasionally), you'll feel totally depleted and discouraged. How long would you keep pouring water into a cracked bucket before stopping?

On the other hand, when cracks are so small that leaks are slow, you might not catch on for a long time. While each tiny trickle is hardly a problem by itself, many of them add up quickly. And they squander substantial energy, without you deriving any benefit at all. Those drip-drip-drips can be the early-warning signs of serious energy problems ahead.

You cannot afford to use up too much of your available air on trivial activities—or to run dry on a regular basis. It's very difficult and time-consuming to recover from massive losses. Many people search fruitlessly for a medical cause or diagnosis when their problem is primarily an energy-management issue. If depletion continues too long without relief (repairs), however, it can easily become a medical or psychological condition as well.

As you pay watchful attention to the ebb and flow of your energy level during the day, see if you can find the source, the epicenter of where the energy drain is the worst. Treat repairs there as a high priority.

Monitor Your Energy Requirements

Constantly losing energy in the same situations, or around the same people, indicates something is amiss. Before starting repairs, figure out what specific front-burner air/energy-consumption issues demand attention first.

How frequent and significant are the specific energy leaks? Where do they show up? Then deal with them one at a time.

Reduce energy wasters:
- Negative emotions—worry, stress, and anger
- Spinning your wheels in indecision
- Repetitious and unproductive activities which produce little or no satisfaction
- Letting the expectations of others call your tune
- Ambivalence, marching in place because of being of two minds
- Trivial or shallow pursuits which consume lots of time or energy without recharging us
- Blowing up or shorting out with minor provocation

Energy management should also include a resolve to expend energy wisely. And deciding so goes beyond the merely personal concerns because your energetic state impacts others. Make sure your increased energy flows freely throughout your entire way of life. It adds a harmonizing influence to your other choices as well.

Of course, younger people have so much energy they assume it is an inexhaustible resource. And they bounce back very fast. So they see little need for air/energy conservation. But even they can exceed their body's capacity to regenerate. A component of energy management which comes with getting older is changing those profligate energy-using habits forged in our youth.

Use the reclaimed energy to:
- Pursue your creative challenges or interests
- Engage in inner exploration to learn more about "who you really are"
- Gain access to your wisdom through your direct hands-on experience
- Work toward creating the kind of world you want to live in
- Liberate your thinking from limiting assumptions and beliefs
- Develop healthier relationships

It gets increasingly difficult to muster sufficient motivation for energy-draining pursuits once you're aware they don't serve you well. In moving toward greater air efficiency, you lose interest in chasing after "fool's errands" or in unnecessary complications. You can simply walk around them. There's little stomach for side issues which divert you from what's providing the air you need.

Flying High on the Proper Fuel

Buoyant energy is not rare, but it is fleeting. Maintaining sufficient reserves pushes those driven by joy or creative pursuits to seek circumstances where it's most available. In addition, you generate large amounts of energy during happy and creative experiences. But it has a short shelf life and you burn through it quickly.

Creative thinking and inspired actions require more of a different fuel than routine activities do. The availability of enough of it generally accounts for the hot-and-cold cycles of creative thinkers or projects. Anyone who figures out how to maintain their optimal energy levels can accomplish their goals more consistently—and with less *down* time.

Like an airplane at takeoff, more fuel is needed to get airborne (up) than to maintain flight. That requires lift-off energy. Staying up involves acquiring adequate supplies, along with decreasing the drag and resistance which waste it.

Energy to Run the Three-story Human Factory

G.I. Gurdjieff was a 20th century spiritual teacher who asserted that people need to do inner work in order to wake up and function consciously. His approach involved the need to work on oneself mentally, emotionally, and physically—all at the same time. His teaching is called a Fourth Way School for that reason.

Gurdjieff described the human body as functioning like a three-story factory. The bottom two floors are physical processes which usually run on ordinary energy. The top floor, which represents higher mental and emotional processes, cannot operate on that fuel. It needs a more refined form (which I've been calling air/energy or buoyant energy). In addition, such third-story functions cannot operate in the presence of negative emotions.

Some activities (like writing a poem) are not inherently better than others (like scrubbing floors). The true value of any undertaking should be judged by whether or not it is done with conscious awareness, while awake. Gurdjieff's approach advocates *doing every activity consciously,* because when you do you're able to tap into even more of the high-octane energy.

The special fuel needed to operate the third-story activities can also be used for routine matters, to run the bottom two floors. But it does not work the other way around. That's why it is unwise to fritter away higher-octane air/energy on negative or mindless activities.

The physical body, being matter, can use either form of fuel, as do routine mental or emotional activities. But intense creativity, joy, and inspiration, which are third-story activities, operate with the enhanced energy only. Increased access to air provides that fuel.

As an added bonus, your efforts to live fully awake generate even more of the vital energy. So staying "up" and awake can become self-sustaining.

Increase your energetic level:
- Discard or ignore low-energy activities and relationships—those which leave you drained or empty
- Notice what *increases* your energy level, your sense of wellbeing, and happiness—seek out more of it whenever possible
- Notice what *decreases* your energy level, your sense of wellbeing, and happiness—avoid it whenever possible
- Seek out high-energy mentors, peers, thinkers (as in reading inspiring books); spend more time with them
- Act with kindness and caring at every opportunity so can both/all enjoy shared air/energy—while creating more of it
- Take time for appreciation, gratitude, and lighthearted fun

The saved energy can be devoted to big problems and challenges, or used to spark fresh ideas.

Binkles Really Feel Good

Binkle—*the energy created when you really connect with someone or something which inspires you (even yourself). It's a zizz!—the smallest bit of upbeat energy which you can sense or share with another person.*

Every binkle is a small pocket of air. Said the other way around, in every pocket of air it's possible to find a binkle. Binkles are a measure of the energy itself, varying from teeny to massive.

A binkle delivers a zizz of highly-charged energy. Some are mildly-pleasant ripples and others are head-to-toe zaps. Repeated binkles can build on each other in a delightful way. How or why it happened is secondary to the sensation and the energy surge. A view which "takes your breath away" or sensing something real and abiding can be sensed as "high binkle" because of the resulting feelings.

I conceived and coined the word "binkle" in 1992. "Binkle" can be a noun or a verb. I consider it the fuel of your creative impulses—as well as the reward for them. Its impact on your state of mind is immediate. You can, on occasion, feel energetic surges without having a clue as to why. But there is a feeling of "just right" about it. That sensation is either present, or it isn't, when something happens. Its presence cannot be faked.

The binkle is a measure of high-octane, lift-off energy—much like a watt or an ohm. Rather than its intensity being registered by an electronic device, *you sense it with your body*. Every binkle is actually a jolt of higher-than-normal energy which can be experienced by the cells. You feel its presence and intensity—from mildly pleasant to electrifying and world shaking.

Notice *a binkle is the energy that is experienced*—not the reason the binkle happened or the situation in which it occurred. Binkles are not the thoughts you have about how you feel. They are not about whether or not you like something. Binkles are no more complicated than *feeling* the sensation itself—the rush of buoyant energy.

When you say something touches you deeply, that's a sign of binkle energy. If you reflect back on your happiest times, you will probably recall that special sensation was present.

Binkles are exactly the same energy which fuels creativity and peak experiences. They are exactly the same energy that fills your heart with joy, or wonder or, dare I say—love. Each is brief, but the sensations can build on each other and grow in intensity. They are the energy of *feeling alive and happy* inside.

Look for them, from the leap of your heart when you sense one, to the residual afterglow of "life is good." Binkles are sensed as bright spots sprinkled through your everyday life—each a "now moment" being felt energetically.

If you question the need for a separate word for this special energy, ask yourself: when you have had a surge of uplifting energy or special moments, didn't you give credit to the circumstances or the other people present? You attributed such a feeling to what occurred, while ignoring the energy responsible for it all.

You treat specific circumstances when the energy was strongest as though each cause is different, rather than noting the presence of *the very same energy* in each case.

It is not your mind which recognizes binkles, or even your emotions, but *your whole self*. Each binkle experience provides a brief moment of sensing yourself altogether whole—with nothing lacking. Binkles are not about reconciling all parts of yourself or of getting them back together. When high-octane energy is felt intensely, you somehow *know yourself to be whole and complete already*.

Binkles start your creative juices flowing and provide a reminder that what you really care about the most *is* important. Vitally important. So even though the word "binkle" may be new, you are already sensitized to what "rings your bell" when you feel it.

Even the youngest child is a master at binkles. It is the fuel children run on, the spark lighting their enthusiastic faces. It is only as we grow older that it seems to be shoved into a smaller portion of our everyday existence. It thrives on high-octane air, so it's possible to get that joy of life back, no matter what your age.

> Note: I wrote a young-adult fantasy about the power of binkles, with gnomes, magic, and the battle of good versus evil in *The Binkle and the Catawampus Compass*, © 2007.

Binkle, Krindle, and Laphe Work Together

To the concept of binkles, add two related notions: krindle and laphe (also coined by me).

Monitoring your upbeat energy:
- Binkle – the *energy* which is felt; the zizz, a moment of sensed perfection
- Krindle – the *meter* or battery which detects and holds the special energy, located within the physical body
- Laphe – (pronounced, "laugh") the sense of being full of binkles; acts as a balanced feeling which is centered within

Krindle—It has long been apparent to me that humans have a specialized gauge attuned to the availability of binkle energy located within our bodies. However, medical science has failed to detect the specific organ function. The krindle is a binkle energy meter and short-term battery.

It detects signs of available binkle energy in your surroundings, rather like a Geiger counter registers radiation. If a person remains binkle depleted for too long, the krindle ceases to function—hence, no binkles.

Laphe—It acts as a self-adjusting shock absorber attuned to binkle energy. It keeps your upbeat energy level on an even keel. Laphe resembles the bubble in a level, indicating whether a person's energy is balanced—"on the level" *or* "off kilter." When your air/energy is high and without stress, you feel a sense of fullness and happiness.

When you are properly aligned with respect to air/energy, there is a sense of being centered and very responsive to energetic changes in your circumstances. To engage life with a laphe approach, first detach from the specific situations, but hold an attentive place within yourself, where you are ready to respond to shifts in the energetic flow.

As you allow the binkle, krindle, and laphe to be engaged in response to whatever is happening, you flow with the energetic currents which eddy around you.

Adopt the Binkle Standard. Forget about your "To Do" list or your "what I always do" approach. Instead, gauge how your day went by using a different yardstick.

The Binkle Standard:
- Spend more time and attention with people or activities which give you binkles
- Spend less time and attention with people or activities which drain your binkle energy away
- Pass them around! Leave a trail of binkle energy wherever you go
- Pause to enjoy how good it makes you feel

Binkles Make You Look Radiant

When my son Ross was a sophomore in college, he took a semester off so he could compete in chess tournaments. That's when he took a job with a large national company as a school photographer for local middle and high schools. We lived in a large enough city it took many photographers to cover them all.

Photographers all received the same training to take pictures the way the company wanted. They all followed the same procedures and used the same company-issued equipment.

You know the drill: on the appointed day, each class lines up to get their individual pictures taken. And person by person, once they smile for the camera the students return to class. About two weeks later students get their proofs so they can order packages of prints. Those who don't like their proofs sit for retakes, to see if they'll get something better than the first time. It's a time-tested process which has gone on for years.

One day, I had to pick Ross up at the company office at the end of the day. While I was waiting for him, I got talking with the lady who handled all the school bookings. She told me what a good worker Ross was and how they considered him their star photographer. But she was also quite perplexed. I could tell there'd been a lot of discussions about him by those on the staff.

"When we send Ross to a school, we never have any problems while he's there. He gets the pictures taken. But we can't figure out what he's doing. Wherever Ross takes pictures, *we don't get hardly any retakes.*"

She was really wondering what Ross was doing different than the rest of the photographers. Not having a certain percentage of retakes (dissatisfied buyers) did not seem possible. Yet Ross was doing it consistently.

I was pleased to hear that, but I was not at all surprised. I knew exactly what Ross was doing because he had told me after he'd been working there several weeks. But there was no way I could explain his method to her. Even if I could, there was no way my telling her could change the training so all their company photographers would do what Ross did.

This happened not long after I discovered the binkle, and Ross was a natural-born binkler. He's a pretty cordial guy, who's open and knows how to connect. People respond to his warmth and sincerity—it's nearly impossible to resist. Ross had said to me:

"I like taking class pictures, but keeping up the pace is hard. You only get less than a minute per student, and most of that is spent getting them positioned and ready. Then I talk to them a bit in order to get them relaxed. I don't take a person's picture until I can get them to binkle. But once they binkle, I get a great shot."

Ross had been photographing people binkling with him. That's what added a warmth and depth to their appearance, and the camera caught it. No wonder students liked the way they looked once their proofs came back. No wonder they didn't want retakes. And apparently that held over the thousands of pictures he took.

Ross was watching for, and captured, the precise moment when the person was suffused with that special energy. So apparently, not only do you feel a binkle, Ross proved it shows on your face too.

Chapter 8
Finding Ample Air Throughout Your Day

Freedom Is Relative

The desire to be free motivates people to try new things and to go in different directions. Freedom allows you to create whatever you can desire and imagine without undue influence by constricting circumstances or other people.

Being free implies an orientation: *free from* or *free to*—away from something or toward something else. Which is carrot? Which is stick? In motivational terms, they're the *push* away from something unwanted, or the *pull* toward what is desired.

Stephen Covey said, "People who exercise their embryonic freedom day after day, little by little, expand that freedom. People who do not will find that it withers until they are literally being lived. They are acting out scripts written by parents, associates, and society."

Your current commitments limit the degree of freedom you can exercise when making subsequent choices. Hanging on to too much personal baggage restricts your options too. Whether it is mental stuff or physical stuff which holds you back, the effect is the same.

Becoming more emotionally aware involves learning about the constructive use of freedom. You find more ways to use it wisely and to invest your efforts judiciously. Choosing without restrictions is not just about selecting from the current possibilities you're aware of. Those are limited by your prior decisions which block taking advantage of something unprecedented. (See BonBon, Ligatures of Devotion, Chapter 6.)

> Being enslaved by the exigencies of life and by our constitution does not preclude the possibility that we can *feel* free. We experience freedom when we choose a path that provides us both meaning and pleasure. Whether or not our subjective experience of work is of freedom depends on whether we choose to be slaves to material wealth or to emotional prosperity, slaves to others' expectations or to our passions.[19]

---

[19]Ben-Shahar, Tal, *Happier, Learn the secrets to daily joy and lasting fulfillment* (New York, McGraw Hill, 2007), 98.

You can also think about freedom in terms of *what it makes possible*. What doors will be opened to you which would otherwise remain blocked by circumstances or what other people want from you? Harriet Rubin said, "Freedom is actually a bigger game than power. Power is about what you can control. Freedom is about what you can unleash."

Freedom *From* Conformity

Freedom really is not free. Nor does it come without strings attached. It comes with responsibilities, even though the popular perception treats freedom as an escape from them.

Rather it offers an *opportunity to choose something different,* something you might be quite willing to commit to. Sometimes it takes you off the beaten track, where most social conventions do not apply. But for many people freedom is not so all-consuming. Yet it can be found in small gestures of great personal value or through their pockets of air (Chapter 13).

Conformity always comes at the expense of greater diversity or originality. People differ greatly as to how much conformity or control they're willing to tolerate, and at what personal cost. Being able to take advantage of what freedom offers requires considerable self-knowledge and courage. As Epictetus (himself a former slave) said two thousand years ago, "No man is free who is not a master of himself."

But the truest measure of your freedom is found not in the large choices but in the small ones. This exercise of freedom is solitary. This exercise of freedom is conducted in split seconds, heralded by no one.

Every moment and event invites you to act. Your choices are between your habitual reactions and something else which is not so constrained. If that opportunity to do something—anything—differently is not seized, the familiar reaction will prevail.

Victor Frankl said: "Between stimulus and response, there is a space. In that space lies our freedom and our power to choose our response. In our response lies our growth and our happiness." Your conscious self is poised to jump into that small space. But the opportunity is lost unless you choose it over what you'd do through habit or inattention. *That's where the air is.*

Democracy Through Action
A BonBon

We don't just vote at the ballot box. We vote in our daily lives as citizens—for those causes and concerns we believe in and against those things of which we disapprove.

We vote with our time—whether we invest it in cultural or civic activities, or in the movies and TV programs we watch.

We vote with our money—with regard to which products and charities get to receive our patronage.

We vote with our kind and supporting words—to a young person making an effort to learn, to an old person making an effort to stay involved.

We vote with our behavior—whether we drive with safety and with courtesy, or whether we are wasteful.

What happens at the polls or through government affects us a lot less than the frequent votes each one of us gets to cast every day. Make your votes count.

Choose the activities which give you pleasure. Cast your ballot for beneficence in your world.

See yourself as a citizen of the universe and vote for its survival and betterment with every choice and every activity. In this way democracy becomes a living force, with you choosing the world you want to live in. You have the power to improve whatever you touch, so why not vote for it?

© 2014, Faith Lynella, from *BonBons to Sweeten Your Daily Life* or *More BonBons and Treats*   http://faithlynella.com

Saga of the Sorry Seal

Woe is me

I'm so sorry. I really hate to interrupt your reading. But I feel the need to share my tale of woe. Maybe I can be a bad example you can learn from.

It wasn't so long ago that I didn't have a care in the world—swimming, eating, basking in the sun. But then I started to think that something was missing in my life.

Is this enough? Am I happy or just stuck in my ways? Believe me, that was not smart. Because the next thing I knew, I wasn't happy or carefree anymore.

My advice to you is: Find the times and places which bring you joy and satisfaction. Then enjoy the heck out of them! Never, never doubt them or criticize them. Don't dream of something you'd like better.

Heed my warning or you'll end up like me. Because I didn't appreciate what I had, the satisfaction I took for granted all went away.

A Lifelong Riddle

I believe everybody is born with the same deep questions about life and meaning: Why am I here? What is real? Is there something more to life? And we each have precisely one lifetime to arrive at answers which we consider satisfactory. However, it's also possible to ignore them entirely. But it's hard to get a sense of purpose that way.

Finding your own answers to the big questions adds a measure of meaning which is yours alone. Grounding your answer in "who I am" and in what you do *is* your life's work. It is as simple as that.

Finding answers for yourself:
- How many aspects of yourself can you discover, claim, and encourage to bloom before you die? (self-knowledge and self-acceptance)
- How many parts of yourself can you use in ways which *reinforce* each other? (making the combination stronger and more effective)
- What can you make or contribute of lasting value?

Looking for those answers delivers something that's true for you, and increasingly relevant along the way. And your discoveries needn't be complete or "pretty" for them to still prove useful. Bear in mind certain fruits will not ripen for a long time. Wisdom and self-mastery come from a vantage point that is the work of a lifetime.

Self-knowledge requires you to assimilate many different aspects of "who I am." Little insights now and then begin to add up to a glimmer of something important. And once they're unearthed, those gains in self-awareness are never lost. First the long-ignored parts of yourself are found, then they're embraced, then integrated, so all of them can participate in the open.

Finding Air in Public Places

We have a right to expect non-toxic air in the places where we work, shop, or amuse ourselves. When we must leave your safe sanctuaries (Chapter 4), we need to be even more sensitive to whether where we go to is air-rich, air-depleted, or so-so (neutral).

The quality of its air/energy is probably what makes a specific place or enterprise attractive to its clientele. The best of them serve as an air oasis—as well as a watering hole. But toxic watering holes exist too (Chapter 9).

On some deep-seated level, each of us seeks out groups, organizations, and watering holes which match the level of air/energy we're accustomed to—just like the other people who go there do. So most places you frequent perpetuate your current energy level, rather than raising it. The test of a particular place's safety for you is whether you leave feeling more recharged or drained (at least most of the time).

Each person has to find a way to deal with insufficient air at work, with their families and close associates, and in the way they're treated by the places they spend their money. But until now, the lack of healthy air in many public places has been treated as non-optional. It was take or leave it. No more.

The distrust of government and our social institutions to help us live better lives has gotten so bad we no longer expect salvation from that quarter. Most institutions do not comprehend air/energy or the human needs which rely on it. Solutions to widespread energy pollution must come from elsewhere—from us.

Undesirable conditions in the public arena are not likely to change as long as they're treated as something which cannot be fixed. But even entrenched ideas we live with collectively can yield when the common perception is challenged.

As an example, America went from us thinking drunk-driving deaths were something we could do nothing about *to* them no longer being tolerated after Mothers Against Drunk Driving took a stand.

They changed what we as a society will stomach. And the change happened rather quickly because their movement gave voice to what we already want—and have a right to expect. Driving drunk is no longer acceptable or condoned. Yes, some continues, but on a much smaller scale—and without the wink of inevitability.

We don't need to live with as much toxic air as we do, either. There still is a necessity for personal doggedness as we fight our individual battles to get what we need. But each of us can and should do more to demand pockets of air, positive energy, and personal respect as fundamental rights. Since we all bear the price of doing without, we should cheer on those seeking more air publicly.

We also need to stand up collectively to insist on changes when existing low-energy policies and practices are deemed no longer acceptable. Our politicians have failed us. Corporate America has failed us and added insult to injury with their customer-unfriendly practices.

Don't let those in authority get away with it. Speak out. Vote for more air. And vote with your money, patronage, and complaints too.

Air in the Workplace

In former times, going to work involved hard labor. By the end of the day, workers were physically tired. Work was hard on the body, but not particularly hard on the mind or emotions. There are fewer jobs like those anymore. Machines have taken on most of the tasks which required so much physical exertion.

Today's place of work appears to be more humane, less strenuous. Most people work at desks, in comfortable stores and offices, with computers, and for fewer hours. A day's work is not so hard on the body, but common workplace pressures take a much higher toll on the emotions and mind. Working conditions are often stressful because there's so little air to be found there.

Air is not a luxury. It is not something that's "nice to have" but less important than "paying the bills," making a living, or fulfilling your daily obligations. For you to deliver your best efforts, there needs to be some air/energy available for you when working. Being paid with dollars alone is not sufficient compensation because money, in itself, is not life sustaining.

In our jobs and careers, we always assumed we'd get paid. But we never, ever, ever, expected what we do for a living would be at the expense of being able to breathe sufficiently while doing so. As it is, most of the time away from work is needed just to shore up the energetic damage from being there—just to go back to work the next day.

Receiving money that lacks any air/energy (let alone if it's toxic to boot) is a bad bargain. It has the marks of involuntary servitude. No wonder so many workplaces are toxic environments and employees hate their jobs. Hint: Healthy working environments have something to do with workers being respected since unrelieved disrespect is a form of toxic air.

If you're spending half your waking hours doing something, shouldn't it be something you enjoy doing? The people who are the best at what they do tend to be the ones who love doing it—they derive considerable air from it. There's a big difference when a person is excited to show up at work. And they do a better job, too.

Whether the causes of low energy in the workplace are due to unrealistic time pressures, inhumane policies, the specific organizational culture, or particular individuals exploiting those around them, this form of systemic abuse can no longer be considered the norm.

Most people have accepted that spending their workday in oxygen-deprived environments is part of the job. Or doing soul-deadening work is the price which must be endured for a salary. We've accepted we must be around low-energy people (even within one's family) who keep us emotionally drained and energy-depleted.

Nobody wants to live like that. It's not what we want and we have to insist upon a say in making it stop. Such a low-air reality is part of an unsustainable *status quo*. It's time to stand up for air-rich working conditions. We need a fresh approach—one that supplies fresh air.

But nothing will improve unless individuals start to recognize pervasive oxygen-deprivation is no longer going to be tolerated. And they must feel strongly enough to make a stink.

By contrast, work we enjoy doing has the ability to energize us. As President Theodore Roosevelt said, "Far and away the best prize that life offers is the chance to work hard at work worth doing." So it's not the work which is soul-deadening, but the lack of air and energy to be found from doing it.

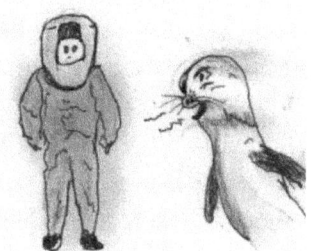

Take Precautions

Consider some form of psychic protective gear when you must enter toxic situations—even if the form it takes is only in your imagination. Prepare yourself by donning a deep sea diving suit before going under the waves. A hazmat suit which shields you from hazardous materials works too.

You might not be able to find air in the specific job itself. But it's still possible to encounter little pockets of satisfaction in that environment from a job well done (up to superior standards, even when it's not required) or with coworkers. Find puffs here and there. Or don protective gear and seek out more ways to detoxify. Listen to your canary.

Maximizing Your Air Supply

You need upbeat energy to function—not barely, not on auto-pilot, but with a happy and buoyant outlook. There are plenty of ways to reduce the stresses which inhibit your air availability. Some approaches rely on psychological or meditative practices. I'm all for them, but the approach taken here does not showcase any particular technique.

Break free of the downward drag of air-deprivation. You can acquire plenty of air just by paying attention and treating your life as the backdrop of a Find the Air Treasure Hunt. Pause to breathe deeply and slowly when things get tough.

The most important change that's needed is to your mindset—by *actively* paying attention to what comes into your life and to make decisions on the basis of how well they support your air needs. Doing so in turn strengthens your ability to attain the whole range of your desires.

While the approach taken here does not depend on particular practices, there are time-tested ways to expand your air and energy perceptions. They work to quiet the emotions and mind, not simply the body.

Practices which maximize your air supply:
- Mindfulness
- Breathing and deep breathing techniques
- Meditation and relaxation techniques
- Yoga and similar mind-body practices
- Self-hypnosis
- Physical exercise
- Time management or anger management techniques
- Stress reduction strategies
- Prayer and forgiveness

Any of these (and others) provide embellishment of the finer points of relaxed breathing. They're helpful, even pleasant, but what makes them effective is changing your habitual reactions. Such approaches may be worth pursuing, but you don't need any of them to reap the benefits derived from having much more air.

While not endorsing any particular practice, it's up to you to make the call about whether any of them is for you. One might be perfect for your lifestyle, while others might not be helpful at all. Any program which you rely on to energize yourself needs to pass the test: There's air there! And you are the sole decider or judge of that. Bottom line—you know something works because it allows you to breathe free, or freer.

In Harmony with Natural Rhythms

We are all responsive to many kinds of rhythms, most of which we have no conscious awareness about. Some are attuned to the cycles in nature, like the daily 24 hours, or the yearly 360 days, or the pull of the tides, or the phases of physical maturity. Many cycles are tied to the rhythmic nature of your own body, whether it be digestion, new cell growth, or the influence of hormones.

Your in-breath and out-breath, coupled with the th-thump of your heartbeat, are smaller and individual versions of such larger patterns of nature. They are aligned to some extent with innumerable pulsations and rhythms which echo back to those larger harmonies of all creation.

Some would say we are aligned to the "breathing of the cosmos." The heart and lungs are situated next to each other, reinforcing the interdependence between the breath and the beating of the heart as they transmit oxygen to your body. You can sense such a connection when you flow along harmoniously with it. Your heart, mind, and body are likewise responsive to larger patterns at work.

The heart's perspective is expansive by design, tending toward the largest, most inclusive, scope possible (feminine, yin energy). Whereas the rational mind is more reductive and analytical as it narrows focus in order to act (masculine, yang energy). And the flesh keeps it grounded in the material world.

The tension between them provides the fullness—which collapses if their complementary tension cannot be maintained. The interplay of these expansive and contractive forces plays out in the act of being alive.

Each of us customarily prefers one of the three modes over the others: action (physical), ideas (mental), or emotions (feeling). However, modern culture is severely biased in favor of the rational perspective and has rigged the reward system in that direction. Yet grounding your best efforts requires that each and all of the modes be brought into concrete expression.

The "make it happen" phase of an undertaking puts a premium on the smooth interaction of all three. A sincere heart tempers the drift toward unbridled practicality and furthers the "innocence of perception" which permits you to stay creative, and fresh.

Tensions among the mental, physical, and emotional components of your nature sustain a dynamic balance—the dance of active give-and-take which prevents you from settling into an overconfident rut. That's what keeps you vibrant in your way of responding to life.

It is worth noting you are likely to give yourself credit for being logical and in control, even when the larger rhythms or emotional influences are determining what you choose. Rational behavior may be more of a figment than a reality in determining what you do. Mental prowess is needed, true, but as a team player. It's not calling the shots.

We Collaborate in Our Becoming

Although you participate in larger rhythms, you are not merely a bystander, relegated to doing as you're told in the larger scheme of things. The particular roles you play are vital and ongoing. Their combination determines the degree of passion you bring to the part. You're building your moral fiber through the decisions and actions you make.

In the process, you alter the world in which you live. That's not just shaping your own individual sphere of influence, but it has an impact on the public sphere as well. Time will tell the value of your contribution. But there is no doubt you're changing yourself and the future by the manner in which you do what you do.

Hark... Who Speaks There?
A BonBon

A while back, when my daughter, Jessica, was a teenager she applied for a job. The owner of the business was outspokenly bigoted and disparaging to women. Jessica was torn between wanting the job and fearing the daily indignities she could expect if hired. She asked me: "Should I take the job?" Here's what I told her.

You have to decide for yourself, and it's up to you to understand why you made that choice. You can take the job for the right reasons or for the wrong reasons. You can decide not to take the job for the right reasons or for the wrong reasons. WHAT you decide is less important than knowing the REASONS for your decision.

Some voice within you (some part of yourself) will become stronger and you will start trusting it more. Other voices within you (parts of yourself) will become weaker and less able to influence your decisions. The choice of which voices you decide to listen to within yourself will build your character and influence each choice to come.

Start noticing what parts of yourself become stronger each time a choice is made. That awareness will make you potent.

By the way, she didn't take the job, but the process she went through continues to influence her daily.

© 2014, Faith Lynella, from *BonBons to Sweeten Your Daily Life* or *More BonBons and Treats*   http://faithlynella.com

Don't Be Fooled by Counterfeit Air

Counterfeit money isn't worth anything. It looks like the real thing at the time. You accept it at face value, as though it is worth having. Later you find out otherwise. You lose twice from counterfeit money, or from counterfeit air. There's a financial loss, followed by the emotional letdown of being fooled and cheated.

Counterfeit air can be a serious problem in relationships. Healthy relationships openly exchange energy—the give-and-take engendered by communication and trust. When a person finds out the other person was not sincere in what they said, did, or promised, it's not any different than being paid in counterfeit money. You did your part, without getting a comparable (agreed upon) return.

If being short-changed happens in a casual exchange, there's probably no serious harm done. You just keep the person at arm's length thereafter, and you keep your guard up a bit more. But when it happens with someone you trust, someone in your inner circle of close intimates, the effect can be devastating. The loss hits you so deeply because it's a form of counterfeit love.

Some kinds of goals and desires can pull a person toward counterfeit air. The attraction of greed, fame, lust, envy, and power over others are temptations of the material world. Don't fall for their showy promises, for what they provide is not solid or enduring. They provide counterfeit rewards. Even if the thing desired seems to deliver as you hoped in the short term, what you gain from it isn't worth much. And it pollutes your existing air supply.

Money is especially tricky because all of us have so many of our hopes and dreams, as well as past successes, wrapped up in it. But as a way to be happy it leave a lot to be desired (Chapter 16).

The more money we have, the more we get used to it, and the more we want... first we fail to enjoy our wealth as much as we ought to. Second, our craving to purchase and possess in ever-greater quantities in order to achieve the same level of pleasure can put us on the path to runaway materialism and acquisitiveness, such that more and more money is spent and less and less happiness is derived from it.[20]

Spot the Hidden Motivations

In situations where there's no air to be found, check into the unacknowledged motivations behind the behavior of those around you. When something (or someone) isn't what/who it pretends to be, you're being manipulated on some level. Figure it out. Trust your discernment to spot the tell-tale clues of insufficient air.

Then work backwards to see what's causing it. Can the superficial appearance of the scene, or the players, be trusted? Or is there a secret motivation in play you're not supposed to know about?

Consider money, power, and self-interest as equivalent for purposes of this exploration. Watch for the double-dealing clues which appear in the particular situation—if they're present. Following the money or power reveals the other party's real priorities and anticipated rewards. It has a way of getting down to noticing what "smells fishy."

When taking a closer look, also notice whether people are depriving you of your energy (you're being vampired). If so, is it being done intentionally or unintentionally? To what extent are they sucking you dry or manipulating you for their own advantage? Watch out for being bamboozled and vamped because they're even more insidious and common than being robbed in other ways.

---

[20]Lyumbomirsky, Sonja, *The Myths of Happiness: What should make you happy, but doesn't: What shouldn't make you happy, but does* (New York: The Penguin Press, 2013), 170.

Fear Wastes Air and Energy

Your energy level reflects your emotional and vibrational level. Fear, in any of its various forms, represents a very low vibration rate. And it reduces the energetic state of whatever it touches. More things to be scared of (and there seems to be no end to them) can push you even lower. You don't function well with negative emotions because they're air-bereft.

An ironic side effect of living defensively is that it seldom makes you safer. Being fearful squeezes the air out of you, leaving you gasping, unable to feel happy or renewed for long. Anger and fear feed a downward spiral which costs you not only peace of mind, but maybe even your mental and/or physical health.

> Unfortunately the mind, in its anxiety for us, tries to make plans for a huge number of possible futures, most of which will never arrive. This constant leapfrogging into the future is a waste of our mental and emotional energy. The most important way we can prepare for the unknown-to-come is to make a reasonable plan and the to pay attention to what is happening right now. Then we can greet what flows toward us with a clear, flexible mind and an open heart, ready and able to modify our plan according to the reality of the moment.[21]

How you respond to what scares us is seldom examined—but the solution can start there. It's not to be found in chasing after the scary stuff. Reacting as usual pushes your buttons in ways which muddy your thinking, so it's no longer to be trusted. Remember, you have other choices which can serve you better—as long as you stay open to them.

STOP – just breathe. Do nothing for a moment. Such a drawn-out pause could be enough to break the chain of inevitability leading to a bad outcome. It disrupts the act-react pattern which usually ensues. You've altered the timing, and in so doing gained a moment of freedom. (See BonBon, Haven't Got the Tim*ing*, Chapter 10)

---

[21] Bays, Jan Chozen, How to Train a Wild Elephant: And other adventures in mindfulness (Boston, Shambhala, 2011), 7.

Lurking, Lurking, Lurking
A BonBon

Lurking, lurking, lurking in the murky murky depths, below the surface, just out of sight is a gnawing, groaning sense of unease. In the dark of the night, when all else is quiet, you barely hear them moaning: "Ooooh... Ooooh..." "What about the bills?" "Ooooh... Ooooh..." "There's nothing you can do about your boss, kids, future, etc." "Ooooh... Ooooh..." Such gnawing refrains flit through your mind, constricting your heart, paralyzing your confidence.

You're being visited by your own subterranean monsters. "Ooooh..."

They are real, sort of, at home in your deep dark recesses, out of your sight, but not out of your mind.

But they cannot survive in the light. Shine some light, some focused attention in there and they are seen to be as concrete as shadows. Their power depends on them staying unclear, barely articulated.

Don't avoid them; that's what keeps them functioning, instilling fear. Confront them. Demand they speak up— state their case, make the fears explicit. Put the spotlight on what they say. They probably are not valid concerns (if they are, by all means deal with them). More likely, they are only immature, not-quite-rational notions.

Say, "Thank you, I hear what you say and will consider your input. Let me handle it, I know what to do."

Once you've heard them, you've been liberated. They lose their power over you. There is nothing further they can do to you. If they come back, say it again, as often as necessary. You REALLY are more potent than your fears, once you see them in the light.

© 2014, Faith Lynella, from *BonBons to Sweeten Your Daily Life* or *More BonBons and Treats*   http://faithlynella.com

AIR AND ENERGY SURVIVAL KIT

- Find something enjoyable—revel in it
- Make something gratifying happen which lifts your spirits
- Breathe long, deep, and slow—as you stop everything else you're thinking or doing
- Unplug and recharge at the same time
- Find a binkle—the energy created when we really connect
- Feel grateful

Chapter 9
Stress is Suffercating

Toxic Thinking Requires House Cleaning

What are you filling your mind with? How much of your thinking is consumed by doubts, worries, anger, and fears? Is it spinning out gossip and discontent? Is it escaping to a fantasy world or wishing for expensive toys and possessions? Is it daydreaming about how things could be—or should have been?

There's very little oxygen to be found in any of that. When such low-energy concerns fill our thoughts, there's not much place for uplifting ideas to roost.

> When our brains get stuck in a pattern that focuses on stress, negativity, and failure we set ourselves up to fail. [We can] retrain our brains to spot patterns of possibility, so we can see—and seize—opportunity wherever we look. In the midst of defeat, stress, and crisis, our brains map different paths to help us cope. [We can find] the mental path that not only leads us out of failure or suffering, but teaches us to be happier and more successful because of it.[22]

If you're feeling dissatisfied about with how things are going, open the windows of your heart and mind to let fresh breezes blow through. Becoming attuned to the discomfort from your unmet air needs can open you to opportunities that bring in fresh air.

---

[22] Achor, Shawn, *The Happiness Advantage: The seven principles of positive psychology that fuel success and performance at work* (New York, Crown Business, 2010), 17.

Start with the jam-packed, airless attic of your head. A vigorous spring cleaning pulls down the wispy cobwebs of things long gone, sweeping out the timeworn, cheerless psychic clutter. Look into the dark corners and move stuff around in there.

Dig out the emotional trophies which rekindle your spirit. Savor your favorite memories of pleasures gone by, tender friendships, and praiseworthy triumphs. Give them a place of attention and honor in your recollections, so they continue to enrich you often. Then jettison the junk.

~~~~~

Watch Out for DIS
A BonBon

Feeling a little disappointed about how things are going, a little disapproval about the way the kids do their chores, some discontent about the situation at work? Gee, it's been tough, just one thing after another, with no end in sight. You can change them *all at once*. These aren't problems, you see—they're mind-sets. And you already have the power to eliminate them any time you choose—Instantly!

First notice what's going on—these are "DIS" words; they start with d-i-s. There are many of them: *dis*agreement, *dis*aster, *dis*cord, *dis*comfort, *dis*couragement, *dis*ease, *dis*may, *dis*grace, *dis*dain, *dis*pute, and on and on. Using such words signals that you are in the DIS place. It is impossible to see accurately while you're there.

You've heard of "rose-colored glasses," which make the wearer see everything as rosy (in glowing terms, too beautiful). In the DIS place you wear brown-colored glasses. Everything looks brown (or muddy if you prefer). Quick! Take them off! They make the world seem awful (offal) and that's the opposite of awe-ful, where you are amazed and uplifted by what you see*.

Once you can see DIS you need to *dis*connect from it. Anything you do next is a step out of the *dis*heartening quagmire. Take a walk. Visit a friend (but don't talk about your complaints—or theirs). Enjoy your kids—or anyone else's. Wash your car (or do something physically demanding). Go out for a sundae. Change *what* you're doing, *how* you're doing it, and *with whom* you're doing it.

Quickly *dis*engage; *dis*tract yourself. Change your mind as quickly as you change TV channels. You'll like the new view better—honest. If you don't *dis*tance yourself from DIS, your life will be melancholy—or *dis*mal.

*This is an example of *frivel*—inspired wordplay

© 2014, Faith Lynella, from *BonBons to Sweeten Your Daily Life* or *More BonBons and Treats*   http://faithlynella.com

How polluted your air supply is reflects how much of your attention is taken up with negative concerns relative to how much is taken up with positive ones. Does the polluted stuff occupy a sliver or a whole lot?

As your air dwindles, you suffercate. But negative environments are not just determined by their quantity, duration, or the percentage of bad air. They are also marked by their intensity and drama. They tend to overwhelm and drown out other ways of thinking. They can short you out, thereby wasting considerable life-sustaining air.

Saga of the Conflicted Seal

I don't happen to know
if I'm coming or going

Stop Expressing Negativity

Negative thoughts and speech can so easily poison your air supply. Think twice before flinging bitter words (or instead deciding to hold your tongue). But negative consequences seldom stop there. Mean words hurt feelings and undermine trust—sometimes past repair.

These are small leaks in the plumbing sense, but they can cause serious adverse outcomes when unrestrained. Sad to say, expressing negativity saps your capacity to be happy—while inflicting pain on anyone who hears it.

All inner resistance is experienced as negativity in one form or another. All negativity is resistance. In this context, the two words are almost synonymous. Eckhart Tolle describes why negativity doesn't serve you well in *The Power of Now*,

> Negativity ranges from irritation or impatience to fierce anger, from a depressed mood or sullen resentment to suicidal despair. Sometimes the resistance triggers the emotional pain body… The ego believes that through negativity it can manipulate reality and get what it wants…. The fact is, of course, that negativity does not work. Instead of attracting a desirable condition, it stops it from arising. Instead of dissolving an undesirable one, it keeps it in place.[23]

Situations where expressing negative thoughts are prevalent act as low-air environments that pull everyone down. They cannot sustain you, so you need sufficient high-air sources or relationships in your life to counteract their draining influence. Whatever safe havens you have deserve more of your involvement than the toxic ones do.

Negative communication which seem so ordinary:
- Gossiping and criticizing others
- Complaining
- Bitching
- Blaming and bullying
- Whining and being vociferously resentful
- Lying and deceiving—by word or omission
- Cursing and swearing—it's not the words which do the damage as much as their tone
- Threatening and intimidating

---

[23]Tolle, Eckhart, *The Power of Now: A guide to spiritual enlightenment* (Notato, CA: New World Library, 1999)

The most destructive kind of negative speech of all is what you say to yourself—because you come to believe its eagerness and give it weight. Unrelieved self-criticism leads to feeling unworthy. Most of us are nice enough people that you'd never say such terrible things to someone's face. But you somehow feel it's O.K. to belittle yourself.

In fact, you feel virtuous to point out your flaws—avidly and repeatedly. It's as though pointing a finger at them distances you from being *that* person. Stop it! It's not accurate; it's not helpful; it's unkind, and it makes a big hole in your air supply. A crucial aspect of becoming air-savvy is replacing negative self-talk with a more loving and supportive way of relating to yourself.

Another variety of negative self-talk takes the form of regrets. They tie you to the past, as they suck the air out of today. As Katherine Mansfield said, "Regret is an appalling waste of energy; you can't build on it; it's only good for wallowing in."

Being kind to yourself pays off with major gains in your energy level. Even better, the steady drain which self-reproach inflicts on your tender psyche winds down. It's replaced by a more accurate and endearing sense of liking yourself.

Sidestep Odious People

Don't Get Energy Vampired

Your life force is precious and you suffercate when it gets too low. So watch out for situations and people willing to suck you dry. They are energy vampires. Their motivations may differ, but whether the drain is large or small, they are dangerous to you.

Pay particular attention to the boundaries you maintain with the people around you. We like to speak freely and wouldn't want an easy give-and-take to be compromised by putting up walls unnecessarily. But you don't want to live defensively either, even though it might be essential to reduce excessive energy drains which can occur in social situations.

Sometimes, in close relationships you've allowed someone to take considerable energy from you for their needs. You were glad to do so—it was the considerate thing to do. While it probably started from a generous and supportive impulse, such a flow cannot be maintained indefinitely. Nor can such an imbalance be the basis of a healthy relationship.

There are two problems—the energy flow is one way, instead of it being a mutual give and take. Second, one party is left drained—repeatedly and as a matter of right by the other. If that's a regular occurrence with anyone who is close to you, it's time to reassert your boundaries or you'll never regain control of your energy supply.

In particular, protect yourself from those prepared to suck your energy away without restraint. Their neediness acts almost like a black hole since you couldn't ever give them all they want. Keep your guard up. Set limits. Start by getting on your own side and recognize your own needs. Send clear signals about how far you will go.

Just to be clear, it's you who must change if you want excessive air/energy demands on you to stop. People who take too much are not likely to cut back willingly, even with warnings. They feel they have some claim on you, so any adjustments would have to come from you drawing the line.

Feeling Stressed Is Evidence of Energy Depletion

There is no question the world you live in is stressful and the pace is non-stop. That is *unless* you cultivate effective ways to deal with it. You gain a measure of protection when your air reserves are on "full." Many of life's problems will bounce off like water on a duck's back. You'll notice them, but your coping capacity can handle it.

Chronic stress reduces your coping capacity—especially if it is prolonged and occurs without interludes of relief. It leads to living in a narrower and narrower band of possibilities. It lacks the healing balm of hope for better things to come. Plumbing and electrical repairs are needed (Chapter 7) since the energy which does come can't be held long enough to escape the downward pull.

Stress acts like a war of attrition—it wears you down. Stress inflicts small dings to your confidence and judgment, which keep you off balance. Gradually you get careless, make poor choices, slip, and then it gets harder still. Stressful circumstances create a war zone where you feel vulnerable with every step you take.

Your air reserves are vital to your protective scheme. Guard your air supply and ration it carefully. It's harder to get recharged when you're under fire and reserves dwindle. So pick your issues and battles prudently. Put the most important matters ahead of the rest. Be clear who your allies are—and how you all can support and replenish each other.

Being stressed and depressed reflect an interaction of low air influences. It ranges from having a bad day to pushing toward insanity. Psychological or mental illnesses which require more than an attitude adjustments, are beyond the scope of this book. But short of that, you can hold worries and the barbs of negativity at bay by cultivating air-rich experiences. It includes making meaningful choices which make you happy.

Martin Seligman, the chief proponent of the positive psychology movement, argues that being happy depends on pursuing *gratification* rather than simple pleasure. The important difference between them rests on you cultivating your individual strengths and virtues, from which you gain staying power. Although Seligman speaks of depression in *Authentic Happiness*, I think his words apply to even more benign influences which are pulling you in that direction.

> One of the major symptoms of depression is self-absorption. The depressed person thinks about how she feels a great deal, excessively so. Her low mood is not a fact of life, but is very salient to her. When she detects sadness, she ruminates about it, projecting it into the future and across all her activities, and this in turn increases her sadness….
>
> Gratification dispels self-absorption, and the more one has the flow that gratification produces, the less depressed one is… The pleasures come easily, and the gratifications (which result from the exercise of personal strengths) are hard-won. A determination to identify and develop these strengths is therefore the great buffer against depression.[24]

---

[24] Seligman, Martin E.P, *Authentic Happiness, Using the new positive psychology to realize your potential for lasting fulfillment* (New York: The Free Press, 2002), 118-9.

Keeping Stress at Bay

Those aggravating things which go wrong during the day, and keep you awake at night, have a cumulative effect on your brain's ability to remember and learn. Science has studied the consequences of stress on the brain. A chronic overreaction to stress overloads the brain with powerful hormones which are meant only for short-term duty in emergency situations.

What's called stress is really a complex of reactions and physiological processes which are hard-wired into our bodies. These are governed by brain structures and reflexes, which developed very early in mammalian evolution. Their activities have a direct and immediate effect on the brain, nervous system, and all organs of the body. The processes involved are much more substantial than mood swings or feeling crappy.

Your reaction to danger triggers the release of a variety of biochemicals which improve the odds of survival. The sympathetic nervous system *(SNS) turns on* the fight or flight response. When a danger finally passes or the perceived threat is over, the brain initiates a reverse course of action which releases a different combination of biochemicals. In contrast, the parasympathetic nervous system *(PNS) turns off the initial reaction* and triggers the relaxation response.

Both systems are attempting to arrive at a metabolic equilibrium between the stimulating and the tranquilizing chemical forces unleashed in your body. Getting stuck in a state of on-going internal imbalance has serious consequences for your brain cells.

Ideally, the complementary SNS and PNS systems can cooperate as needed. The two of them carefully maintain metabolic equilibrium by making adjustments whenever something disturbs this balance. However, all of this occurs at a reflexive level and without conscious control. Deep breathing and efforts to relax can help to bring them into balance.

The corresponding roles of the SNS and PSN are elaborated upon by Craig Lambert in *Harvard Magazine*.

Happiness activates the sympathetic nervous system (which activates the 'flight or fight' response) whereas joy stimulates the parasympathetic nervous system (controlling 'rest and digest' functions). 'We can laugh from either joy or happiness,' Vaillant said. 'We weep only from grief or joy.' Happiness displaces pain, but joy embraces it.[25]

An on-going state of internal imbalance results if either of the systems dominates the other without relief. It can cause serious problems for your brain, emotions, peace of mind, body functions, and overall health. If some of the stress hormones remain active in your brain for too long, it injures or kills cells in the hippocampus (in the limbic system and midbrain) which are needed for memory and learning.

Chronic over-secretion of stress hormones adversely affects vital brain functions, especially your memories. Too much can even prevent the brain from laying down new memories or prevent access to already existing ones. The interaction between those systems also influences your emotional responses in significant ways.

As you develop greater air-awareness, you can become better able to correspond to what your body requires and is experiencing overall. As the caretaker of your physical and emotional wellbeing, it is incumbent on you to make the kind of choices, and learn the kind of skills needed, to minimize the stressful influences you're exposed to.

Identify Your Danger Zones

Just as you identified your safe havens and recharge places (Chapter 4), you should also ascertain your places of greatest air vulnerability. You want to keep increasing the number and variety of your recharge places, while reducing the number of places and situations where you're vulnerable to drains. They you'll experience fewer leaks and less time immersed in them.

Being air-aware sensitizes you about where caution is warranted. Also factor in whether a particular drain is minor or massive, whether it is occasional or it gets you every time.

---

[25] Lambert, Craig, "The Science of Happiness," *Harvard Magazine*, Jan-Feb 2007.

There are two ways to look at where to apply corrective efforts. On the one hand, massive leaks do the most damage, but they are also likely to be harder to deal them. It could be too difficult to tackle them head on to begin with.

On the other hand, smaller leakages could be reduced or eliminated more easily. In that case, it's possible to steadily whittle down the range of risky places or situations one by one. Therefore, each gain builds on those before. And you're more capable of taking on the bigger, scarier ones. The important thing is to start taking immediate steps to repair your plumbing and wiring so they don't get worse.

Really dangerous situations (toxic air) should be avoided when possible. If there's no getting around it, approach it like a deep-sea diver going under the waves. Don protective emotional gear and limit the duration of exposure to it. Deal with it (or them) cautiously and from a distance.

Keep your guard up:
- Recognize situations, places, and people who are risky energy-wise
- Take precautions and practice evasive moves so you're not caught off guard
- Stay alert and poised to act
- Avoid being spread too thin or in too many directions so you're constantly off balance
- Consider the ramifications if existing leaks remain unrepaired
- Take small air/energy victories as you find them

You don't need to live on high alert, but don't lull yourself into ignoring whatever depletes you on a regular basis. What can defeat you is not just "out there," but is also in your complacency. Even if circumstances are highly risky and fear-inducing, you have the resilience to deal with them—if you only can sustain the will. But living defensively also consumes considerable energy and runs you dry if such conditions continue unabated.

Extreme Fluctuations Are Harmful

Being around someone (or something) who is alternately hot and cold is crazy-making. A person who is always negative and low energy is unpleasant, but also a known quantity. So it's relatively easy to steer clear of them. But someone who is safe one day and unsafe the next is much more difficult to deal with.

They show extremes of behavior, like being over-demonstrative in their affection one time, then neglectful and severely punishing at others. When a person has to be around somebody erratic, it makes them doubt they're reading the signals correctly.

For example, the inconsistent behavior of someone like a battering husband is hard for family members to deal with. The mixed signals are disorienting because a person cannot trust their assessment of the situation. Is the beating an isolated event? Am I partly responsible? Am I reading too much into it? He's so nice to me/us the rest of the time. Can I rely on his promises to stop (or get help) this time?

Psychologists know the worst way to raise a child is for a parent to show alternately hot-and-cold emotions toward the child, or for them to apply alternately strict and permissive standards. Contradictory signals not only make children feel insecure, but they're fearful about how to respond to them. Such second-guessing stirs up all kinds of trust issues on the young psyche that might never be resolved.

Looking for Air in All the Wrong Places

We need air/energy and can barely function without enough of it. If people can't get all they need in healthy ways, they'll get it anyway they can. Some approaches could be excessive and inappropriate—even to the point of addiction.

Being addicted is at the "I can't stop myself" end of the spectrum of what is an otherwise widely-accepted human activity (with a few exceptions). Any further step taken along that line risks taking the person out of the normal range and closer to the highly-perilous end.

An addict is extremely unreliable except for their one-pointed desire to get their fix. Beyond a certain point, the hooked individual cannot go back to the relatively normal middle ground. Or they have become so identified with the maladaptive behavior it won't let go of them.

Addictions represent compulsive behavior which is pursued to relieve psychological pain. Whether the addicted person is driven by pleasure or the desire for safety, they feel they have no other choice except to get relief. They are unable to stop the behavior which gives them a dopamine hit and temporarily turns the pain off. (Dopamine is a neurotransmitter in the brain which is tied to the pleasure and reward centers.)

The compulsion which drives addictive behavior is primal—not accessible to the rational mind. What makes the behavior addictive is the need for it gets established in the limbic system, the hypothalamus located in the midbrain. (It is sometimes referred to as the reptilian brain.) Once it happens, the addiction never really goes away. Whether or not the addicted person resists those cravings for their fix, they spend the rest of their life yearning to have it again.

Addictive needs can take over a person's thinking, to the extent it relegates every other priority from job, to family, to self-respect to being expendable. Once a person can no longer turn off a particular need except to satisfy it, getting more comes to dominate all other aspects of their life. They keep repeating the behavior which gave some form of relief in the past. However, the downsides and disruptions to other routine concerns are out of proportion to the benefit to be derived from it.

Short of being addicted, I consider over-reliance on any particular "drug of choice" as a "too muchness" issue in certain regards (Chapter 8). If you see signs of over-dependence on only one source of air/energy, you're at greater risk of taking the need too far. While that alone doesn't make a person addicted, it does argue for pulling back and taking a second look.

Dealing with entrenched addictions is way beyond the scope of this book. My greater concern is for those who are fundamentally O.K. but they're leaning too heavily on a single source of relief. The person is deriving all their air needs from just one kind of fix—to the exclusion of a variety of sources.

The primary fix squeezing out their other air sources creates a vicious circle. Finding high-air sources of many kinds and in many places offers a critical boost away from addictive tendencies.

I once heard an alcoholic hurts 20 other people. I don't know if it's true, or if there are exceptions. But I do happen to know addictive behavior leaves a trail of misery in its wake. And such behavior can be recognized by the effect on its victims. People who are ruled by their addictions are toxic in the extreme to those they touch.

Those who are consumed by their addictions suck up all available air, heedless as to whom they hurt—or how badly. Normal social standards regarding appropriate behavior no longer apply as far as they're concerned.

People who love, like, or rely on an addict (or an addict-in-training) are very vulnerable energy-wise. Their own need for air is extremely high because of being constantly drained by the person who is out of control.

Anybody who has toxic people and situations sucking the air out of them regularly should treat the situation as an urgent wake-up call. (And it needn't get extreme before doing something about it.) Someone can care about the excessively-draining person, but should don protective gear in their presence.

The Dampening Effect of Fear and Self-doubt

Fear provides a valid protective function because it sounds the alert as to possible dangers. Fear also constricts the flow of energy and the hopefulness which makes a person willing to take chances or act kindly. Yielding to remembered (or imagined) fear freezes individuals and organizations in indecision or helplessness—at the very time their best analytical skills are needed.

Fear generally signals movement toward a lower and slower energetic state. When you encounter a threat, you slow down considerably and go into heightened alertness, taking in environmental details which are usually dismissed as unimportant. Any little thing can set the alarms off. Such reactions lack proportionality since the person acts in an all-or-nothing fashion.

Fear-based responses are prone to over-reaction. How likely you are to respond at such times is only marginally influenced by your rational intelligence, social conventions, or what we've learned through experience. While your beliefs and morality cannot control those reactions, they can throw up enough resistance or ambivalence to curb its impact somewhat.

In the same manner, when you let your self-doubts or self-criticism run rampant, you undercut your ability to assess things accurately. It also burns through your air supply quicker than need be. It throws you off and makes you timid. You cannot lead from your strengths or take your best shot from there.

The immediate dangers from being defensive and not on your own side are not so much "out there" from something which could hurt you, but in the way you allow it/them to shrink your range of possibilities, and to impair your judgment.

A defensive orientation is distrustful, valuing safety over considering other possible alternatives. It is averse to making changes or taking chances. Once fears and doubts run the show, you wind up ensnared in a web of self-imposed limitations that perpetuate feeling stuck.

When you are angry about your own behavior (or ashamed of yourself), you're functioning without sufficient air. And this is a toughie because you carry that outlook around with you. Your feelings about yourself are not like other toxic air that you can stay away from. Self-revulsion, unworthiness, and shame make for a toxic brew that pulls you down and keeps you down.

Not Feeling Good about Yourself

"No one can make you feel inferior without your consent," Eleanor Roosevelt said. Yet a lot of suffercation is self-inflicted. For a variety of reasons, you ride roughshod over your own feelings and behavior. You set impossible or contradictory demands, and then berate your unavoidable failure to meet them. That's mean. You do more than consent to your mistreatment; you are the relentless perpetrator.

In *Daring Greatly* Brene Brown explains the difference between guilt and shame.

> We often use the terms *embarrassment, guilt, humiliation* and *shame* interchangeably. It might seem overly picky to stress the importance of using the appropriate term to describe an experience or emotion; however, it is much more than semantics…
>
> Guilt = I did something bad.
> Shame = I am bad….
>
> When we apologize for something we've done, make amends, or change a behavior that doesn't align with our values, guilt—not shame—is most often the driving force. We feel guilty when we hold up something we've done or failed to do against our values and find they don't match up. It's an uncomfortable feeling, but one that's helpful… Guilt is just as

> powerful as shame, but its influence is positive, while shame's is destructive. In fact, in my research I found that shame corrodes the very part of us that believes we can change and do better...
>
> People believe they deserve their shame; they do not believe they deserve their *humiliation*...
>
> Embarrassment is the least serious of the four emotions. It's normally fleeting and it can eventually be funny. The hallmark of embarrassment is that when we do something embarrassing, we don't feel alone. We know other folks have done the same thing and, like a blush, it will pass rather than define us.[26]

Based on the twelve shame categories Brown identified in her research, she found a strong gender difference between what makes men and women suffer most keenly. Much of it is reinforced by cultural norms which we feel we must measure up to—however imperfectly.

Nobody seems to be spared. The beautiful person, who fate has smiled upon in so many ways, is still likely to suffer from not feeling "good enough" in one way of another. Or a person might adopt an approach that's so egotistical they can barely be endured by others. Or the person's posturing could have the opposite effect of what they intend, so they appear to be faking it.

> The primary trigger for women, in terms of its power and universality is the first one [on Brown's list]: how we look. Still. After all of the consciousness-raising and critical awareness, we still feel the most shame about not being thin, young, and beautiful enough... Motherhood is a close second. And (bonus!) you don't have to be a mother to experience shame. Society views womanhood and motherhood as inextricably bound; therefore our value as women is often determined by where we are in relation to our roles as mothers or potential mothers.[27]
>
> Basically, men live under the pressure of one unrelenting message: do not be perceived as weak... Men are caught in a

---

[26] Brown, Brene, *Daring Greatly: How the courage to be vulnerable transforms the way we live, love, parent, and lead* (New York: Gotham Books, 2012), 73-4.
[27] *Ibid.*, 86-7.

double bind…it's not just 'Don't be perceived as weak,' but also 'You better be great and all powerful.'[28]

We've set ourselves up for failure since many of the standards people in our culture aspire to are both unrealistic and transitory, even if you somehow manage to reach them. Self-rejection and criticism are not useful motivators when it comes to making your circumstances better. In fact, they are usually done *instead of* making things better.

Greater self-knowledge shows your failings do not define you and there is much about yourself which is fundamentally right. Get on your own side, not defiantly, not defensively, but because you belong there. Besides, *that's where the air is*.

---

[28] *Ibid.*, 92-4.

Chapter 10
Engage in Healthy Air Practices

Disasters and Air Pockets

Hurricanes, earthquakes, wild fires, and other natural disasters are dramatic, large scale, and destructive. They often involve whole communities and take many lives. In the aftermath, search and rescue teams fan out to find survivors. Through the media lens, the world watches. Hopefully... Fearfully... We hold our breath...We collectively rejoice for those who are found alive—against long odds.

More often than not, the key to survivors being found alive resulted from them finding a pocket of air during the long hours of waiting. Those who watch rescue efforts over TV and social media breathe a shared sigh of relief at their good fortune. In such human dramas we're all again reminded of the fragility and preciousness of life.

Afterward, a lengthy period of agonizing recovery follows before things return to normal. In fact, much of what was considered normal could be gone for good. There will be suffering, but it might call up a communal spirit to share the burdens, which can be awakened at such times. How well the community rallies and pulls together is decisive for a solid recovery.

After a job loss, close death, serious illness, divorce, or cataclysmic setback you need to regroup. In many ways, your individual adversities resemble natural disasters because your solid ground (what you always trusted) is shaken and pulled out from under you. In short order, your world tumbles down. The smoothness of your recovery could depend on having enough pockets of air in place which can withstand the blow.

Having spent years getting your protections in place, how well do you handle the re-discovery that none of those puny efforts keep you safe from earth-shaking events? There are many forces you cannot change, which are beyond human control. But you can take precautions and be better prepared for them. You can rise above the ravages of fate by the way you pick up the pieces.

It's never too soon to cultivate additional air reserves for difficult times. Just as we all need more air in times of trouble, look around your circle of friends and associates right now. Some people near you (in proximity or your intimates) are suffering from air-deprivation. It's very likely you could be a pocket of air *in their lives* and their dark days.

Playing that role actually creates more air for both of you. Don't wait for bad things to happen to be supportive energy-wise.

Your true power is often revealed *after the fact*—by how you individually (and collectively) respond to misfortune. That's equally true whether the devastating problems are your own, or you're in a position to provide some relief to those worse off. What latent character traits of yours rise to the occasion during difficult times?

Do you assist gladly? Or reluctantly? Or not at all? Do we take a single step or continue to assist until the tide is turned? Do you feel yourself getting stronger as you find more ways to pull together? Can we develop a groundswell of public collaboration from sharing the suffering and saving each other? That would make for a high-air recovery indeed.

Alligator Watch
A BonBon

When you're up to your ass in alligators, it's hard to remember you came to drain the swamp. Author Unknown

Sometimes alligator attacks seem like they'll go on forever. No sooner than you've dealt with one crisis, than there's another, then another, then another. Each attack insists on being taken seriously and handled NOW. Alligators seem to come in bunches—triumph over one and there are more in line.

When beset by the need to "put out the fire," speed and endurance are critical. Your ability to do anything the "right" way, let alone the "carefully planned" way is a routine casualty. The assaults are draining and soul deadening—"If I can just get through this, then…" Anything that's less urgent gets pushed into "then…." Life as you'd like to live it inevitably goes on "hold." If you dare wonder "How much more can I take?" you needn't wait long to find out.

Fortunately, such trials help us to find strengths seldom used and to discover what matters most. The need to find "those things that endure" becomes paramount. Trivialities fall away, and you get to find out who your true friends are. These discoveries are the upside of the downside.

As you drag on, enduring, struggling, fending off whatever form the alligator of the moment takes, what could possibly seem like progress? As long as there's yet another alligator, it's got ya! Take heart—look at what you've been through, and survived, and discovered (although the value of that comes later, in a more reflective mode).

Notice that you're now only up to your knees in alligators. Can ankles be far behind?

© 2014, Faith Lynella, from BonBons to Sweeten Your Daily Life or More BonBons and Treats   http://faithlynella.com

~~~~~~

Don't Shirk the Small Stuff

There's an old joke: How do you eat an elephant?
One bite at a time.

Don't be fooled by the immensity of a challenge. The sheer size of the difficulty alone should not be enough to prevent achieving what you set out to do. Just get started and take one step, or bite, after another. Sooner or later, if you keep at it you'll get done.

In that spirit: How do you survive when everything seems too hard or hopeless?

One breath or pocket of air at a time. Some may come easier than others, but take satisfaction along the way because you're finding enough to hang on. Little bites, little steps, little puffs of air can make all the difference. Shawn Achor tells us,

> Psychologists who specialize in goal-setting theory advocate setting goals of moderate difficulty—not so easy that we don't have to try, but not so difficult that we get discouraged and give up. When the challenges we face are particularly challenging and the payoff remains far away, setting smaller, more manageable goals helps us build our confidence and celebrate our forward progress.[29]

---

[29] Achor, Shawn, *The Happiness Advantage: The seven principles of positive psychology that fuel success and performance at work* (New York: Crown Business, 2010), 139.

Develop Your Unique Voice

Every human is programmed with an inborn urge to find his or her own sense of identity and purpose. We long to make a difference, just by being who we are. Such a drive includes finding your own inimitable voice, which sets off the fortuitous merging of your heart's desire and your ability to make your mark on the world.

Expressing your personality in an authentic way means whatever you do displays a unique flavor all your own. Your identity is an amalgam of inner and outer characteristics and quirks. The form it takes is a tangible demonstration of your actions and priorities.

Psychologist, Dr. Robert Firestone said "You are not going to find the meaning of life hidden under a rock written by someone else. You will only find it by giving meaning to life from inside yourself." What's right about you shines through you and is expressed by every word and deed. But it's easy to lose sight of your true value when life dings you.

As you learn to function from your authentic self, you also discover you are "*more than* you thought," rather than "less than you feared." There are many ways you are already living up to your ideals and life purpose. It reflects the degree of alignment between your practical side and your higher nature.

Everyone has difficulty identifying their most distinctive and essential qualities. Your core traits are so deeply entrenched and omnipresent, you don't realize how unique they are to you. So you fail to accurately judge your own particular strengths. Until you discover and claim your one-of-kind point of view you'll muddle along with mediocre moves—even while holding a fistful of winning cards.

As writer Hugh Macleod points out, "Part of being a master is learning how to sing in nobody else's voice but your own... Put your whole self into it, and you will find your true voice. Hold back and you won't. It is that simple."

Each life purpose is custom made for and by a particular person—a combination of their specific circumstances, worldview, character, and the choices they've made. Yours fits you perfectly, just like a suit tailored to fit feels quite different than one picked off the rack. A person who is aware of their uniqueness and purpose signals that as well.

Sometimes, what a person calls their purpose seems generic, like "feed the poor" or similar sound-good ideas. Half-baked and unfocused notions describe a worthwhile desire rather than a unique approach to a goal. Ask yourself, what makes a particular desire yours, done precisely *your way*?

Is there a burning passion, an urgency, a sense of needing to get started? That's a clue. Act on it right now! Acting from such a fired-up sense of purpose coalesces into specific activities which are different than anyone else's.

On a similar note, is there an insistent urge which keeps coming up no matter how often or ruthlessly you've shut it down? Could it be your wee small voice? Maybe you should pay attention to what it has to say to you, or to offer you.

One way to escape the limbo of wondering about your life purpose (before it's found and become evident to you) is to jump in as opportunities present themselves. Take action on moments of inspiration, even while it's not yet clear where the circumstances are headed. In committing to *do something* and taking the initial steps, circumstances are invited in. Many of us discover our purpose only after we're firmly embarked on it.

If you grab on to what fate puts in your path, you could find yourself led step by step to where you need to be—even as your sense of direction builds in ardor and clarity.

At some point, you could look back and see a path you've made (and are making) which is yours alone. Don't worry about how to add your distinctive style and flavor as you do so. It would be nearly impossible to keep them out.

Living a Life of Meaning and Purpose

Part of what makes each of us unique includes our one-of-a-kind mix of talents, skills, and motivations. These depend on which gifts and/or strengths have been cultivated. Gifts and talents are inborn, so a person has a particular one, or not. Even so, they will not bloom without prolonged effort.

But strengths can be developed by anyone. Normal infants are born with the *capacity for all the strengths*. Then the combination of the person's preferences and enthusiasms, coupled with what their world reinforces for them, leads each to choose some strengths over others. Beyond that, it is a matter of drive and diligence as to how far a person takes them.

But your innate capabilities do you little good unless you put them into practice. You gain a sense of meaning when you cultivate those abilities closest to your heart and share them with the world. Take pains to make choices that will display those distinctive skills and priorities. As Brene Brown said,

> *Squandering our gifts brings distress to our lives.* As it turn out, it's not merely benign or 'too bad' if we don't use the gifts that we've been given; we pay for it with our emotional and physical well-being. When we don't use our talents to cultivate meaningful work, we struggle. We feel disconnected and weighed down by feelings of emptiness, frustration, resentment, shame, disappointment, fear, and even grief.
>
> Most of us who are searching for spiritual connection spend too much time looking up at the sky and wondering why God lives so far away. God lives within us, not above us. *Sharing our gifts and talents with the world is the most powerful source of connection with God.*
>
> *Using our gifts and talents to create meaningful work takes a tremendous amount of commitment...* No one can define what's meaningful for us. Culture doesn't get to dictate if it's working outside the home, raising children, lawyering, teaching, or painting. Like our gifts and talents, meaning is unique to each of us.[30]

---

[30] Brown, Brene, *The Gifts of Imperfection: Let go of who you think you're supposed to be and embrace who you are* (Center City, Minnesota: Hazelden, 2010), 112-3.

My Life Matters
A BonBon

My life matters; and because I know that, everything I do matters. I have a responsibility to prefer the worthwhile above the superficial and make the choices which reflect that I can tell the difference.

In each little activity of the day, it is possible to discover that there is meaning and there is a meaningful choice to be made. The more I discover and seek out that truth, the more I learn that NOTHING I do is insignificant.

© 2014, Faith Lynella, from *BonBons to Sweeten Your Daily Life* or *More BonBons and Treats*   http://faithlynella.com

---

Self-reliance is rooted in an awareness of your own deep-seated strengths. Yet, without keeping them at the front of your brain, you're vulnerable to your every change of mind and every shift of social convention.

In order to trust yourself you must first *know* yourself (deeply and accurately), then *value* yourself for your essential qualities, and finally respect yourself enough for them to guide your steps. You're worth all the effort required. For it can rightly be said about your relationship with yourself, "'til death do you part."

Make some lists. Don't bother to make a list of things which need fixing about yourself. You've done that before—lots of times. And it didn't do anything but tear you down. The brain is good at criticizing, and you've spent too much time dissatisfied with various aspects of yourself. Enough already!

Instead, make a list of "What's Right about Me." That's a nearly-impossible list to make since none of us thinks about "who I am" in that wonderful way. And it's not the list your ego would write that's all braggy and self-centered—it's tuned to me, me, me! And as it shouts, it drowns out the genuine voice of your most heartfelt nature.

It's easy to overlook your quiet strengths and puff out your chest because of other peoples' opinions of yourself. But such a superficial view doesn't get to your core identity. The list of what's right about yourself is best written from your heart, for it can recognize your essential value.

Making such a list could take some time. But start on it and keep adding to what you find. As you recognize more of your under-appreciated essential qualities, a more accurate view of your gifts and strengths develops. You'll see the air pockets residing within yourself. Surprise! They're linked up with embracing what's right about yourself.

Saga of the Superficial Seal

What do you think? Is this my best side? Doesn't my fur glow in this light?

Scrap Played-out Air Pockets

Just as the need to find more air pockets is ongoing, so is the need to cull them when they no longer serve up what you need. Many pockets are a single-time experience. Or a favorite could start to provide stale or toxic air. Or you no longer like how something makes you feel.

We all have fond memories of special times and special places. You can't help wanting to go back and reconnect with the delicious feelings they bring up. The best of them engender precious, air-rich sensations—especially if there's a lot of love involved. How good it feels to hold those reminiscences dear and tap into them over and over. They're still alive for you. That's healthy.

Some memories are joyous trophies to keep close to the heart. Some are bitter-sweet, a mix of happy and sad, so you're both attracted and repelled by them. Many more are ho-hum, destined to gradually fade away. For it is the intensity of the emotions felt at the time they happened which keeps certain heart-warming recollections sharp and clear.

Some memories are train wrecks, recent enough that thinking about them re-ignites the pain and sense of loss. The blood is still flowing. Tread carefully with those. Over time, today's tenderness and emotional anguish will recede. But the experience should not be forgotten. You're not really done with a setback until you can see and accept the larger-scale consequences (and growth) which come from it. (See BonBon, Getting All You Pay For, Chapter 6.)

When revisiting memories, hold this specific query in mind: Is there *still* air there for me? Which make you stronger and happier? Which open up old pain? Take note of unresolved issues you still haven't made peace with. In either case, you will find grounds for satisfaction by taking a closer look. Such milestones show how far you've come, along with a sense of how much was completed or left behind.

Previously safe places (both actual and mental) can become toxic or cease to serve up air. However, previous pleasant associations with them could also keep you from noticing which ones have lost their potency. If you find yourself no longer being happy or energized from things you used to enjoy (or with someone in particular), give such a change of heart credence.

What's gone could have been outgrown or the lack of interest could mark a phase completed. Treat them as signs of progress as you move on, and have no regrets. However, if the interests or relationships are sound, give them an extra measure of concern, so you don't take them for granted.

Certain stale air sources may need cutting back in order to preserve your overall air integrity. The severity of the energy drain associated with them indicates how abrupt or total the clipping needs to be. Observe caution and healthy air practices as you begin.

Former air pockets which are now toxic to you:
- Bad mental and emotional associations of former train wrecks
- Being controlled by an unsupportive person, group, obligation, or attitude you used to consider acceptable
- Dishonest and/or degraded ethics which you used to use or tolerate from others
- Friends or relatives you can no longer trust or respect
- Happy experiences which you took for granted or those which drift into regrets you continue to stew over

Make amends where you can. Drop the dead horses you've been dragging along, and learn from your mistakes. Now let all that go and move forward.

Once you're paying attention air-wise, you can fix those which can be repaired, or move away from those that can't be. Staying on top of needed repairs prevents developing a serious plumbing problems later (Chapter 6).

This is mostly about making an attitude adjustment, but it calls for ongoing vigilance. As Max Planck said, "When you change the way you look at things, the things you look at change."

Gratitude Is an Intentional Act

By being grateful you put a spotlight on the many things going right in your life. And they're even more vital to you during the rough patches. Such an outlook looks past the ups and downs which color your days. It's about choosing where you put your attention.

Feeling full of gratitude and appreciation can only be done *intentionally* and *consciously*. They are the very opposite of habits. The two of them often came together and reinforce each other. Either can deliver an uptick of air/energy, whether in small amounts or large. They make your day brighter by bringing your focus to the good stuff, the innumerable ways the world keeps going around despite the difficulties.

Habits are performed on auto-pilot and without forethought. What's the difference? Habits go on, even when (and especially when) you're not thinking about what you're doing. By contrast, when something is done intentionally and consciously, your attention is fully engaged. The moment you stop paying attention to what you're doing it stops and reverts to the habitual response. You fall back to the normal, "non-grateful" way of seeing things.

Feeling grateful comes easy when things go your way. Can you also be grateful when you've been stabbed in the back, or when there's not enough money to cover the bills? It's not difficult to be thankful when you're feeling fit and energized. But how about gratitude when your body hurts past endurance and there's no improvement in sight?

Benefits associated with gratitude practice (that's backed up by scientific research):
- Aids the immune system
- Lowers the heart rate and improves a person's moods (and the survival of their marriage)

- Increases the sense of happiness, good will, and wellbeing
- Increases hours of sleep and feeling more refreshed by it
- Builds resilience, flexibility, and optimism

Gratitude and appreciation both operate on a very high-energy vibration rate which add context and meaning to a particular concern. They magnify and intensify whatever happenstance in which they occur. Either of them involves a stepping back from the particular experience, as you notice how it fits into a bigger picture. In doing so, you feel a surge of buoyant energy.

Gratitude and appreciation amp up your consciousness level so you feel good about things. And those around you can feel that additional air as well from how you treat them. Those upbeat energies also temporarily override the influences which drag you down. Jan Chozen Bays tells us

> Appreciation practice is an investigation. Can we find anything, anywhere, in this moment, that is cause for appreciation? We look, listen, feel. Anything? When we take a little time, we may find that there are many things to appreciate, from being dry, clothed and well fed, to encountering a kind store clerk or the warmth of a cup of tea or coffee in our hand.
>
> One category of things to appreciate is that which we experience as positive, such as having food in our belly. Another category of things to appreciate is the things that are absent, such as illness or war. We don't appreciate their absence until we've suffered their presence.[31]

Pause several times a day to think about all you have to be grateful for. It's a great way to start each day. Or you might reflect back on the day's high points at bedtime. Tell friends, partners, and family members something you appreciate about them at every opportunity. Now do the same for yourself.

---

[31] Bays, Jan Chozen, *How to Train a Wild Elephant: And other adventures in mindfulness* (Boston: Shambhala, 2011), 163.

Attend to Reminders and Blessings

Becoming air-aware doesn't come naturally to start with. Each of us has too long a history of being air blind—relating to things based on appearance and our expectations, rather than on its energy level. So it's helpful to develop practices which keep you more attentive to your air/energy levels throughout the day.

Several of the methods I endorse are appreciation practice (above), bestowing blessings (next), and setting up never-sleeping reminders, which pull your attention back to something important, even after you forget.

A never-sleeping reminder is established by allowing a certain common experience to serve as a reminder for something else. One event triggers a particular response in you, which energizes you each time it happens. There needn't be a direct connection between the two events, except as you've established in your mind. It doesn't depend on anybody else's participation. And you can stop it whenever you wish.

If I Could Only Remember...

Here's an example. When my daughter Jessica was about 20 she totaled three cars in the space of a year. Of course, three accidents were expensive and terrible. But that seemed secondary since in each case she was able to walk away without injury because she was wearing her seatbelt.

I wasn't a fan of seat belts before then, and had resisted wearing one myself. My gratitude over her survival was so great I never wanted to forget. I didn't simply start wearing my seatbelt, but I established a never-sleeping reminder for myself. Each time I fasten my seat belt, I say a prayer of thankfulness because my daughter is still alive.

To this day, I always pause for a moment as I snap the belt, to allow that sensation of appreciation to rise up in me. It is not a matter of thinking about it or doing anything more than shifting my attention away from where it would otherwise be. The act of fastening my seat belt triggers the fullness of gratitude in me all over again.

By the way, we found out what caused the accidents and she got the help she needed. She had a previously-undiagnosed sleep disorder which was taking her brain off-line briefly without her actually dozing off. Fortunately, those days are gone, but I continue to rejoice that my daughter is still alive every time I fasten my seat belt.

A few ideas:
- Each time I see a pregnant woman I am grateful for my own children, and I say a prayer for her and the child to come
- Each time I see a person in a wheelchair or on crutches, I am grateful I can walk
- Each time I see a very old person I rejoice that I have lived so long and I send good wishes their way

The Gentle Art of Blessing
Pierre Pradervand

On awakening, bless this day, for it is already full of unseen good which your blessings will call forth; for to bless is to acknowledge the unlimited good that is embedded in the very texture of the universe and awaiting each and all.

On passing people in the street, on the bus, in places of work and play, bless them. The peace of your blessing will accompany them on their way and the aura of its gentle fragrance will be a light to their path.

On meeting and talking to people, bless them in their health, their work, their joy, their relationships to God, themselves, and others. Bless them in their abundance, their finances... bless them in every conceivable way, for such blessings not only sow seeds of healing but one day will spring forth as flowers of joy in the waste places of your own life.

As you walk, bless the city in which you live, its government and teachers, its nurses and street sweepers, its children and bankers, its priests and prostitutes. The minute anyone expresses the least aggression or unkindness to you, respond with a blessing: bless them totally, sincerely, joyfully, for such blessings are a shield which protects them from the ignorance of their misdeed, and deflects the arrow that was aimed at you.

To bless means to wish, unconditionally, total, unrestricted good for others and events from the deepest wellspring in the innermost chamber of your heart: it means to hallow, to hold in reverence, to behold with utter awe that which is always a gift from the Creator. He who is hallowed by your blessing is set aside, consecrated, holy, whole. To bless is to invoke divine care upon, to think or speak gratefully for, to confer happiness upon—although we ourselves are never the bestower, but simply the joyful witnesses of Life's abundance.

To bless all without discrimination of any sort is the ultimate form of giving, because those you bless will never know from whence came the sudden ray of sun that burst through the clouds of their skies, and you will rarely be a witness to the sunlight in their lives.

When something goes completely askew in your day, some unexpected event knocks down your plans and you too also, burst into blessing: for life is teaching you a lesson, and the very event you believe to be unwanted, you yourself called forth, so as to learn the lesson you might balk against were you not to bless it. Trials are blessings in disguise, and hosts of angels follow in their path.

To bless is to acknowledge the omnipresent, universal beauty hidden to material eyes; it is to activate that law of attraction which, from the furthest reaches of the universe, will bring into your life exactly what you need to experience and enjoy.

When you pass a prison, mentally bless its inmates in their innocence and freedom, their gentleness, pure essence and unconditional forgiveness; for one can only be prisoner of one's self-image, and a free man can walk unshackled in the courtyard of a jail, just as citizens of countries where freedom reigns can be prisoners when fear lurks in their thoughts.

When you pass a hospital, bless its patients in their present wholeness, for even in their suffering, this wholeness awaits in them to be discovered. When your eyes behold a man in tears, or seemingly broken by life, bless him in his vitality and joy: for the material senses present but the inverted image of the ultimate splendor and perfection which only the inner eye beholds.

It is impossible to bless and to judge at the same time. So hold constantly as a deep, hallowed, intoned thought that desire to bless, for truly then shall you become a peacemaker, and one day you shall, everywhere, behold the very face of God.

And of course, above all, don't forget to bless the utterly beautiful person YOU are![32]

---

[32] Pradervand, Pierre, *The Gentle Art of Blessing: A simple practice that will transform you and your world* (Hillsboro, Oregon: Beyond Words, 2009)

We've all been on both the giving and receiving end of such blessings. My hope is that each of us can engage in even more of both the granting and receiving end since feeling blessed makes a palpable difference in the world. To my way of thinking, there's binkle energy and love in every blessing. And air, too.

Air and Time Are Intertwined

Time is a sister of attention in that it flows along. But you only notice those parts of it which have an impact on you at the moment. Humans have a love-hate relationship with time because we seem to be in a perpetual battle to stretch it out, slow it down, or pack more into it.

Shortages of time are very much like polluted air. You feel constricted, rushed, and driven by them both. Too little time keeps you off balance, struggling to make the hours, and minutes, and days stretch far enough. Jim Rohn said, "Time is more valuable than money. You can get more money, but you cannot get more time."

Time is a factor in many of the concerns which matter to us. But you need to spend both your time and attention in ways which will bring those sought-after fruits into your experiences.

> Take time to work—it is the price of success
> Take time to think—it is the source of power
> Take time to play—it is the secret of perpetual youth
> Take time to read—it is the fountain of wisdom
> Take time to be friendly—it is the road to happiness
> Take time to love and be loved—it is the nourishment of the soul
> Take time to share—it is too short a life to be selfish
> Take time to laugh—it is the music of the heart
> Take time to dream—it is hitching your wagon to a star
> Anonymous

Your Larger Rhythms Set Your Speed

Each of us has developed our natural rhythms as to the way you do things—gradual or rushed, precise or relaxed, painstaking or drifty, etc. It's *how* you proceed. In a sense, they're all equivalent because nobody's speed is better or worse than anybody else's. Your speed is an integral part of your personality and the way you relate to the world. But you don't notice your tim*ing* because it is so much a part of your behavior.

Speeding up your timing, or slowing it down, have the same effect—they break auto-pilot. In that sense, a tiny break is as useful for shifting gears as a large one. Each time you relax and take a deep breath, it disrupts the current timing. The disconnection acts as a restart and opportunity to do something more harmonious.

Your conscious self is not subject to the habitual nature of your timing. So put it is at the tiller—guiding your behavior moment by moment. Imagine all the air to be claimed in any activity where you tinker with your timing intentionally.

Haven't Got the Tim*ing*
A BonBon

We will give up our time much more willingly than we will ever give up our TIMING. We carefully dole out our time like money, spending some on this or that, more here, none there; but we consciously spend it. We know we're making trade-offs, trying to satisfy the competing demands on our time, our energy, our lives, hoping there will be enough to go around.

It's full of tough choices, but we understand about spending time, carefully portioning out our hours and minutes.

In each thing we do we express our timing. The rate at which I do a thing is "the way I do it." We don't question our timing because it is invisible to us. It has become part of who we are and whatever we do.

We have gradually consigned most of our timing options to the blind operation of habit. In the process, we have lost our power to alter our speed except under extraordinary situations (such as great danger).

Yet, if we can change our timing, we can increase our ability to alter the way events impact us. Whether we speed up or slow down, whether we make a large or small change, we have altered our customary reaction pattern. In so doing, we have gotten our finger back on the controls. Now we can choose the rate at which we respond and thereby have reasserted a degree of control in life usually denied us.

We can DECIDE to match or alter the speed at which our choices are made and then consciously choose how to proceed. In that small measure of freedom, we find we can make freer, more relevant choices.

Our timing is a small matter, but we are governed by it. Try taking back control of it and you'll really see who is in charge. It is hard work to wrest a fragment of change in timing, and no victory lasts. But watch your timing; it's your direct path to freedom.

©2014, Faith Lynella, from *BonBons to Sweeten Your Daily Life* or *More BonBons and Treats*   http://faithlynella.com

Sensing the Larger Rhythms

Being attentive to your own air and energy levels alters your fundamental relationship to the passage of time. You still move from activity to activity and thought to thought. But you start to attend to the tempo which connects you to the larger milieu within which you operate.

While they are larger and impersonal, you begin to see your very personal place in the larger context that's present in each moment.

You can relax into that pace and energy in a way that's compatible with your own desires. Kent Nerburn said "We all have to learn to listen. Our spirits are harpstrings, played upon by the winds and the light and the passing of the hours. We must learn to hear their music, and let them raise melodies in our hearts."

Sensing the tempo acts as a reset—ceding a nonexistent control of the future to a harmony in the here and now. Disengage. Breathe. Relax. Rejoice. There's plenty of air.

Elastic Time

Being in synch with time is a matter of being aligned with larger rhythms—allowing yourself to flow with them and submitting to their speed and direction. Increasing air-awareness signals an ability to correspond more fully to the larger dynamics. Build the muscles whereby you can switch to time being more elastic. Time really isn't fixed; it can be stretchy and bendy.

You've had occasional experiences of time being elastic—when there was more than enough, when you did prodigious feats in a trice, when time seemed to stand still so you could accomplish all you wanted to. Those are examples of entering non-linear time. It is not part of our 3-D reality because the rational mind can't comprehend it.

But you've experienced it when you've stepped outside your normal mindset. Non-linear time is a parallel possibility which runs through your days. And when you leave your customary point of view behind because you're focused on something bigger, you sometimes can hitch a ride.

It takes you to the timelessness of time. When you go within or flow effortlessly along with larger rhythms, the customary limits of time cannot hold you. Air/energy in its most concentrated and pristine forms becomes your booster rocket.

Chapter 11
Enjoy Passion, Joy, and Flying High

Your Passion Is a Super-big Air Pocket

Americans have a high opinion about the "pursuit of happiness"—getting to do what we're passionate about. It has been idealized as the brass ring which allows the rest of life to make sense. We assume that if only we could follow our passion, everything else would fall in place. That's a tad simplistic and seldom true—but it is what we want.

Still, we feel considerable conflict about passion as well—and rightly so. By its very nature, passion is excessive; it lacks moderation. Unrestrained passion leads to extreme mood swings and outrageous behavior. So much unrestrained, fiery intensity released at once can (and often does) lead to negative outcomes. Nor can it be sustained indefinitely, so there's a letdown at some point.

The ideal is to become passionate about being alive, for that possibility is with each of us at every moment. Emily Dickinson recommends you "Find ecstasy in life; the mere sense of living is joy enough." Passion adds the exclamation point to whatever we do.

Pay attention to what makes your heart sing, your eyes light up when you speak about it, and your ideas their most scintillating. That's tangible evidence of your being in touch with what animates you. At such moments, your heart, mind, body, and spirit are united in a combined sense of passion which corresponds to your deepest sense of who you are. That energy is palpable and exhilarating!

When you're flying high, your heart, mind, and body respond avidly to the uplifting impulse in its own manner. But each of them has a different way of indicating its agreement. Savor each of them: the mind seeing things click into place; the body pulsing with vibrancy; the heart feeling the emotional richness of each experience; the spirit harkening to what is eternal. Don't leave unclaimed "air on the table."

I Wanna Have that Wanna-Happen Energy
A BonBon

> Once in a while, a project or idea comes together of its own accord. It's so seamless, spontaneous, and rapid I just have to hang on. There's a singleness of purpose that pushes aside whatever else competes for my time, attention, or energy.

Something in me recognizes "it's got a mind of its own." What it is trying to do is counter-intuitive, which means I wouldn't have thought to do that in a million years.

Wanna-Happen Energy puts me in unresisting overdrive. This is Clear Sailing Energy, but riding on a schooner instead of a dinghy. It takes over my Do List. But it doesn't stay there long because what needs doing is so quickly accomplished. Then the whole thing is off to what's next, because it *wants to happen*. If it joins up with the buoyancy of Lift-off Energy, there could be a game-change. Things really start to move!

The energetic surge pulls me right along. Yet this process isn't hurried so much as incredibly efficient. Unerringly, no thought or motion is wasted or off-track. I get even more oomph from doing the work—without feeling drained at all. I'm energized! I'm almost giddy about *getting to do it* because it feels like such a privilege to be involved.

This state of affairs resembles a blueprint just waiting to be made tangible—no trial and error or fumbling around. Somehow, on some level, it's apparent this isn't half-baked or a pile of unrelated pieces. But it exists as a whole, with just a bit of assembly required of me.

This is not Breakthrough Energy since there are no barriers or logjams to be breached. Nothing stands in its way. The force of it overrides existing everyday rhythms and routines, as it proceeds toward its driving purpose.

You feel a rush of joy and delight as Wanna-Happen Energy is going on. But after it passes there's a saddened letdown. Not yet! . . . Oh no. . . is it over?! You realize that whatever just happened was an event—something special to be pondered and reflected upon. But wondering about hows and whys can't explain it—or bring it back.

That burst of energy didn't arise from you, but you gladly played your part. Now your role is to watch with reverent appreciation to see what comes of it. But you certainly can't help wishing for some more of that Wanna-Happen Energy again.

© 2014, Faith Lynella, from *BonBons to Sweeten Your Daily Life* or *More BonBons and Treats*   http://faithlynella.com

Passion Is Red Hot

Passion can be spotted by its intensity—it is hard to miss it. Passion refuses to sit quietly in the background or bide its time. It demands attention—pronto! Lacking that, a project is merely an interest or obligation, one among many, which is slipped in among the responsibilities of life.

Passion enflames you and carries you away. Its energy cannot be controlled. It takes you over—heedless of the costs which might follow. Passion comes from the Latin word, "passio," which means to suffer. Such feelings can be so intense they are painful.

Unbridled passion often leads to intense suffering, sooner or later. Although passion can bring dreadful suffering, it also brings intense joy and pleasure. At the time it surges through you the feelings are wonderful! Jubilant! Indescribable! But whether it leads to joy or pain depends on what happens next.

Passion is not a gift without strings so much as a potent energy to be mastered. Doing that is not the same as it being suppressed or stifled, however. It is possible to learn to channel passion's powerful force to your advantage, without being overwhelmed by it. And when its force is coupled with a worthy purpose, things happen.

There is a sexual connotation to passion as well. By the manner in which human beings are wired up, intense outbursts of creativity are connected to sexual energy. Given how much pleasure can be generated through either one, the pull can be all-consuming.

Passion adds spice and variety—arousing your interest and single-minded drive. Vincent van Gogh said, "I would rather die of passion than of boredom." Passion is never boring. It is also feared by bystanders because of the way it disrupts the *status quo*.

Some highly-creative individuals rely on its high-intensity lift so much they treat it like a drug that's needed to spur the creative process. After being so "high," a person often encounters problems handling their return to a commonplace condition once it's over. They careen between the highs and lows in a most unstable way.

An aspect of achieving mastery involves being able to cope with the ups and downs of passionate engagement somewhat smoothly. Passion releases dopamine and energizing hormones that have drug-like qualities on the brain. Some people come to need the hit it brings so much it unleashes a tendency toward addictive behavior in them.

There's no brake on it, and conventional social standards or relationships cannot keep passions in line. No wonder why following your bliss or passion has such an impact. It's the full-color version of a black and white movie.

The Most Important Thing

Whatever your primary passion or sense of life purpose might be, put it ahead of all your other concerns. Don't settle for a life of dull mediocrity, which has allowed everyday obligations to beat your passion out of it.

What you're most passionate about fires you with an over-riding drive to be fully engaged with it. It's exhilarating! As Oprah Winfrey advises, "Passion is energy. Feel the power that comes from focusing on what excites you."

This classic story is about the search for God, but is also true for your calling (what calls to you intensely) or whatever you're most passionate about.

A hermit meditating by a river is interrupted by a young man. "Master, I wish to become your disciple." "Why?" asks the hermit. The young man answers, "Because I want to find God."

The hermit jumps up, grabs the young man by the scruff of his neck, drags him into the river, and plunges his head under water. After holding the man down for a minute, with him kicking and struggling to free himself, the hermit finally pulls him out of the river. The nearly-drowned man coughs up water and gasps to get his breath.

When he eventually quiets down, the master asks, "What did you want most of all when you were under water?"

"Air!"

"Very well. Go home and come back to me when you want God as much as you just wanted air."

Finding a Passion of Your Own

The joy and satisfaction from doing what you love should not be treated as an afterthought, or a lesser motivation, when you're making significant life choices. For that, more than any other factor, could determine whether you stick with what's chosen as an obligation, or you have a life you truly enjoy.

Your passion drives you since it is the embodiment of your core identity. It expresses who you are in a unique and will-not-be-denied way. Howard Thurmond, the civil rights leader, said, "Don't ask yourself what the world needs; ask yourself what makes you come alive. And then go and do that. Because what the world needs is people who have come alive."

The height of passion toward an activity is to feel, without a particle of doubt, it is what you were born to do. Usually you'll be better at that particular thing than almost anything else you could be doing. Even if the execution of it is not masterful, the satisfaction from doing it is enormous.

What makes someone pursue one urge or field of endeavor with passionate enthusiasm, rather than all the others? Whatever gets you excited and stirs you deeply could be leading you to precisely where you belong. Your wee small voice becomes a loud and passionate one, when it is heeded. And it is nudging you in certain directions where you can shine.

Many influences are at work in helping you find your purpose—most without your conscious awareness. The choice as to whether to respect your deepest desires is rather personal. What is *your* heartfelt predilection? And what do you allow to stand in the way of bringing it to life?

Falling into your passion is easy for the fortunate few who discover theirs serendipitously. Searching for your passion, on the other hand, is a challenge for the rest of us. And it is not easy. If you expect it to be, you will be frustrated. The two most common trip-up issues involve: 1. searching in your head instead of your heart, and 2. a misplaced focus on money.

When one pursues the question "what is your passion?" most people who are still looking for theirs expect an immediate answer from within. When one doesn't appear, they force the issue with their minds, searching every accessible memory of past experience in the left-brain hemisphere. Options appear and the sorting begins. Unfortunately, the rational brain can't recognize what's original, unique, or inspiring. And it totally distrusts passion.

So when you're advised to "look deeper within yourself," what those advisors are really saying is pay attention *elsewhere* within. The right brain is a parallel processor (versus the left brain serial processor) and home to visions, inspirations, connectedness vs. separateness, and the chemistry of bliss. You receive its messages through feelings, often coming in whispers rather than shouts.

The only way to access what it has to tell you is to disengage from the linear thinking which dominates the left brain and logic. Some people meditate. Some people garden. Some people escape to nature. Be still and attentive; you will eventually be granted the realization you seek.

Expecting your passion to pay the bills is an iffy proposition, however. It can work for a few, but having a passionate calling does not imply that doing it will be income producing. Passion and money serve different masters and call upon very different skill sets.

There are many additional factors involved in launching your own business. And what drives your passion is not very likely to fit within the highly-structured job descriptions of an established organization.

Trying to turn a passion into a business or livelihood can easily kill the excitement about it. The yucky and repetitive parts can easily eclipse the enjoyable aspects of the creative experience. Having to deal with all the business considerations might start to feel like drudgery. So you could stop enjoying it so much.

Once a person's passion gets tied up in their financial survival, the motivations for doing what they love are totally altered. While some individuals manage to pull off combing creativity and commerce, it's not the only way to fully engage it.

Being Led by Your Heart's Desire

The clarity of your heart's desire beckons on the horizon. It calls to you in tantalizing ways. While what the heart wants is energized and directed from within, it needs to be anchored in the outside, practical world if it is to ever be more than a dream.

The animating idea must be grounded in action. To quote Balzac, "It is easy to sit up and take notice. What is difficult is getting up and taking action." The potency of your clarity of vision and commitment to act draw the desired outcome into tangible existence.

You aren't handed a life's purpose. It's not whispered into your ear by God, a fairy godmother, or even your higher self. It is discovered through expressing your enthusiasm and excitement as you do what feels most meaningful for you. *There's air there.* And the breadcrumbs which help you to find it, that are dropped along the way, have been the very same pockets of air you've been finding to sustain yourself step by step.

The idea is made tangible by collaboration of imagery (heart), intellectual how-to (head), and your efficient feet on the ground (physical). Your life purpose is not simply your preferred interest. It is intimately tied to your core identity. The amount of passion to sustain it must be intense, for that's what provides the power for it to outlast all obstacles. Care so much about whatever yours is that you commit to it without hesitation.

According to Anne Morris, "The irony of commitment is that it feels deeply liberating. In work, in play, in love, the act frees you from the tyranny of your internal critic, from the fear that likes to dress up and parade around like rational hesitation. To commit is to remove your head as the barrier to your life."

As you creatively work to achieve what your heart considers possible, the world will be well served by what you can do with it. What you achieve with your heartfelt and passionate desire to make things better is your most valuable legacy.

What your heart requires:
1. Make a commitment to what you desire most—your life goals or sense of purpose. It's not one among many desires, but your primary one. It expresses your core identity.
2. Don't "settle" and prematurely take what the everyday world offers, or to satisfy what other people want you to do. Hold out for what has greatest value to you.
3. Trust your inner wisdom about it and respond to its prompting without delay—that's your wee small voice at work.

Also, don't feel you can have only one per lifetime. We grow, change, outgrow, and reinvent our point of view, so what animates us also evolves. Austin Kleon advises that you not settle for a single passion. "Don't throw any of yourself away. If you have two or three real passions, don't feel like you have to pick and choose between them. Don't discard. Keep all your passions in your life."

Saga of the Passionate Seal

Seals have feelings too. Just because I don't talk about them doesn't mean my life is nothing more than swimming around or eating fish. I'm not philosophical, but I am sensuous. I am immersed in a world of sensuous pleasures.

I love! Love! Love! the way the water slides over my fur as I dive. I'm in heaven from the freedom, the buoyancy, the fluidity, the effortless gymnastics as I twist and glide. Not every fish or sea urchin tastes the same; some are nothing short of gourmet delights.

The life I lead allows me to have few distractions from what brings me the most pleasure. It fully fills my days with sensuous satisfactions. Even when I'm stretched out on the bank, the sun's rays caress me in ways that make me deliriously happy from the top of my head to the tips of my flippers.

My life may seem unexciting to you. But what you see me doing happens to be how seals act when we're passionately satiated.

Ask Not for Whom the Bus Comes...
A BonBon

And Jesus walked along the lake. And he came upon some men who were fishing and said unto them, "Follow me."

And one of the men said unto him, "Would you mind coming back when the fish aren't biting?"

And so he left.

Opportunities present themselves in many guises. Some are humdrum, as easily caught as waiting for the next bus. There will be many other choices along soon.

Some other opportunities have the possibility to be life changing. If it's not embraced quickly and with the right spirit, it will be gone—never to return for you. If you should miss it, decline it, ignore it, that indicates that it's not much of a priority in your life. It's the bus not taken.

Who knows if there will be another one as providentially designed for you. The question to ponder—can you tell the difference?

© 2014, Faith Lynella, from BonBons to Sweeten Your Daily Life or More BonBons and Treats   http://faithlynella.com

Joy "Hides" in the Midst of Life

What brings you joy? Where does it come from? Make a list of where you find the most joy these days.

Write them down. Keep writing…

Got it? Good. Whatever you noted down, it's much too short a list, too narrow a view. It just scratches the surface. Those are the obvious places where happiness is easily found, *the ones that you don't miss.*

You're surrounded by untapped joy-filled possibilities. There are many, many more ways and places to tap into what could be energizing and uplifting for you. What about all the other places you haven't ever noticed? Or those that call for some prior effort on your part? Once you can recognize those unexplored opportunities, you've multiplied your joy harvest.

A person attuned to the joy to be had *will always be able to find some.* Pay attention to the energizing feelings that come along with it. A ho-hum experience can turn joyful and special simply by your sheer desire to embrace it.

Another way of finding more joy is by looking for the numerous ways that you systematically *tune it out.* Like binkles (its closest relation, Chapter 7), joy is there to be found and en*joy*ed just by your taking the time to notice what else is happening around you. Look at your world with fresh eyes and an open heart—see what you find…

Feeling stressed indicates *resistance to joy.* When feeling "down," your joy resistance is most evident. That's exactly when hearty (as in heartfelt) doses of joy and pockets of air can do you the most good. They also counter-balance the largely negative emotional roller-coaster ride sucking your energy away.

Brene Brown's research led her to see that even those who have suffered greatly find they can discover joy in small ways.

I learned about joy and light from people who have spent time in sorrow and darkness.

1. **Joy comes to us in moments—ordinary moments. We risk missing our joy when we get too busy chasing down the extraordinary.** Scarcity culture may keep us afraid of living small, ordinary lives, but when you talk to people who have survived great losses, it is clear that joy is not a constant. Without exception, all the participants who spoke to me about their loss, and what they missed the most, spoke about ordinary moments....

2. **Be grateful for what you have.**

3. **Don't squander joy.** *Every time we allow ourselves to lean into joy and give in to those moments, we build resilience and we cultivate hope.* The joy becomes part of who we are, and when bad things happen—and they do happen—we are stronger.[33]

Keep a Joy Journal, a Joy-nal (more frivel)

Bothering to notice and sink into joyful experiences as they come along brings more of them. Whether it's more in quantity, quality, or frequency is for you to decide. But at the very least, you'll discover there's much more happiness and joy available to you than you've bothered to notice.

Jot down the energy-boosting events you feel as they happen. Watch for little things which make your heart leap. Paying attention to what uplifts you adds a double dose of energy. Writing them down helps you spot patterns or additional joy you might have overlooked at the time. Keeping your mind focused on joy even tunes out the background hum of negative distractions.

Couple your attention to joy with a binkle journal for noting down what brings you air and energy. As air and energy gain more prominence in your day, your life feels more vibrant—and burdens fall away.

---

[33] Brown, Brene, *Daring Greatly: How the courage to be vulnerable transforms the way we live, love, parent, and lead* (New York, Gotham Books, 2012), 125-6.

What's less prominent in an air-rich life?
- Drama and acting out
- Sense of needing to be in control—instead, one *flows* with experiences
- Negative emotions or outbursts
- Struggles of all sorts for there is greater ability to rise above troubling events
- Predictability—though to be honest, things seldom went as expected
- Linear thinking and black-and-white standards
- Obligations to material objects and non-nourishing relationships
- Time and space restrictions
- Cultural taboos and sacred cows

Passion Between People Can Be Illusive

What first comes to mind is a lover—the love of your life, a soulmate. With passion so intense often comes intimacy, and possibly sex. If nobody fits that role for you, there's likely to be a severe longing for somebody who could fill the bill.

But you can have a passionate love for certain individuals who aren't past or present lovers. A parent's love of a child, or a grandparent's love for grandchildren, etc. Those can be powerful and long-standing ties. But blood ties are not always loving or intimate ones, no matter how much a person insists their family is the most important thing in their life.

Your family ties represent a mixed bag. When you say (and who doesn't?!) "I love my family," there are some individuals you indeed love with all your heart. But there are others who you can hardly stand. Admittedly, when the family unit is threatened by outside forces, everyone closes ranks and lays their individual issues aside.

But those who are closest to you also have the most history with you—some of which could be painful or unsettling. Work through any unresolved issues with each of the significant people in your life carefully, so the fragile bonds of caring aren't tarnished or broken.

In the interest of air security, sort through your feelings toward family and close associates, person-by-person to find the existing air in those relationships. Those safe havens are your recharge faces and places.

The best and most reliable of them should be recognized as significant air pockets. Invest the emotional effort to appreciate those individuals—loudly and often. Keep that trust and caring nourished at the emotional level so it endures and grows stronger still.

The intensity of passion declines. It has to or you'd burn out. So much fire cannot be maintained indefinitely—nor should it be. It should be allowed to morph into forms which can be sustained in the ebb and flow of life. It also requires a protective structure like the flame within a lantern.

Grounding your passion in multiple ways assures it remains a vibrant force for you. If that isn't done, its force flashes on and off, leading to an all-or-none or feast-or-famine existence.

On one level, so much front-burner intensity settles into something more ordinary, more day-in and day-out. There's a risk in doing so, however. It's just too easy to adjust to what has been gotten and stop appreciating it or them. The psychological term for it is adaptation. Sonja Lyumbomirsky describes it this way.

> One of the clues that lets you know you've adapted to your partner is that you've ceased to appreciate her. Truly appreciating someone means valuing her, being grateful for her, savoring your time with her, and remaining keenly aware of the goodness she has brought into your life… [Studies have found] that people who persist at appreciating a good turn in their lives are less likely to adapt to it.
>
> Appreciation is vitally important for several reasons. First, appreciating our relationship compels us to extract the maximum possible satisfaction from it and helps us to be grateful for it, relish it, savor it, and not take it for granted. Second, we come to feel more positively about ourselves and to feel more connected to others. Third, our expression of appreciation motivates both us and our partners to bolster efforts to take care of the relationship. And, finally,

appreciation helps prevent us from getting too 'spoiled' and from paying too much attention to social comparisons and experiencing envy.[34]

Don't Take Relationships for Granted

An important life task is learning to keep what you love alive so it doesn't lose its vibrancy. In relationships, you might take someone for granted. The desires and goals that you wanted so badly before they were yours gradually gets shoved to back burner and never get the attention they clamor for.

You figure "someday I'll get around to it." But you seldom do, so its/their specialness fades and fades. Who knows whether you'll feel regrets down the road. But by then the daily opportunities to embrace them, or it, have passed.

Of course, acknowledgment is not just for lovers. Each of us blooms brighter when we feel its warmth. Expressing gratitude and appreciation provide the essential air/energy for a relationship. There's a palpable desire for them that is a sub-text for whatever is being spoken of. Those with whom you've forged a close bond deserve no less.

The saddest song I know is "Cat's in the Cradle" because it shows the life-shrinking cost of lost opportunities.

Cat's in the Cradle
Harry Chapen (1974)

My child arrived just the other day
He came to the world in the usual way
But there were planes to catch and bills to pay
He learned to walk while I was away
And he was talkin' 'fore I knew it, and as he grew
He'd say "I'm gonna be like you dad
You know I'm gonna be like you"

And the cat's in the cradle and the silver spoon
Little boy blue and the man on the moon
When you comin' home dad?
I don't know when, but we'll get together then son

---

[34] Lyumbomirsky, Sonja, *The Myths of Happiness: What should make you happy, but doesn't: What shouldn't make you happy, but does* (New York: The Penguin Press, 2013), 24-6.

You know we'll have a good time then

My son turned ten just the other day
He said, "Thanks for the ball, Dad, come on let's play
Can you teach me to throw," I said "Not today
I got a lot to do," he said, "That's ok"
And he walked away but his smile never dimmed
And said, "I'm gonna be like him, yeah
You know I'm gonna be like him"

And the cat's in the cradle and the silver spoon
Little boy blue and the man on the moon
When you comin' home son?
I don't know when, but we'll get together then son
You know we'll have a good time then

Well, he came home from college just the other day
So much like a man I just had to say
"Son, I'm proud of you, can you sit for a while?"
He shook his head and said with a smile
"What I'd really like, Dad, is to borrow the car keys
See you later, can I have them please?"

And the cat's in the cradle and the silver spoon
Little boy blue and the man on the moon
When you comin' home son?
I don't know when, but we'll get together then son
You know we'll have a good time then

I've long since retired, my son's moved away
I called him up just the other day
I said, "I'd like to see you if you don't mind"
He said, "I'd love to, Dad, if I can find the time
You see my new job's a hassle and kids have the flu
But it's sure nice talking to you, Dad
It's been sure nice talking to you"

And as I hung up the phone it occurred to me
He'd grown up just like me
My boy was just like me

Pushing to the Point of Exhaustion

Passion drives you to keep going when you would otherwise quit. Lazy, bored, and unmotivated people do not burn out. They don't care enough to bother. They don't feel something vitally important is at stake. When things get rough, they give up or drop the ball. Too bad... They are unwilling to gird up their loins and redouble their efforts just because things aren't working.

By contrast, those who have a clear goal they're burning to reach "come hell or high water" refuse to stop. For those driven by passion or vision, apparent failure is not seen as an acceptable outcome. Instead, setbacks are treated as a place to recharge, re-strategize, and regroup in order to begin again. They have a longer-range objective.

Individuals who keep pushing ahead, despite overwhelming odds or limited resources, are likely to achieve their goals in the end through hard work and diligence. They are usually high-energy, capable, and ambitious. So what if something is harder than expected? They're geared for such challenges because they think achieving what they foresee requires no less.

But such determination makes them prime candidates for burning out. Passionate drive cannot be sustained very long unless it is replenished, without there being high personal costs. It doesn't reflect poorly on your level of commitment for you to stop and reassess your strategy and pace in a cooler frame of mind.

Where you invest your creativity and passion is where you derive a sense of identity, value, belonging, and meaning. So who wouldn't give it their all? Of course you should. But don't forget to recharge as required. Otherwise something within you will short out.

I've treated the saying "It's always darkest before dawn" with a barely-suppressed anticipation. The worse things would get, the closer it must be to flipping over. Surely with things this difficult, we're about to see the dawn. But I'm rethinking that approach.

To put it in air/energy terms, when your reserves have been used up, it might not be anywhere near dawn or fresh air. Be prepared for the drought to be longer or darker than you expected or prepared for.

Just as emergency preparedness dictates having flashlights, bottled water, and extra batteries on hand, getting your pockets of air in order will be life-sustaining at the point when you run dry. One way to get prepared is to stay positive. You don't let a few clouds darken the whole sky. Expecting the best nudges you to try more things and take more risks. Shawn Achor said:

> Studies have shown that optimists set more goals (and more difficult goals) than pessimists, and put more effort into attaining those goals, stay more engaged in the face of difficulty, and rise above obstacles more easily. Optimists also cope better in high stress situations and are better able to maintain high levels of well-being during times of hardship—all skills that are crucial to high performance in a demanding work environment.[35]

When the pressures on you are greatest, you no longer have accurate judgment about what is, or is not, possible. Or it's something which might be possible with extreme measures, but is it worth the candle? You're torn between pushing on no matter what, or saying "that's enough." Which is the wiser course, given what's known when the choice is made? Which of the possible outcomes are you prepared to live with?

You must accept certain limits, even while being open to other factors which could alter the equation. Is this course of action worth it, even with added hands, resources, or a tailwind of fortuitous circumstances? Is this the right time or setting for what's driving you?

Stay open to the possibility that the goal or motivation established at the beginning might have been accomplished in a different way, or that it's not as important as it once was. If the costs to your coping capacity can't be sustained, you need to give credence to the physical, mental, or emotional signals which insist they can't go on like this. You need relief; you need air!

Even passion has its limits. Sometimes, no amount of effort or determination can make things happen, or happen soon enough, or in the way you want them to. It might not be your personal failings which stand in the way.

---

[35] Achor, Shawn, *The Happiness Advantage: The seven principles of positive psychology that fuel success and performance at work* (New York, Crown Business, 2010), 98.

But also, the timing or interaction of many elements you don't control are required for the process to play out. Those cannot be forced.

As the anxiety of impending failure builds, you might start to lose it, over-react emotionally, and suffer total exhaustion. What's required at such times, even more than additional digging in and digging deep, is for you to give yourself permission to step back often enough and long enough to restore your equilibrium and confidence.

In the process, additional air pockets which could replenish you come into focus. Stepping back is not a failure of desire or of execution. It is an essential accommodation to the realities of bringing energy into matter—and your intention into tangible manifestation.

Chapter 12
Find Air in Your Inner World and Emotions
The Biggest Air Pocket Is Inside Yourself

Your inner world is the Fort Knox of energy and air for you. There is more to be found by going within than from any combination of external air pockets. Of course, the ideal is to have access to plenty of air inside yourself, as well as from outside. Access to your Fort Knox depends on developing an alignment between your highest qualities (inner) and your behavior (outer).

As you become sensitive to air/energy's crucial role in your life, you'll tap into those inner reserves more readily and easily. A rich inner life is like having a bank account you've been making deposits into every day of your life. But when the pressures of living get in the way, the log-in or password sometimes gets misplaced.

Your essence resides inside and does not change according to outside circumstances. It is the "who I am," or more precisely, "who I *really* am." Usually what you know about it is by snatches since you can't see it directly. You discover your core identity through the variety of ways it reveals itself as you go about doing the business of living. But your essence is the part of yourself most directly connected to unlimited air/energy.

According to Tal Ben-Shahar,

> The core self comprises our deepest and most stable characteristic—our character. It comprises the actual principles by which we live, which are not necessarily synonymous with the ones we claim to follow. Because we cannot observe a core self directly, the only way for us to know a person's character is through its manifestations, through the person's behavior, which *is* observable.[36]

Your essence should not be confused with the ego, which provides the public face you show to the world—and yourself. But the ego serves your intellect and self-image, which are in flux—changing according to the dictates of circumstances. Whereas, it is your core, or essence, which is solid and unchanging, for it represents your spiritual reality. As such, it is aligned with unlimited energy.

---

[36] Ben-Shahar, Tal, *Happier, Learn the secrets to daily joy and lasting fulfillment* (New York, McGraw Hill, 2007), 114.

Within Is a Big Place

Going within yourself takes you to your inner sanctuary, your place of peaceful refuge in the trials of life. The ideal is to feel at ease in both your inner world and your outer world. And the likelihood of that goes up the more they are aligned. Colin Wilson wrote, "The road that will take us forward is also the road that will take us inward."

Many unclaimed air/energy pockets become available once you went within and discovered more about yourself that you never bothered to notice or appreciate. So much of what influences your behavior used to be dismissed as trivial, irrelevant, or wrong.

As you explore parts of yourself you've never fully laid claim to, set out with the curiosity and wonder of an adventure, the way young kids do. There are marvels to be found… Put your rational mind and sense of responsibility on back burner now and then, as you go inner-world spelunking.

There is some confusion about the inner world because it does not neatly connect up with the geography of the everyday world. Words like soul, essence, core, authentic identity, and higher centers are not identical. And most of what's said about them is rather sloppy because language doesn't contain specific terms or reference points able to nail them down. Further complicating any discussion on this topic, a person's inner world is so subjective that they use those terms without meaning the same thing at all.

Despite there being very real differences in their meaning, I will not even attempt to draw distinctions between them. So even though I use those terms (or quote others who do), I am not referring to their specific differences, but instead to what they have in common. For our purposes it is enough to know those state are accessed from within. That is in contrast with other kinds of knowledge we have about our external world. And the distinction between your inner and outer world is really all that's required to take advantage of an air-rich life.

However, I quote Jeffrey Maitland to indicate that there's going within, and then there's going even deeper within. Most of the more arduous inner work spiritual adepts do is to get to that next level. "Our center is not our core. In a sense, the center is a gateway to our core. In being centered, you are at once given access to the core of your being… finding your core is also the beginning of finding the core of being."

From Dragons to Princesses
Rainer Maria Rilke

We have no reason to harbor any mistrust against our world, for it is not against us. If it has terrors, they are our terrors. If it has abysses, these abysses belong to us. If there are dangers, we must try to love them, and only if we could arrange our lives in accordance with the principle that tells us that we must always trust the difficult, then what now appears to us to be alien will become our most intimate and trusted experience.

How could we forget those ancient myths that stand at the beginning of all races – the myths about dragons that at the last moment are transformed into princesses? Perhaps all the dragons in our lives are only princesses waiting for us to act, just once, with beauty and courage. Perhaps everything that frightens us is, in its deepest essence, something helpless that wants our love.

So you must not be frightened if sadness rises before you larger than any you've even seen, if an anxiety like light and cloud shadows moves over your hands and everything that you do. You must realize that something has happened to you. Life has not forgotten you; it holds you in its hands and will not let you fall. Why do you want to shut out of your life any uneasiness, any miseries, or any depressions? For after all, you do not know what work these conditions are doing inside you.

Self-mastery demands you come to see your true self, beyond just considering your superficial appearance. You accept in grace and humility that as much as you know about yourself, it only scratches the surface. There's always more to be found—worthwhile stuff.

However, it must be understood that mastery, like wisdom (its sibling) is not simply about how much you know or how sophisticated your insights are. That's cumulative, built from years of direct experience. For that awareness you must yield to the immensity of what is unknown (and can't be known), as you let something wiser within guide the self-discovery process.

Self-knowledge represents a divergence from cumulative understanding. You discover that there's more to you than you thought. Yet much of what's well-known about yourself simply don't matter a hill of beans compared to those deeper discoveries. The universe inside yourself comprehends your identity, priorities, and beliefs from a more encompassing view.

Love after Love
Derek Walcott

> The time will come
> when, with elation,
> you will greet yourself arriving
> at your own door, in your own mirror,
> and each will smile at the other's welcome,
> and say, sit here. Eat.
> You will love again the stranger who was your self.
> Give wine. Give bread. Give back your heart
> to itself, to the stranger who has loved you
>
> all your life, whom you ignored
> for another, who knows you by heart.
> Take down the love letters from the bookshelf,
>
> the photographs, the desperate notes,
> peel your own image from the mirror.
> Sit. Feast on your life.

Reclaim Your Lost Bits

In all things, you should strive to be true to "who I am." Seeing yourself clearly requires an honest and discerning eye—without aggrandizement or defensiveness. And true to life, the more attentively you engage the experiences which come your way, the more accurately you can read the signals about yourself and the world you inhabit.

You are the embodiment of countless facets of yourself—some claimed, some rejected, some familiar, some totally unsuspected. While certain aspects are conscious, many others are not. Some of them you like, others you don't. Some can be discovered only because they show themselves indirectly, revealed by covert observation of your attitudes or behavior.

If you want to be the master of yourself, you need to invite as many of those parts of yourself as possible to the party.

According to Gary Zukav, "If you are not conscious of all the different parts of yourself, the part of yourself that is the strongest will win out over the other parts. Its intention will be the one that the personality uses to create its reality." In that case, all the other parts of yourself are relegated to being bit players in your ongoing drama. The whole of you is an ensemble cast—let each part strut it's stuff. You'll be the richer for it.

Self-discovery calls many unrecognized sides of yourself "out of the woodwork." They bring out a broader range of your abilities and unconventional ways of seeing things than ever before. Whether or not you like all they represent, each of them holds a sliver of your identity. So refusing to see certain ones leaves a hole. Greater self-knowledge fills in those holes, those gaps.

Dostoyevsky wrote:

> Every man has reminiscences which he would not tell to everyone but only his friends. He has other matters in his mind when he would not reveal even to his friends, but only to himself, and that in secret. But there are other things which a man is afraid to tell even to himself, and every decent man has a number of such things stored away in his mind.

These are not shameful secrets but unfocused regions of your identity that are still unclaimed. Even though you know little about them through your conscious awareness, they are already wired into your air/energy system. That's why improving self-knowledge increases your air/energy level—and *vice versa*.

Flow with Your Emotions

Emotions hold massive amounts of air/energy. They're fluid, ever-changing, and versatile.

The words "flow" and "fluid" suggest flowing flexibly with them. One of the reasons to go within is to access your emotional awareness. Your emotions certainly are a natural force which refuses to be denied. When riled up, they flood out your less-flexible, rational processes.

Learning more about what makes you tick leads to many more ways to relate to your emotional responses than you're using now. Emotions may not be rational, but neither are they random since they have a "logic" all their own. That's learned by willingly flowing with them. They are rooted in the mid-brain, the limbic system, which does not use language or respond to logic, which arises in the intellect.

Your mind, body, and emotions each have its own sphere in which its particular abilities work the best. All three contribute to your ability to flow and be appropriate in your response. When one of them doesn't fully participate, its particular functions have to be performed in some fashion by the other two modes. But that's less than ideal.

Learn to decipher this non-verbal, non-rational language. You'll discover what the emotions understand is miles faster, less ambivalent, and more trustworthy than what the intellect can discover on its own. That's also true for what the body knows. But first you must open the door and invite your body and emotions to speak to you.

~~~~~~

In Praise of Blubbering and Yammering
A BonBon

Everyone experiences life in three ways—logically, emotionally and physically. Early on, we learned to let the logical side do the talking. It's good at it and people are more likely to pay attention.

Since our logical side controls the mouth it assumes it calls the shots. But it edits out information that doesn't make sense to it—information that isn't rational. What it deletes is primarily related to the body and emotions.

When our emotional side tries to speak up and be "logical" it blubbers. When our physical side tries to speak up and be "logical" it yammers. Neither of which comes across as articulate—but that doesn't mean the body and emotions don't have anything worth saying.

Neither blubbering (hurt feelings) nor yammering (body hurts) come across as persuasive or coherent. To the extent their message gets through at all, it's likely to be embarrassing for both the speaker and the listener. The point is almost always lost because it's made so ineptly.

Our logical side wants to leap in and tidy up the information since it, too, doesn't "get it." That's why the blubbering or yammering started in the first place.

So here's the dilemma—whether to persist with belaboring the issue that's putting you in a poor light, or to drop it—let it go, resolved to "forget the whole thing."

When it comes to verbal expression the body and emotions are woefully inept—they're accustomed to keeping quiet. So when they do speak out—however awkwardly—pay attention. Listen. Trust there's something being said that your logical mind didn't notice or can't address. But it's something you need to be aware of, nonetheless.

Respect the sincerity of what's being expressed, however illogically. Don't attempt to turn it off. Listen beyond the words, for the underlying message. Muzzle your own smooth-talking logical point of view that's eager to edit or correct. Consider the blubbered or yammered information relevant, since there's a core of truth in it—truth that would be so easy to ignore.

It takes courage to let yourself blubber or yammer. It takes even more courage to listen and respect the perplexing message. Yet you'll be amazed by what you'll discover about yourself on those channels you've assumed carried only gibberish or static.

Tune it in, don't tune it out.

© 2014, Faith Lynella, from *BonBons to Sweeten Your Daily Life* or *More BonBons and Treats*   http://faithlynella.com

---

As either-or thinking, which is favored by the mind, is finding itself no longer the only game in town, three-centered awareness (with heart, mind, and body working together) will take its place more and more. You learn how to think with your heart and to feel with your mind.

As the three of them increasingly play nice together (three-centered), they have no difficulty interfacing with your higher nature (or your higher angels). The four-centered state builds on the three working as a team. Only now they are melding into an integrated unit. *There's mega air there!*

When you allow your inner states to express themselves, you don't get to cherry-pick which of them are acceptable and to your liking. They all have something to offer and can shed additional light on your character and circumstances. Each has its appropriate role and place. But your rational or egotistical priorities often get in the way of authenticity.

Khalil Gibran said "Keep me away from the wisdom which does not cry, the philosophy which does not laugh and the greatness which does not bow before children."

Emotions Are Energy Reservoirs

Emotions are energies which support inner knowledge, social connections, and healing. According to Karla McLaren in *Emotional Genius, Discovering the Deepest Language of the Soul*:

> Emotions are now categorized, celebrated, vilified, repressed, manipulated, humiliated, adored, and ignored. Rarely, if ever, are they simply honored. Rarely, if ever, are they seen as distinct healing energies in their own right.[37]

Each of us has a lifelong discomfort in dealing with our emotions. Before we even acquire verbal skills, we've learned how to stifle our feelings—to stop expressing them out loud. By five years old, we're already skilled at hiding or distorting our emotional reactions in social situations. It's not surprising we come to distrust them, rather than paying attention to what they have to say.

You can't simply transform a particular emotion into a different or preferred one by changing its name. Calling a pig a dog doesn't make it one. Calling your anger acceptance doesn't make it so. It just leads to more emotional confusion—denial or repression, coupled with wishful thinking.

Trying to change a disliked feeling into one you like better is quite different from accepting or transforming it. Transformation comes after accepting and embracing something which was previously rejected. That's what healing and unifying are all about.

The Mindful Path to Self-compassion Christopher K. Germer said,

> How do you care for your emotional state? The compassionate way is to befriend painful emotions—to stop fighting them. There are many words for this: empathy,

---

[37] McLaren, Karla, *Emotional Genius*, (Columbia, CA Laughing Tree Press, 2001), 7.

concern, kindness, care, forgiveness, mercy, benevolence, thoughtfulness, tolerance, supportiveness, acceptance, understanding, friendliness, sympathy.[38]

We usually think of these terms as ways we should treat other people. But the person who needs them the most, and is probably doing without from you, is yourself. Finding a respectful and loving way to treat yourself will satisfy a lifetime of longing. That alone trumps any other pocket of air. As such, you are no longer in doubt as to your true value. Priceless. Trustworthy self-knowledge and self-acceptance grow from that discovery.

A Fresh Start at Self-acceptance

Each of us has already accepted the parts we like about ourselves. And that includes what we like to do unapologetically and in public. The unclaimed parts of your nature reside in the shadows and in ambiguity. Those unaccepted and/or unacceptable aspects of yourself remain problematic for you as long as you pretend they don't exist.

Either you expect to outgrow them, hope they'll improve or go away on their own, or you periodically go on virtuous vigilante hunts to stamp them out. But even the unacceptable parts of yourself are there for a reason. They're valid and genuine aspects of your essential nature.

Each of them is intimately connected to you, and together they comprise your uniqueness. Accept the fact that it is all worthy of acceptance. As JOSEPH CAMPBELL SAID, "THE PRIVILEGE OF A LIFETIME IS BEING YOU WHO ARE."

One of the things I like best about getting older is I'm no longer driven to "fix myself." I've arrived at a place where the aspects of myself I used to think were not good enough are as dear to me as the parts I considered laudable since all of them work together as a package deal.

After many years spent trying to "perfect my act," I like the person I've become, including how my quirky and dissimilar parts hang together. I've not simply made peace with that; knowing it makes me happy. I enjoy the time I spend in my company and sharing a joke with myself (maybe an inside inside joke).

---

[38] Germer, Christopher K., *The Mindful Path to Self-compassion: Freeing yourself from destructive thoughts and emotions,* (New York, The Guilford Press, 2009), 106.

A side-effect of greater self-acceptance is a sense of timeliness. It puts you in a natural flow with the forces of life. That helps you feel peaceful and calm—life's nourishing and steady reassurance as you plod along.

Control Is the Wrong Issue

Most people try to figure out how to "handle" their emotions—usually by suppressing them or redirecting them to be more acceptable. It begs the question, should or can they be handled at all?

Only the intellect thinks so. Your emotional nature certainly doesn't want to be controlled or manipulated. Besides, suppression doesn't support your higher purpose in the long run.

Every emotion is both valid and useful to help you understand your behavior. Each of them reflects crucial seldom-recognized aspects of your identity. There are not some emotions which are good (acceptable) and others which are bad (unacceptable). You need to find a way to come to terms with what you considered the undesirable emotions you've labelled "wrong" and left unclaimed. They represent further areas of self-discovery and potential pockets of air.

According to an ancient Indian fable, every person has within them three elephants—Mind elephant, Body elephant, and Emotion elephant. The Emotion elephant needs to run free because it alone can take the person where they want to go. It's the only one which can be happy. However, that elephant *cannot be trained or disciplined.*

The Mind elephant and Body elephant can be trained. A person must teach both of them discipline, so they can *run alongside* the Emotion elephant, and confine it a little. Notice both the Mind elephant and Body elephant must be trained. That's where your efforts at self-control need to be applied. It is fruitless to try to control the Emotion elephant directly.

Accept Your Vulnerability

Brene Brown's research on shame and vulnerability, show why that side of your nature must be acknowledged in order for you to have access to the emotions you crave the most. Brene Brown said:

> Our rejection of vulnerability often stems from our associating it with dark emotions like fear, shame, grief, sadness, and disappointment—emotions that we don't want to discuss, even when they profoundly affect the way we live, love, work, and even lead. What most of us fail to understand … is that vulnerability is also the cradle of emotions and experiences that we crave. Vulnerability is the birthplace of love, belonging, joy, courage, empathy and creativity. It is the source of hope, empathy, accountability, and authenticity. If we want greater clarity in our purpose or deeper and more meaningful spiritual lives, vulnerability is the path.[39]

Being in synch with all of yourself allows you to decipher your feelings, rather than being cowed by them. That's not the same as refusing to feel them or shutting them off. Keeping open to what the various ones have to express permits you to comprehend the fullness of your experiences more completely.

Tune In the Emotion Channel

Emotional energy supports your ability to survive in the world. Make peace with your full array of emotional states, for each of them serves a specific and necessary function for you. They allow you to listen to your deepest intelligence—which uses symbols rather than words. It does not kowtow to the left brain's logical view of events.

Be alert to your emotional responses as they arise, not to edit or suppress them, but to include that awareness in how you operate. It is relevant and remarkably timely. Stay curious about why you reacted in a certain way. There's much more going on than you think there is.

---

[39] Brown, Brene, *Daring Greatly: How the courage to be vulnerable transforms the way we live, love, parent, and lead* (New York, Gotham Books, 2012), 33-4.

Maintain as much detachment as you can manage, without getting defensive. Paying close attention to your unfiltered (prettied-up) reactions as they can expose your underlying motivations—the ones you're less than clear about. Anything which helps you see them, face them, or comprehend them leads to your making better choices.

Words are a rather slow and inefficient way to communicate about your feelings. But they're often the best we can do. On the other hand, emotional symbols deliver complex messages much faster, intensely, and accurately than words can. Such symbols can include sensory input which trigger meaningful associations: a sound, a smell, a taste.

All those sensations can sometimes bring a recollection back full-blown from the distant past. Symbols can deliver a multi-faceted emotional message in an instant, along with its full energetic whack.

Blaming someone else for what you don't like, or making excuses for yourself interferes with getting to the real underlying reasons you do what you do. Look beneath the surface and see what else is "speaking" to you in your environment and from other people. You'll be amazed.

As you become more aware of the intricate interplay between your energy and emotional states, you sense and respond to signals you used to ignore. Those act as an early warning system to alert you to move away from what you don't want.

Find the air-deprived bits of yourself and provide them/yourself what's needed. Until you accept those rejected aspects of your nature which you don't respect, you cannot respond appropriately to what they need. That leaves you air-deprived and at the mercy of their unrecognized means of satisfying it. In other words, they act outside of rational control.

For example, that could be the "childish" part of yourself that you think you "outgrew," or that acts irresponsibly. Yet it has an uncanny ability to find air/energy pockets in lighthearted ways. It is seldom respected or appreciated, yet it is in charge of wonder, curiosity, and play in your life. How can you reject that side of yourself—the one who never doubted that you could do anything, even fly—without losing something vital?

Get more sides of yourself aboard as full-fledged and "worthy." It confers helpful advantages:
1. You free up copious locked-up air/energy which was used to keep the lid on them

2. You get to participate in the fresh air pockets where they have unhampered access
3. The unclaimed sides of yourself have always demanded their particular flavors of air—even if it was unrecognized; so now satisfying them can be aboveboard rather than covert

Because you couldn't own up to those ill-defined desires (especially to yourself), such needs were satisfied in less-than-direct ways. They were showing up as distractions or problems to solve, rather than as accepted or reasonable needs. Now some of it is out in the open.

As an example, the desire to feel dependent and looked after (the child of a caring parent) never really goes away. The competent-adult self wants no hint of such dependency. So the dependent side distorts what it asks for from others. One might get sick, knowing on an unconscious level that being dependent is acceptable at such times. The desired attention (and care) is only offered to sick adults.

Of course, none of that thinking is conscious, and would be denied if someone dared to suggest such a thing. But when looking for air, it's important to recognize what rewards (air) might be available from behavior we do not acknowledge. In this example, there's a pocket of air which comes with being sick—despite the obvious downsides.

So much of life doesn't correspond to what makes sense to the mind. There are times when it should be left behind, as you let other sides of your nature take their turn at making choices. Feeling free is a holiday from being responsible. There's also considerable air to be found just by breaking free of the very restrictions we assume to be the way we should live.

~~~~~~

Jailbreak
A BonBon

Logic is a jailer. It keeps us functioning with preset limits and punishes us for escaping. It constructs restrictive and confining mental structures more solid than brick and mortar. Try spending a little bit of time every day eluding it. Carve out time and areas in your life where the "right way" or the rational way have no influence. Find lots of "wrong," awkward, silly, irrational ways to do the most familiar things.

Logic is over-rated. There are a zillion things in which it is not helpful at all. And it is so seldom fun. Abandoning it is often fun and fraught with surprises. So take a holiday from your intellect, first in small doses or activities. Then let the freedom creep into more and more of what you do. Break out of your own routine. Sure, you'll be "back to normal" soon enough.

Fear not, you can always get back and reclaim your briefly abandoned mental structure. But like any holiday, you return with fresh insights, a renewed and broadened awareness. You return with added flexibility, aware of more choices, even within your familiar limitations.

Back to jail? Maybe, but is it really a prison when you hold the key? Or does it become a prison only because you fail to use your key?

© 2014, Faith Lynella, from *BonBons to Sweeten Your Daily Life* or *More BonBons and Treats*   http://faithlynella.com

~~~~~

Chapter 13
Discover Air in Simple Pleasures

Feeling Fully Alive

Every person alive seems to be on a lifelong quest to find something which can make them happy. But what that might be seems undefined and elusive. You say, "If only it were this way, I would be happy" or, "If only I had that, I would be content." While your attention is off looking for it, you overlook the little opportunities for satisfaction coming to you each day.

It is often the small comforts and simple pleasures which make you feel "all is right with the world." It could be anything. Maybe it's a favorite food which transports you to a childhood recollection of feeling safe and loved; or it's an unexpected kindness which makes your day; or it's seeing the first crocus of spring.

Occasionally, reflect back upon your air/energy level at times when you were happiest. You felt energized, disengaged from time, and on top of the world. Sometimes, it seems like "walking on air." Your feet didn't seem to touch the ground because the rush of uplift energy was enough to defy gravity.

In the moment when you experience the simplest of pleasures, you aren't thinking about your quest for happiness—or worrying you might never find it. You are simply enjoying the fullness of the experience and feeling intensely alive.

You know that, however briefly, you want for nothing. You have no agenda, or more accurately, you're in a space where those concerns don't matter. It is also effortless. That's not surprising since air/energy resonates with your life force.

Albert Einstein makes the choice abundantly clear: "There are only two ways to live your life. One is as though nothing is a miracle. The other is as though everything is a miracle." In moments of highest inspiration, you sense the miraculousness of every little thing.

Great things and small are seen as equally important because scale falls away. The fact they exist at all is the common denominator—what gives them splendor. Each object of creation is recognized to be real, vital, precious, and significant.

You recognize your life is overflowing with it! According to William Morris "The true secret of happiness lies in the taking a genuine interest in all the details of daily life."

Embrace the miracle which is life—and all the tangible ways it touches you. That includes appreciating anything which your senses reveal about the world. Sink into the countless little gems of pleasurable experience that come to you at any moment of the day. As you tumble into those small moments of quiet enjoyment, you discover that pockets of air are virtually everywhere.

Afternoon on a Hill
Edna St. Vincent Millay

I will be the gladdest thing
Under the sun!

I will touch a hundred flowers
And not pick one.

I will look at cliffs and clouds
With quiet eyes,
Watch the wind bow down the grass,
And the grass rise.

And when lights begin to show
Up from the town,
I will mark which must be mine,
And then start down!

Engage All Your Senses

There isn't much thinking going on when little things are speaking to you. It's all sensation coupled with the emotional flavors which are sparked. Your senses lead the way, and they express is noteworthy.

This is your body, your flesh letting you *feel the world* it's intimately connected to. Secondarily to the sensory awareness, the mind contributes its recollections and the emotional associations bubble up.

Don't *Smell* the Roses
A BonBon

"Stop and smell the roses." How often have you heard that one? Please don't just smell them. There's so much more to be experienced—a world untapped in every blossom.

Discover a totally new relationship with flowers, the stuff of nature, or whatever is around you that's seldom noticed or appreciated. Start by *deciding to notice*. Make what's usually in the background of your busy life front and center. Pay attention, now. Focus the full horsepower of your sensory apparatus on a single flower, for instance.

Hold on. Wait… don't rush this.

What do your eyes see? Shift magnification, noting shades of light and shadow, the colors, the textures, the closed still-unpopped buds, the wobble in the breeze, its rootedness into the earth, the bugs crawling on the stem or buzzing around it.

Touch it—gently now. Is it warm from the sun? Moist from the dew? Do the bloom and leaves gently yield to your fingers, while being springy on the bud, yet tough and resisting in the stem? Can you imagine how much more a blind person would be "seeing" with their touch?

Listen. A flower may be silent, but it grows in a world that's anything but. Bend down—eye to eye, ear to bloom, with it. Stand still, your ear as close as possible. Get quiet, really really quiet. Turn off the hum of mental chatter, your personal Muzak. Can you hear the flower now? The buzz of insects, the chirp of birds, the rustling of the wind in nearby branches, the purposeful footsteps of someone going by, the hum of traffic in the distance. You might even hear the rubbing of the fabric in your clothes as you breath in and out. Quiet? No way!

O.K., *now* smell it. Really do it right, with your eyes closed—slow and deep. Don't just smell the blossom, but also the leaves, buds, seedpods, noting how the various parts seem the same—and different. Compare the part that's in the sun with the same part that's in shadow. Is it mustier? Crush a leaf or a petal and inhale the essence released. Let your mind run free. What associations come bubbling up? Are you transported back to grandmother's garden? What emotions flood in?

Taste it. Knowing that some plants are poisonous, think twice about chewing and swallowing. Build on what your nose unlocked. Is the taste familiar? Like an herb? Bursting with succulent life force? Roll it around in your mouth and explore its texture with the tongue, against the lips. Notice all the associations and emotions unleashed. Drag it out.

Five senses—infinite observations. And that's just the beginning—that's the flower as each sense takes it in. Now step back (physically and mentally) so you can experience the whole flower with the whole of you. Doesn't awe and wonder bubble up? Don't you, for a moment, feel the magic of "seeing" like a young child? There are no ideas about the flower—just the enjoyment of it, as you respond to its delicate beauty.

Take a quick check out of the corner of your eye, in the back of your mind. Life's problems are nowhere to be found—for the moment. They're eclipsed by the splendor of a flower, along with your taking the time to put something else ahead of them.

That's just one flower, but an encounter very worth your time. It's one that every flower offers—and any object that's experienced sincerely can provide.

© 2014, Faith Lynella, from *BonBons to Sweeten Your Daily Life* or *More BonBons and Treats*   http://faithlynella.com

When you step out of your habitual way of taking in the world, you can visit a stillness and fullness which are every bit as real as your usual one. But also, you are at peace. Dag Hammarskjold said:

> In the point of rest at the center of our being, we encounter a world where all things are at rest in the same way. Then a tree becomes a mystery, a cloud a revelation, each man a cosmos of whose riches we can only catch glimpses. The life of simplicity is simple, but it opens to us a book in which we never get beyond the first syllable.

The more intense the emotion and physical sensations which are associated with an event when it happens, the clearer and more complete the recollection can be after the fact. That's why you can revisit the bright spots which moved you deeply so fully, but you don't recall humdrum activities (even though much more time is spent doing them).

Compare your routine way of getting by with an out-of-this-world day, when everything seemed vibrant and wonderful! All your senses were fully engaged. Each element is charged with meaning. Every detail stands out and can later be brought to mind and savored over and over again. *There's air there.* Open yourself to such sensuous delights and let them carry you away.

Look Beyond the Ordinary

Just because things are familiar does not mean they are not special as well. You make them special by focusing your full-beam attention upon them. You make something special by recognizing there is much more to it than it appears to be. When you allow yourself to be one with any particular thing, the experience enlarges you and fills your heart with awe.

Being fully engaged with life can carry you to a place of stillness—where serenity, joy, and lightness reside. It might take you to uncharted territories, where you could unearth rare gems of insight about yourself. For at such moments, *it all is important*!

It is a world where everything is charged with meaning. It takes curiosity and courage to let those free-flowing energies take you where they will. You have to keep your usual desire to be in control at bay.

You're just along for the ride. But that's when freedom and playfulness frolic. Friedrich Nietzsche said "Underneath the reality in could we live and have our being, another and altogether different reality lies concealed." And yet, we sometimes get to visit.

Intrinsic Motivation—Just for the Pleasure of It

Intrinsic motivation means doing something for the sheer pleasure of doing it. The true worth of such activities cannot be justified by merely considering what it produces. On one level, that's irrelevant. The thing was done primarily for the simple pleasure of being totally involved in the experience.

The reward from such activities is immediate and totally subjective. The payoff in satisfaction you feel happens right now—not eventually. The rest of the world has been pushed aside while it happens. The satisfaction won't last, but it was worth it. Such activities will have a quality of play about them.

It doesn't matter much what anybody else thinks about it. It also does not matter much if there's something tangible to show for it. As James M. Barrie, the author of *Peter Pan* said, "Nothing is really work unless you would rather be doing something else."

Intrinsic motivations (within yourself) are contrasted with extrinsic motivations which come from outside yourself. Extrinsic motivations are a mix of carrots and sticks used to reward (or control) behavior: money, desirable possessions, fame, social approval, power, threat of punishment, and coercion. When something is done for the pure satisfaction of doing it, all those "benefits" are secondary.

Your responsible side is likely to treat something done just for the fun of doing it like getting an extra dessert—not something for every day. Or doing what you like might be treated as a reward for "eating the yucky stuff" which you *had to do*.

Of course, what anybody does for pleasure or recreation is a matter of taste: from puzzles, to gardening, to climbing mountains, to bird watching. It rings their bell.

What those activities have in common, they are not done primarily as a job, or for money, or as a responsibility, or to produce something. This is for time out of harness—as well as the air and satisfaction which come in the process.

In that sense, there is no difference between making real pies or mud pies if it lifts your spirit. But make no mistake, taking time to have fun or make something beautiful without any concrete rewards beyond that, is still worth doing. It can be a critical driving force of your behavior. Such playfulness is time well spent, no matter how old you are.

Make a Space for Grace
A BonBon

God comes in the little spaces between—between activities, between thoughts, between people. That's the brief moment where there's a "space for grace." It's not felt as grand and glorious, but close and intimate—because God becomes alive to us that way. That's really how we connect—not through large gestures but in the wee, small, personal and intimate ones.

But for that to occur, we must leave space that's unfilled with other matters. Make space between all those jostling concerns

sucking up your attention and energy. Make space for the presence of God, and it will be filled.
- Space between events bring peace and freedom (though brief).
- Space between people brings respect, and often love.
- Space within yourself brings joy.

P.S. Make a space for Binkles!
Every space IS a Binkle!

© 2014, Faith Lynella, from *BonBons to Sweeten Your Daily Life* or *More BonBons and Treats*   http://faithlynella.com

The Present of the Present

There's no explaining why certain things you love to do are delightful for you. Doing them is a gift you give to yourself. There's a disengagement from whatever else is going on as you sense the moment's satisfaction. The sensation might only last a flicker, but it could be enough for a super-quick recharge of upbeat energy. And when conditions allow, the sensation can be extended to a full-fledged respite.

Whenever any of those just-for-me moments arises in you, pause and let your heart feel full. "Sometimes it's the same moments that take your breath away that breathe purpose and love back into your life." Steve Maraboli tells us. Draw the sensation out. If it comes from memory, allow the deeply-satisfying original experience to come alive for yourself once again.

However, there's a danger in living in the past, thinking things which happened before, (or the people involved) are more important than the here and now. While the past can be a trap for some, others are busy daydreaming about what they expect the future to bring them. Either route is O.K. as a time out, as a breathing space. But too much of either should send off warning bells.

The mind works in such a way as to drop out unpleasant details of prior experiences. Or it projects future hopes with a false veneer of perfection which makes them seem more desirable and unblemished than the world you're actually living in. Who wouldn't prefer to take that? But it's a phantom.

Hanging out in the past or the future for your satisfaction is at the expense of all the air/energy to be had here and now, as you live and breathe. Every now moment is an infusion of oxygen. The truth is, pockets of air can only be engaged right now. Even if you're wrapped up in recollection or anticipation, that's the very thing you're *choosing to do with this moment.* It's *instead of* other things left unchosen at this time.

While the past (as memories) and the future (as dreams or aspirations) can provide air briefly, it's closer to stale air. It's a step removed from this very moment, the only time in which you can actually feel life pulsing in you.

As you focus on the little things, you re-discover feeling completely alive is less about what happens to you than the quality of your response to it. Your bright hopes or joyous recollections serve you best by lighting the twinkle in the eye and reminding you of what you already know. Now *that's* here and now.

As Richard A. Bower said, "The call to simplicity and freedom is a reminder that our worth comes not from the amount of our involvements, achievements, or possessions, but from the depth and care which we bring to each moment, place, and person in our lives."

Arrive in a State of Grace

When your highest awareness becomes grounded within the everyday world, it appears as grace and gracefulness. Grace adds an element of luxury, of "something special" wherever it appears. Its presence reveals the alignment of your ideals within practical reality.

Expediency would treat grace's added sparkle as expendable or an optional enhancement. But grace is not simply a matter of appearance; then it would be merely pretty or pleasing. It also includes a dollop of extra air/energy—a sense of just-rightness.

Where grace is evident, your mental, emotional, and physical sides all feel at peace. Observers sense a grace-infused experience as being true and beautiful. But just as important, on a deep level it gives them air.

Equating truth and beauty attests to the presence of grace. "Truth is beauty and beauty is truth and this is all you need to know," as John Keats said. Such an alignment also signals plenty of lovely possibilities flirting for your attention. Grace, graciousness, and gratitude open the door. Then what will you make of them?

Looking for signs of grace:
- Charm and charming (sincerely heartfelt)
- Refined and courteous
- Beautiful and lovely
- Benevolent and merciful
- Displaying generosity of spirit
- Joyful and at peace
- Dignified and distinguished (but without pomposity)
- Lithe and flowing

Every one of these signs of grace acts as an intersection of multiple layers of significance—from the most ordinary to the most profound. Each of them carries a dynamic energy charge which can be sensed physically. Often the signs are accompanied with a binkle zizz or a moment of quiet enjoyment. Like manna, each sign of grace can only be fully experienced as it arises—this very moment.

Glorify the Small Stuff
A BonBon

It is easy to overlook the very small things that are right in life, that lift your spirits without fail, that make you pause and catch your breath in amazement. They nurture you and make you smile—if only on the inside. They appear like flashes of light that flit in and out of notice—but in tiny ways and quiet ways. Their presence makes your life go more smoothly—what a happy thought!

But we put much more concern and energy into those things that don't work as we like. Focusing on disappointments and let-downs is not an intelligent way to portion out our time and attention. It's better to spend it on the small stuff that gladdens the heart.

The light of attention is powerful. Detach it from the loud and jarring events that embroil you in turmoil. Instead, focus it on the delightful little things that light up your eyes. Glorify them! Treasure them! Give your simple pleasures extra awareness so they occupy a larger and more influential place in how you live.

Recognize them as they happen and feel blessed. Pause to savor the silent strength you draw from being attuned to their presence. Embracing the precious wee experiences fills you with gratitude. That creates a brief pocket of tranquility, which can be stretched o – u – t for as long as you can hold onto it.

Gratitude is a mindset that brings its friends, Grace and Joy with it. Notice, enjoy, share, treasure—these are verbs, action words. Doing them is your part. But in doing your part, the splendid little things you noticed are enticed to show themselves as being much more significant than they first appeared to be.

They come out and dance with you. By opening yourself to what is small and simple, you discover how much your life is filled with delights that have been too long ignored.

© 2014, Faith Lynella, from *BonBons to Sweeten Your Daily Life* or *More BonBons and Treats*   http://faithlynella.com

~~~~~

We can all benefit from following the advice of Mother Theresa, "Not all of us can do great things. But we can do small things with great love."

Get Hooked on Being Still

I choose to add nothing further to these quotations about stillness because of the paradoxical fact that talking about silence violates it.

- Within stillness is held unrecognized potential. Inherent in that which is quiet, still, and empty is the creative possibility of everything. All of the creativity that we experience arises out of that great mystery, that great stillness, that great void. ~ Cheryl Haley

- You need not do anything. Remain sitting at your table and listen. You need not even listen, just wait. You need not even wait, just learn to be quiet, still and solitary. And the world will freely offer itself to you unasked. It has no choice. It will roll in ecstasy at your feet. ~ Franz Kafka

- When stillness takes you, there is no more drama in your life. You observe it all from a distance, but there is no part of you that is interested in playing the game anymore. The stillness is too captivating. It wells up inside you, breaking over you in wave after wave, bringing such peace that you can no longer put anything into words. ~ Richard Rudd

- All the masters tell us that the reality of life—which our noisy waking consciousness prevents us from hearing—speaks to us chiefly in silence. ~ Karlfried Graf Durckheim

- I could see the ways in which silent prayer was listening to God and dialogue was listening to others. Somehow I knew there was one more piece to listening. That's when I began to practice reflection, listening to my inner voice. ~ Kay Lindahl
- Silence is a fence around wisdom. ~ German Proverb

Drawing Upon Quiet Energy

When I discovered the binkle back in 1992, I loved the zizz of energy associated with it. The binkle awareness and sensation (Chapter 7) became a lens through which I view the world, other people, and my own experiences. With almost no effort, I gravitate toward that positive energy—and away from lower-energy alternatives. I assess almost everything as to whether it has binkles.

Binkle energy is so central in how I live I was surprised to discover several years ago that I was only looking at one side of that coin—the upbeat and effervescent side. What I had, until then, been unaware of was the other side of the coin—the quiet and peaceful side of binkle energy. Binkles are also the energy of peace and stillness. It has a deep, subterranean, calmness that's close to your inner core.

The peaceful form of binkle energy connects to the bottomless, placid pool within which is so deep it doesn't ripple the surface. It is quiet and without the need to express itself (I guess that's how I missed it.). Yet quiet binkles energize the deeper self since it is the energy attuned to your essence. Its force can fuel the three-story factory, but it also feels no need to call attention to itself.

So now I've found the binkles of tranquility—the other face of the binkle. How could I have failed to see it before?! Of course, I've my share of peaceful moments, but never recognized there was binkle energy there as well. Now I do, and have no preference for one side of the coin or the other. They both provide me air in abundance.

Seal Crossing

Your Plug-in Stations which Never Fail You

Each of us has our favorite ways of getting a lift when we need it most. You eagerly look forward to getting renewed during the time involved. These are among the most available and common. Any of them can fit into a busy life and help you keep your equilibrium. Of course, you've found some additional ones as well (Chapter 4).

◊ Air Resides in Alone Time

Solitude and going within allow you to step off the treadmill long enough to catch your breath. Any tranquility to be found provides a respite from the cares of the world. How you act when alone could reveal a very different side of yourself than the socializing side. Alone time can access a deeper side of your personality, one which usually gets lost in the shuffle.

Time spent alone for quiet renewal is chosen *because* it is relatively free of distractions. It resembles a vacuum because if it isn't protected from the press of daily concerns, that space gets filled up with monkey chatter or incessant claims for your attention.

Paul Tillich points to the ambiguity of being alone. "Language... has created the word 'loneliness' to express the pain of being alone. And it has created word 'solitude' to express the glory of being alone."

To my way of thinking, the key difference between loneliness (a minus) and solitude (a plus) reflects whether being by yourself is by choice, and whether you're deriving air from the solo experience.

Being alone can provide a reflective space in which you enjoy being yourself—and with yourself. This could be a time to come to know yourself better, or in less familiar ways. Or it's time for letting out the aspects of your nature which stay hidden from everybody else. It can be for communicating with "the you other people don't see." In fact, as caught up by life as we all get, you don't get to see yourself this way very often, either.

Being in that unfilled space is sometimes meditative, even if it's not a formal practice. As Lance Smith says, "The practice of meditation isn't about escaping to some magical inner realm devoid of life's problems. It's about progressively opening your heart and clearing your mind enough to engage life directly, to be more fully present in a kind, helpful and peaceful way."

◊ Air Resides in Your Relationship with the Holy

Your efforts to go within take you to the place where you can access the spiritual dimension. Inspired and high-air/energy experience nourish that side of your nature. Your spiritual side is always available to you, although your conscious connection to it comes and goes. More accurately, it is constant and unfailing, but it's human nature to forget or lose our orientation.

Every person has a sense of the holy because it is ingrained in our nature. But we differ greatly as to the extent to which we outgrow it with the innocence of childhood or how tightly the intellect keeps it under control. For some, it is largely a matter of a particular religion, and it works for them. But feeling spiritual does not depend on a person being religious. It coexists within all creation, and that's why even the smallest things can open that reality to you.

◊ Air Resides in Books and Libraries

For me, nothing can compare to curling up with a good book for uninterrupted reading. I cherish the books and authors who have touched me deeply. I count favorite authors as my friends, and the great thinkers who I've read and re-read as my mentors. I'm eclectic in my interests, as happily absorbed in a wide variety of fiction genres as technical research for my next book. In my mind, libraries are holy places, the cathedral to the wealth of the human spirit.

I like the idea that while you're reading this book you and I are sharing this moment and these very ideas. Books add a timeless dimension to our connections. Your own bookshelf probably says as much about who you are as a diary would, for these are companions of your heart and mind. When we read, we revisit favorites and find new friends.

Movies are great, but seldom can engage the imagination as fully as reading does. But either of them takes us out of our solitary lives, to see a different view of reality when we ride the magic carpet of imagination. We find ourselves stretched from those adventures, as we find common threads which tie us to the universality of life's challenges.

At the heart of every book or movie is a story. It is our stories that speak to us on so many levels—stories which remind us of our shared humanity.

We pass along our stories, retelling them for the enjoyment they bring, and for the memories they rekindle. We create our own stories (only some of which we share with others), but we also eagerly partake of the stories of those we know.

Stories pull you into a timelessness, almost back to your years of childhood when you believed every word. As Ben Orki said, "Stories can conquer fear, you know. They can make the heart bigger." And what bigger pleasure is there than to read stories to children?

◊ Air Resides in Creative Activities and Imagination

The urge to create and make enjoyable things is innate and universal. The satisfaction it gives is indifferent to scale, so large or small endeavors can be fully satisfying. According to John Updike "What art offers is space—a certain breathing room for the spirit." What's equally true is that whether it's called art or not, what you create has air in it.

Beginners with poor execution can partake of the same enjoyment as a master, when each puts their whole self into the experience. Find ways to be creative, whether it is making a pie, decorating a hallway, or dancing a jig. It makes you feel more human and more alive.

◊ Air Resides in Nature

The natural world is our true home—nourishing us in every possible way. We draw sustenance from the natural world, from the kaleidoscope of the weather on our days, and the green and growing things which surround us. Our animal companions pull us away from our human foibles and vanities. Natural wonders add to the richness of existence. Kent Nerburn said:

> The greatness of nature can overwhelm the insignificant chatter by which we measure most of our days. If you have the wisdom and the courage to go to nature alone, the larger rhythms, the eternal hum, will make itself known all the sooner. When you have found it, it will always be there for you. The peace without will become the peace within, and you will be able to return to it in your heart wherever you find yourself.

Never forget, we all breathe the same air. As such, when you're aware of sensing it, you're connected to something larger than your puny problems, without their limitations or barriers. The simplest pleasure is in touch with the cosmos.

John Muir said, "When one tugs at a single thing in nature, he finds it attached to the rest of the world." And so are you. And so are we all.

Gardening is the number one hobby in the U.S. Yes, time tilling the earth can be done for food, for landscaping, or just to add beauty all around us. But don't discount the down-to-earth satisfaction which comes from having your hands in the dirt and watching things grow. Those activities, too, connect a person to something timeless as they fill the heart with wonder.

◊ Air Resides in Playfulness

Whether or not it is called recreation, certain activities have the ability to re-create the innocent spark which delights in play. Children are unrestrained in their ability to find a way to play, wherever they find themselves. Adults tend to add structure and call it hobbies, or sports, or vacation, or time away from it all. The purpose is the same. Just make sure you get all you need or you'll find yourself running on empty. In *Little Bets*, Peter Sims writes,

> A playful, lighthearted, and humorous environment is especially helpful when ideas are incubating and newly hatched, the phase when they are most vulnerable to being snuffed out or even expressed because of being judged or self-censored. The imagined possibilities become the basis for little bets, just as comedians improvise to develop new material. Plussing [to build upon and improve ideas without using judgmental language] then forms the basis on which to build ideas toward perfection.[40]

◊ Air Resides in Walking and Exercise

Moving your body involves your physical self. Too much time sitting or staring at computer devices make you stiff and stuck. A deep breath demands you flex your body. Do both often for a puff of re-energizing air.

We differ as to how much physical activity we feel the need for. Whatever your body cries out for should be given. If your body doesn't feel good, you don't feel good. And you might as well enjoy those times as well. Don't go climbing mountains (and extreme sports) just to prove you can.

---

[40] Sims, Peter, *Little Bets: How breakthrough ideas emerge from small discoveries* (New York: Free Press, 2011), 75-6.

Walking had an added benefit; it helped me to think. Nietzche wrote, 'All truly great thoughts are conceived while walking,' and his observation is backed up by science; exercise-induced brain chemicals help people think clearly. In fact, just stepping outside clarifies thinking and boosts energy. Light deprivation is one reason that people feel tired, and even five minutes of daylight stimulates production of serotonin and dopamine, brain chemicals that improve mood. Many times I'd guiltily leave my desk to take a break, and while I was walking around the block, I'd get some useful insight that had eluded me when I was being virtuously diligent.[41]

◊ Air Resides in Your Pets and Animals

In a too-complicated world, our critters take us at face value and reflect back the affection we shower on them. All that other stuff doesn't matter to them—or to you—when you're on their life-is-simple wavelength. Other demands upon you might seem daunting, but looking after them, is eminently doable.

Our pets hold a special place in our affection because they so often bring us joy. Caring for animals takes you out of your self-centeredness. Their guileless trust and dependence make you feel larger somehow. As a friend of mind would say, "I want to be the person my dog thinks I am."

◊ Air Resides Where Your Heart Is

If your heart swells with gladness, there's a sparkle in your eye, and you sense your own good fortune, *there's air there*.

---

[41] Rubin, Gretchen, *The Happiness Project: Or, why I spent a year trying to sing in the morning, clean my closets, fight right, read Aristotle, and generally have more fun* (New York, Harper, 2009), 25.

Chapter 14
But What About Me?
Taking Stock of Your Air Resources

NOTICE: This chapter can be omitted entirely if these brief questionnaires aren't of interest. All of the other chapters in the book can stand alone without this one.

If you want to print this chapter for ease in completing the questions, it is reproduced here:

http://pocketsofair.com/self-surveys

Learning More About Yourself

This chapter is comprised of a variety of surveys, points to ponder, and questionnaires. They are offered in the spirit of self-inquiry. There are no right or wrong answers. These are provided to encourage you to look beneath the surface.

These will help you to adapt the information more precisely to your situation. But not until they're put into practice can they crank up the air for you. So don't stop when you've answered these. Don't stop once you compare your answers with those your friends get—like in a magazine quiz. Put them to work for you.

These can give you a better understanding about how to apply what you've read. You'll also be more likely to remember it, since questions like these personalize the information to you. That in turn could spur you to action, to actually engage in an air-rich existence.

DISCLAIMER: No claims are made regarding the objectivity of these measures, or about how well they reflect any particular qualities a person might have. Nothing here implies these are objective, scientific, or better than other measures available.

What do they add up to? Who knows?! How much they help you depends a lot on how well you know yourself already, and whether or not you have other psychological measures to compare with them.

As with any analytical tools, the actual scores and answers are less important than how openly, honestly, and completely you're engaged with the questions. These surveys could be taken more than one time and yield different results each time.

Air Beats Data

Most surveys and questionnaires (scientifically tested or not) are primarily intellectual pursuits. So are these. So do not trust any answers or conclusions from them too much. They are limited in scope and these are a patchwork of measures.

Logical analysis is limited in what it can measure. If does do not take into account what your emotions know or what your body knows. Whereas, when you sense *there's air there*, all three of them are engaged. So trust your unfailing ability to respond to pockets of energizing air. Trust your own discernment and wisdom in such matters.

If this chapter helps you to understand yourself better, all well and good. But nothing here should take the place of your evolving air-finding capability. Trust the combination of your mind, body, and emotions working together to find the air/energy you require.

Check Out Your Plumbing and Wiring
Your Energy Diagnostic Spots Untapped Supplies and Leaks

Perform the kind of assessment that the power company would do for your house. Only this assesses your body's energy as it surges and crashes. So the urgency to find any leaks or shorts is even greater. (See Chapter 7.)

Tally Your *Incoming* Energy Resources
- Where are you getting energy from now?
- How reliable is its availability? Is it steady? Up and down? Unpredictable?
- How much of your daily time and effort does it cost to stay energized—up to speed?
- Where can you tap into additional energy sources? How hard will they be to develop? The tangible and intangible costs?
- Can you reap more energy from what you're already doing?
- Look at the longer term. What needs to be done *right now* to develop available supply lines for yourself down the road?
- Where can you build in greater efficiency (or eliminate inefficiency)?

Evaluate Your Energy *Leakage* (out-flow)
- Where is your energy being wasted? Used inefficiently? Permitted to leak away unclaimed?

- What does it produce? For yourself? For the big picture or other people?
- How consistent is the drain on yourself? Is there a loss every time that such-and-such occurs?
- How massive is the loss? A trickle or a total wipe-out?
- How soon do you notice the energy drop? At the time? Later, when you're "tapped out?" Even before it happened (because of a gnawing sense of dread or *déjà vu*)?
- How much power do you feel you have to alter the demanding situation? Or avoid it entirely? Are you willing to do so? Or why not?
- Can the situation be repaired by re-defining your boundaries? Limiting its scope? Changing the players (including yourself)? Renegotiating the rules?
- Does the leakage touch your core, high-priority concerns? Fixing central issues is more complicated (often painful); but the need is likely to be urgent.

Running Out of Gas

These answers are totally subjective, so nobody but you would arrive at these answers. They're asked so you start to pay more attention to these concerns over time.

What happens to you emotionally when you run out of gas? Physically? Mentally?

How often does it happen?

How debilitating or inconvenient is it?

Is it gradually or abruptly, and without warning?

Is there something or someone in particular who drains you every time?

Can you find a better way to deal with it—or make it less likely?

Where does most of your air and energy coming from?

What are your **favorite** things that give you a respite and/or air? Make the list as long as you can.

What are your **least favorite** things? They're things you actively dislike that are in your life now. Make the list as long as you can, with the intention that you'll whittle it down.

Rate each of your recharge source and/or places

How consistently and reliably does it energize you?
Gives a lift, but not by much
Sometimes, but it's hot and cold

Now do the same with the people who are close to you (also see below).

The People in Your Life

A. Define Your Personal Bulls Eye

Take stock of your circle of personal contacts. Start from being totally egocentric, since you really are the center of your world. Imagine a series of concentric rings around yourself, like a bulls eye.

You are the center dot.
1. **The first circle** Those closest to you, who you trust totally.

   This is your core support circle. Any rejection or betrayal from someone in this group is a catastrophe.
2. **The second circle** People you really like and respect.

   You have a cordial bond with them, but it hasn't been tested through "hell and high water." So far, they've done nothing serious to make you distrust them.
3. **The third circle** Friendly but a mix of close and distant, with both trusting and disappointed events with them. This group is uneven—keep your boundaries in place.
4. **The fourth circle** Casual acquaintances.

   These can come and go without rocking your boat much. And that's by far the largest number of people you know. It's more likely to contain your extended social circle or those you don't see very often.
5. **The outer circle** People who know you or who you know, but without a personal relationship. It could be as loose as popularity, gossip, or reputation. One step up from perfect strangers.

On a piece of paper and make a list of the people who are in your closest-in circle (#1). Next list the ones in the second circle. Don't bother with the others unless you want to.

You're attached to many family or friends by a long history of shared experiences. But that's no longer enough for them to be in Circle 1 or 2. Have you found any shifts in or out of that core support group lately? Watch for it, more is coming.

Vibrational alignments will carry greater weight as to who we attract—and who drifts away. The attachments or relationships you took for granted will change. And some will exist on a whole different basis later.

As Binkle Sources—
Energy coming in *or* Energy Going Out

Returning to those people on your lists, consider them in terms of whether they're binkle sources for you. When it comes to getting recharged, which people are draining to you? Which are energizing?

Note the Direction the Energy Flows:
    A Energy flows both ways about equally
    A+: Dynamite—WOW! Both directions and lots of it
    B: More going from you to them
    C: More going from them to you
    D: You alternate; the flow is one way but you take turns as sender or receiver
    E: It doesn't happen; low energy

Maybe the people in your closest rings aren't the ones you're getting your energy from. Go back to Chapter 7 and see what this tells you about your energy-management (plumbing and wiring) issues.

What's Your Natural Intuitive Style?

The following self-survey is provided courtesy of Patricia Troyer[42]

Everybody is intuitive, and the following questionnaire will not only help you see how naturally intuitive you already are, but which level of intuition you're a natural at and which you might want to work with next: physical (P), emotional (E), mental (M)—in other words, how to fly your plane, not just look at it and rev its engines.

---

[42] Patricia Troyer, *Reconnecting and Tuning In: Recognizing Pure Intuition* (Stone People Publishing Company, 2012)

Do you tend to be more physical, mental, or emotional in your automatic natural reactions. They are all intuitive, and there's no level of intuition inferior to another. Just start from where you are, and go one step at a time.

_____ I look at all possible sides when solving a problem. (M)
_____ I need specific details to solve a problem. (P)
_____ I get easily caught up in other people's problems. (E)

_____ I can tell when someone is being dishonest. (P)
_____ I am never sure whether people are telling the truth. (E)
_____ I can sense when someone is lying to themselves. (M)

_____ I prefer people who are logical and realistic. (E)
_____ I prefer people who are imaginative and creative. (M)
_____ I prefer people who take immediate action. (P)

_____ I like being around people who take their work seriously. (E)
_____ I like being around people who are spontaneous. (M)
_____ I like being around people who do what's expected of them. (P)

_____ I prefer having a daily schedule. (P)
_____ I prefer letting each day just flow on its own. (E)
_____ I prefer working from a To-Do List. (M)

_____ I avoid daydreaming. (P)
_____ I enjoy daydreaming. (E)
_____ I often slip into daydreaming. (M)

_____ I prefer having rules and instructions to follow. (P)
_____ I prefer finding ways around rules and instructions. (M)
_____ I prefer having as few rules as possible. (E)

_____ In a crisis I'm more likely to be excited but act in control. (M)
_____ In a crisis I'm most likely to feel anxious. (P)
_____ In a crisis I'm most likely to do nothing. (E)

_____ I analyze a situation before taking action. (M)
_____ I follow my "gut instincts" and act quickly. (P)
_____ I ask for advice from others before taking action. (E)

_____ I like "knowing" the answer, even if I can't prove it. (M)
_____ I like logic, reason, purpose. (E)
_____ I like taking action to find the answer. (P)
_____ I like dreams. (E)
_____ I like facts. (P)
_____ I like creating from ideas. (M)

_____ I like seeing patterns. (M)
_____ I like logic and analysis. (P)
_____ I like things to stay the same. (E)

_____ I like possibilities. (E)
_____ I like specific plans. (P)
_____ I like seeing the big picture. (M)

There are no right or wrong answers, just ways to pin your natural style. Add statements of your own as you discover things about yourself.

Are You Happy Now?

Take this diagnostic test and find out.

Happiness, you may have heard is relative. It turns out it's also quantifiable, thanks to the University of Michigan's Christopher Peterson, author of *Primer of Positive Psychology*. His Authentic Happiness Inventory Questionnaire uses 24 multiple-choice questions to gauge responders' level of bliss. But to make things easy for you, he was kind enough to boil down his test to 10 essential questions, scored against a maximum of 50 points. So go ahead, grab a pen. You'll find the grading key below.

Choose the response that best describes you:

1. A. I feel like a failure.
   B. I do not feel like a winner.
   C. I feel like I have succeeded more than most people.
   D. As I look back on my life, all I see are victories.
   E. I feel I am extraordinarily successful.

2. A. I am usually in a bad mood.
   B. I am usually in a neutral mood.
   C. I am usually in a good mood.
   D. I am usually in a great mood.
   E. I am usually in an unbelievably great mood.

3. A. I feel cut off from other people.
   B. I feel neither close to nor cut off from other people.
   C. I feel close to friends and family members
   D. I feel close to most people, even if I do not know them well.
   E. I feel close to everyone in the world.

4. A. I am ashamed of myself.
   B. I am not ashamed of myself.
   C. I am proud of myself.
   D. I am very proud of myself.
   E. I am extraordinarily proud of myself.

5. A. Time passes slowly during most of the things that I do.
   B. Time passes quickly during some of the things that I do and slowly for other things.
   C. Time passes quickly during most of the things that I do.
   D. Time passes quickly during all of the things that I do.
   E. Time passes so quickly during all of the things I do that I don't even notice it.

6. A. I have little or no enthusiasm.
   B. My enthusiasm level is neither high nor low.
   C. I have a good amount of enthusiasm.
   D. I feel enthusiastic doing almost everything.
   E. I have so much enthusiasm that I feel I can do most anything.

7. A. I am unhappy with myself.
   B. I am neither happy nor unhappy with myself—I am neutral.
   C. I am happy with myself.
   D. I am very happy with myself.
   E. I could not be any happier with myself.

8. A. If I were keeping score in life, I'd be behind.
   B. If I were keeping score in life, I'd be about even.
   C. If I were keeping score in life, I'd be somewhat ahead.
   D. If I were keeping score in life, I'd be ahead.

E. If I were keeping score in life, I'd be far ahead.

9. A. I experience more pain than pleasure.
   B. I experience pain and pleasure in equal measure.
   C. I experience more pleasure than pain.
   D. I experience much more pleasure than pain.
   E. My life is filled with pleasure.

10. A. I do not enjoy my daily routine.
    B. I feel neutral about my daily routine.
    C. I like my daily routine, but I am happy to get away from it.
    D. I like my daily routine so much that I barely take breaks from it.
    E. I like my daily routine so much that I almost never take breaks.

Grading Key: A = 1, B = 2, C = 3, D = 4, E = 5.
Add the scores to find your total happiness level.

Greater than 38: You're in the top 10 percent of Americans, happiness-wise. **Greater than 34**: You're in the top 25 percent. **Less than 24**: You're in the bottom quarter. **Less than 18**: You're in the bottom 10 percent.

Satisfaction With Life Scale (SWLS)[43]

The SWLS is a short 5-item instrument designed to measure global cognitive judgments of satisfaction with one's life. The scale usually requires only about one minute of a respondent's time.

Below are five statements that you may agree or disagree with. Using the 1 - 7 scale below, indicate your agreement with each item by placing the appropriate number on the line preceding that item. Please be open and honest in your responding.

- 7 - Strongly agree
- 6 - Agree
- 5 - Slightly agree
- 4 - Neither agree nor disagree
- 3 - Slightly disagree
- 2 - Disagree
- 1 - Strongly disagree

____ In most ways my life is close to my ideal.

---

[43] ©Ed Diener, Robert A. Emmons, Randy J. Larsen and Sharon Griffin as noted in the 1985 article in the Journal of Personality Assessment.

____ The conditions of my life are excellent.
____ I am satisfied with my life.
____ So far I have gotten the important things I want in life.
____ If I could live my life over, I would change almost nothing.

- 31 - 35 Extremely satisfied
- 26 - 30 Satisfied
- 21 - 25 Slightly satisfied
- 20   Neutral
- 15 - 19 Slightly dissatisfied
- 10 - 14 Dissatisfied
- 5 - 9 Extremely dissatisfied

Scale of Positive and Negative Experience (SPANE)[44]

Please think about what you have been doing and experiencing during the past four weeks. Then report how much you experienced each of the following feelings, using the scale below. For each item, select a number from 1 to 5, and indicate that number on your response sheet.

1. Very Rarely or Never
2. Rarely
3. Sometimes
4. Often
5. Very Often or Always

____ Positive
____ Negative
____ Good
____ Bad
____ Pleasant
____ Unpleasant
____ Happy
____ Sad
____ Afraid
____ Joyful
____ Angry
____ Contented

---

[44] © Copyright by Ed Diener and Robert Biswas-Diener, January 2009.

Scoring:

The measure can be used to derive an overall affect balance score, but can also be divided into positive and negative feelings scales.

Positive Feelings (SPANE - P):

Add the scores, varying from 1 to 5, for the six items: positive, good, pleasant, happy, joyful, and contented. The score can vary from 6 (lowest possible) to 30 (highest positive feelings score).

Negative Feelings (SPANE - N):

Add the scores, varying from 1 to 5, for the six items: negative, bad, unpleasant, sad, afraid, and angry. The score can vary from 6 (lowest possible) to 30 (highest negative feelings score).

Affect Balance (SPANE - B):

The negative feelings score is subtracted from the positive feelings score, and the resultant difference score can vary from -24 (unhappiest possible) to 24 (highest affect balance possible). A respondent with a very high score of 24 reports that she or he rarely or never experiences any of the negative feelings, and very often or always has all of the positive feelings.

Flourishing Scale[45]

The Flourishing Scale is a brief 8-item summary measure of the respondent's self-perceived success in important areas such as relationships, self-esteem, purpose, and optimism. The scale provides a single psychological well-being score.

Below are 8 statements with which you may agree or disagree. Using the 1-7 scale below, indicate your agreement with each item by indicating that response for each statement.

- 7 - Strongly agree
- 6 - Agree
- 5 - Slightly agree
- 4 - Neither agree nor disagree
- 3 - Slightly disagree
- 2 - Disagree
- 1 - Strongly disagree

---

[45] © Ed Diener and Robert Biswas-Diener, January 2009.

____ I lead a purposeful and meaningful life
____ My social relationships are supportive and rewarding
____ I am engaged and interested in my daily activities
____ I actively contribute to the happiness and well-being of others
____ I am competent and capable in the activities that are important to me
____ I am a good person and live a good life
____ I am optimistic about my future
____ People respect me

Scoring:
Add the responses, varying from 1 to 7, for all eight items. The possible range of scores is from 8 (lowest possible) to 56 (highest PWB possible). A high score represents a person with many psychological resources and strengths.

Questionnaires Related to Positive Psychology

If you want to work through a variety of questionnaires and current research on wellbeing, visit

http://www.authentichappiness.sas.upenn.edu/Default.aspx

Authentic Happiness is the homepage of Dr. Martin Seligman, Director of the Positive Psychology Center at the University of Pennsylvania and founder of positive psychology. That is a branch of psychology which focuses on the empirical study of such things as positive emotions, strengths-based character, and healthy institutions.

That website has many different questionnaires and has had more than 2 million users from around the world. You are free to use all of the resources available there for free.

Search the Internet

Of course you can find many more self-analyzing tools by doing some online searches for relevant terms. Just don't get so caught up in the quest that you rely on that kind of information at the expense of your own best judgment.

Chapter 15
Treat People and Relationships as Pockets of Air

Start with Kindness and Go from There

Kindness is the basic courtesy every person owes to others. Kindness is somewhat more than a social convention because the need for it applies to all cultures, all the roles we might play, and all our forms of interaction. "Kindness is more important than wisdom, and the recognition of this is the beginning of wisdom," according to Theodore Isaac Rubin.

Going beyond kindness toward someone is optional. But to do less is insulting. And it is felt as such because it triggers a recoil deep in the psyche. The world is sensed as a less-inviting place. Unkindness severs a strand which binds us to a common humanity and to the more naïve side of one's nature that expects the world to be a friendly place.

Any flavor of unkindness violates the social contract and the quality of the air we share. In all likelihood, the wound is minor and soon dismissed. But being treated poorly hurts and makes you put your guard up. And it costs you air and energy.

Just as we prefer being treated kindly, we should take care about what we're dishing out. There's considerable air to be found with those whose camaraderie, good wishes, and trust have been time-tested. And as we learn early on, family members are a mixed bag. Some of them are unfailingly caring and supportive, while others might not be.

We take our cues from the treatment of those around us. Is your social life largely air-rich or deficient? Or does it lurch all over the place, energy-wise? Take note of the energy level of those closest to you, for theirs will have a direct influence on your energy as well.

~~~~~

Be the Kind Kind
A BonBon

Life need not be complicated:

> **When in doubt—Be kind.**
> **When *not* in doubt—Be kind.**

When difficulties abound like a swarm of gnats, taking your frustration out on those around you won't make your situation better. Only worse—less caring.

> When life seems like a mucky muddle—devoid of purpose—there's no good that comes from blaming or complaining. From dropping the ball.
>
> All the philosophies and religious principles in the world are mere lip service if they don't make of us a more caring person. Just because it's tough to do,… or rejected,… or misunderstood,… or seems to be futile…
>
> That's no excuse. No excuse at all! It's still what needs doing—all the more so.
>
> Kindness rebuilds the whole, indifferent world—one thoughtful gesture at a time. Challenge by challenge. Person by person. Moment by moment. Isn't that enough?!
>
> Stick with it—Or you'll be AWOL   Absent Without Love.
>
> © 2014, Faith Lynella, from *BonBons to Sweeten Your Daily Life* or *More BonBons and Treats*   http://faithlynella.com

In order for us to get closer to one another depends on one person feeling attracted to what they see and feel in someone else. How well do we know them? How accurate is what we know? Does it only scratch the surface, or does it instead recognize the person's underlying qualities?

We both need each other and influence each other in innumerable ways. For example, hanging around resourceful and energized individuals makes us resonate with those same energies within our own self. Just as being around lowlifes and negative types very often brings us down.

> Our essential hunger is not for food but for intimacy. When intimacy is missing in our lives, we feel isolated from other beings, alone, vulnerable, and unloved in the world.
>
> We habitually look to other people to fulfill our needs for intimacy. However, our partners and friends cannot always be there for us in the way we need. Luckily a profound experience of intimacy is always accessible to us—all it requires is that we turn around and move toward life. This will require courage. We have to intentionally open our senses, becoming deliberately aware of what is going on both

inside our body and heart/mind, and also outside, in our environment.[46]

There are many ways for us to get closer. Some depend on close proximity or deeper emotional ties. Some depend on finding common ground based on overlapping backgrounds or interests. Most develop by degrees, as the level of trust grows. But to get really close and intimate requires self-exposure. We have to drop our guard a tad.

We seek out those who are on our wavelength, who care about what we care about. However, that's not just about us finding others who agree with us and have similar ideas and values. But they also operate at an energy level that's compatible with our own.

Saga of the Social Seal

Can you see me? I'm the one in the middle.
From my photo album

What we say aloud to each other is usually less influential than how we treat each other. Recognize most communication is non-verbal, delivered by gesture, tone, and emotional signals which are much more expressive than words alone can ever be. We sometimes say the most when we speak the least. And all of that effects our energy level as well.

Martha Beck reminds us, "Basic human contact—the meeting of eyes, the exchanging of words—is to the psyche what oxygen is to the brain. If you're feeling abandoned by the world, interact with anyone you can."

---

[46]Bays, Jan Chozen, *How to Train a Wild Elephant: And other adventures in mindfulness* (Boston: Shambhala, 2011), 11-12.

When you're feeling lonely or sad consider it a reminder to recharge. Make something happen that you like. Start exchanging experiences and air with somebody right away, right where you are. However, someone else isn't essential because you can always elect to tap into the high-air parts of yourself.

There's No Substitute for Communication

Genuine communication involves each person expressing and receiving—a two-way experience which calls for a certain level of receptivity by all parties. So listening matters too. Stephen Covey said "When you really listen to another person from their point of view, and reflect back to them that understanding, it's like giving them emotional oxygen."

- Dialogue = two people (or more) exchanging information with each other
- Monologue = one person expounding on what they think; however, two or more people could be doing it at the same time (instead of a dialogue)

Monologues seem to considerably out-number dialogues—especially the open-hearted kind. If solid relationships are important to you, work harder to adjust that ratio. One-sided "conversations" squeeze out the air we like to expect when we open ourselves to speak.

> Listening is not a passive activity. It's not about being quiet or even hearing the words. It is an action and it takes energy to listen… Once we become aware of listening as a choice, we will notice that we have many opportunities to practice choosing to listen in our daily lives.
>
> The second way to define listening is that it is a gift—in fact, one of the greatest gifts we can give another is to listen to her or him with total attention. Think about a time when someone was truly listening to you—not figuring out what to say next, wishing you would hurry up so she or he could speak, or mentally reviewing a to-do list. The person was simply there, listening to you. You felt understood, refreshed, whole connected, healed.[47]

---

[47] Lindahl, Kay, *Practicing the Sacred Art of Listening: A guide to enrich your relationships and kindle your spiritual life* (Woodstock, VT: Skylight Paths Publishing, 2003), 5-6.

We form connections with a particular person on a variety of levels, which then develop further through a dance of mutual self-disclosure. It is likely to be repeated and reinforced over time.

While casual contacts do not require a high degree of self-exposure, there are those in your life who do. Are they getting what they require from you? Or *vice versa*?

One of the challenges you face is to find the correct balance between your relationship needs and your individual needs. Getting them to be less in competition assures you'll have more air/energy for satisfying them both.

Bring Down the Drawbridge

Communication isn't happening if one or both parties have their drawbridges up. There's no engagement or interaction possible then. It doesn't much matter what the sender/speaker says because no message can be received. The receiver is not "open" to it.

The message might be considered unacceptable because of its tone, who sends it, or the nature of the message itself. Until there's a more amenable approach that courts the recipient's trust or self-interest, both parties will stay within their self-protective fortifications.

"Most conversations are simply monologues delivered in the presence of witnesses," according to Margaret Millar.

In other words, the speaker shows no regard for the drawbridge being open. Typically, a person has their say, heedless as to whether it has been heard. (It's in the wrong glass.) Then they expect an appropriate reply, which isn't forthcoming.

Throwing out more logical arguments, or angry threats, after that only makes the impasse worse. That's not persuasion; that's not dialog. It certainly isn't engagement, let alone a two-way street. Those only happen between two people who have established at least enough trust to hear the other out.

Way too much attention is paid to crafting the message and polishing the speaker's point to make it persuasive so the receiver responds as desired. But not enough is paid to the recipient's receptivity to it. In fact that prerequisite is largely ignored. Yet a person has every right to block what they let into their interior world.

The speaker should take the drawbridge issues into account if he or she wishes to avoid an impasse. This is one of the most fundamental signs of respect, yet it's too seldom offered as the "knock-knock" which makes us *want to hear* what someone else has to say.

More often than not, a person has their say, but the recipient doesn't receive it, and that's the end of it. Nothing happens on the personal level because both parties failed to connect. No bridges were built between them on which to secure a particle of trust or understanding. That's why considering the mental drawbridge from the beginning may alter the approach taken. It's worth a try.

Consider what different tactics might be required to communicate to a person who isn't receptive to you or what you're trying to say. On some level, their drawbridge is up. If you want the message to reach them, you can't go blasting in or screaming "your truth."

It's necessary to precede the message with some signal—a knock-knock which isn't adversarial or over-bearing. If helps if your own drawbridge is down as well.

What kind of overture is needed to gain enough trust to get someone to lower their drawbridge a crack? That's the equivalent of the salesman's toe in the door. But it's not as good as being invited in. It's not the same as genuine engagement.

Some form of sincere and respectful preliminaries need to be observed to establish trust, and then to keep it oiled. Going to the trouble counters the corrosive rust which keeps the drawbridge closed. Some form of lubricant is crucial to true communication.

If you want better communication, start by looking at the underlying drawbridge issues, rather than the message content. Yet almost all the effort is spent on perfecting the message which won't be heard. Or the blame is heaped on the person who remained within their safe area with their bridge up.

In my opinion, the fault for not being heard should be placed at the door of the one who thinks speaking their piece is all that's needed for them to talk to somebody. When there have been hurt feelings or past slugfests between the parties, even more care is required.

The drawbridge is a slice of a relationship—a point in time. Sometimes it's up; sometimes it's down. For the individuals involved to continue to grow in their trust for each other, they can't take each other for granted. But if a person does not respect the one they're trying to relate to, that they won't be let in.

Besides, we've all been burned too often by gotcha logic, sales gimmicks, one-upmanship, and self-serving manipulation by those who led us down the garden path. So anything that smells like slick talk or psychological tricks put you on guard. You know you're at risk of being "had."

You may not be able to sort out the sophistry designed to mislead you. But you do not need to. It's enough to be able to tell that *there's no air there*. Tread lightly and humbly because when it comes to communicating, being "right" is not the point. Insistence on being right or vindicated guarantees the other person's drawbridge remains closed to you.

Why Bother to Speak at All?

What is the motivation behind the exchange? What is it trying to achieve? Most conversations are at the level of housekeeping (did you take out the trash?) or basic news. But the kind of communication which caring relationships need requires something more.

There's an emotional component—or the expectations of one at least. It also calls for a higher degree of attention and listening.

Simone Weil said, "Attention is the rarest and purest form of generosity." We become engaged and open to someone else's give and take. With any form of communication, much more is conveyed without words than with them. And the tone and attitude of the speaker could be decisive.

The emotional connotation is entirely different in each case: commerce, instructions, admonitions, affection, etc. Is the conversation to get to know each other better? If so, to what extent? And how much self-exposure or vulnerability does each person need to make to get there?

John D. MacDonald (as spoken by Travis McGee) said:

> The dividing line [between friend and acquaintance] is communication. A friend is someone to whom you can say any jackass thing that enters your mind. With acquaintances, you are forever aware of their slightly unreal image of you, and to keep them content, you edit yourself to fit. Many marriages are between acquaintances. You can be with a person for three hours of your life and have a friend. Another one will remain an acquaintance for thirty years.

It is equally true that in order to be a friend to your own self, you must allow any "jackass thing" to come out of your lips without it bringing out your preemptive editor or judge, who shuts that questionable line of thought down. Justification (which includes any flavor of self-justification or self-criticism) does not serve the truth. And it is a slippery slope downward which you're wise to steer away from.

The Paradox of Being Heard

Many years ago, I was given a paradoxical riddle to solve: You must deliver a message to a person who can't hear it. Huh?!

Therein lies the challenge for us all. As with resolving any paradox, the solutions only comes after you look at the impasse in a new way. You find a change in your point of view which turns what appears impossible on its head.

I've spent a lot of time pondering this riddle, and trying out approach after approach. That's part of what led me to comprehend the importance of the mental drawbridge because it looks at the *context* of an exchange or relationship. It takes into account the degree of openness between the individuals.

We've assumed the merit of our argument will be persuasive. If somebody will just listen to our idea, or hear us out, or give it a try they'll agree with us. So too much emphasis has been placed on the message, but hardly any is paid to the context. Nor have we devoted enough effort to building trust solid or earning the right to speak on certain matters.

You need to show considerable sensitivity whenever you presume to give your opinion on what somebody else should know, or do, or want. That is not about your expertise or the accuracy of what you know. But it is about speaking to somebody about their inner world and things which touch his or her heart. If that's what you're going to do, it's wise to tiptoe.

What Does a Kind Word Cost?
A BonBon

What perverse aspect of our character makes us want to thwart those close to us—to withhold the thing they hunger for? What makes us withhold something which we have in our power to give freely? Each of us, in many verbal and nonverbal ways, communicates to those around us what we really want. Usually it is simple: notice me, appreciate me, respect me; tell me I'm pretty, or strong, or liked.

The message is sent out, riding on each comment, gesture, request. We do not need to know a person well to recognize that hitchhiking message—it screams at us. It says: "This is what I need from you." And then, what do we give them? ANYTHING BUT THAT! Why is that? Do we get power from withholding?

When I was a teenager, whenever a reward or recognition came to me, my mother would say "You couldn't have done it without me, could you." Obviously, the answer was, "Of course, I couldn't have done it without you." I never gave her the satisfaction of that response.

It took many years and a good dose of maturity to see that giving my mother that satisfaction in no way diminished me. Several years ago I tried an idea that enriched both our lives. I resolved that in every conversation with her, I would find a sincere way to say the words, "I couldn't have done (whatever it was, and it didn't matter how minor it was) without you."

Before long something very intangible but longstanding between us relaxed, and we found a more solid basis for our relationship.

It didn't take long for me to see that withholding appropriate responses to another hurt me more than it hurt them. A kind response to another's need is easy to do and requires so little—only a willingness to respond to another's need.

© 2014, Faith Lynella, from *BonBons to Sweeten Your Daily Life* or *More BonBons and Treats*   http://faithlynella.com

NOTE: *My mother is dead now. I am so pleased with what my change of heart did for our relationship during her remaining years.*

What I had yet to learn, as shown in this BonBon, was that putting someone else's feelings ahead of my self-interest did not diminish me at all. As empathy grows, it becomes possible to find a more caring reaction to replace customary ones. Your ways of treating others can produce more air for you both when you want it enough. And it does not depend on how they treat you back.

Each of us needs the warmth and air which come with close relationships. But relationships are living entities. They can die of neglect. When you water them with caring and appreciation they bloom. Just as hostility or indifference hasten their demise.

> We all know what warms our partner's heart if we stop to think about it, but when people are angry and hurt, they gradually stop doing whatever makes their partner feel warmly toward them… It's usually the simple things we 'forget' to voice. The longer couples are together, the easier they fall out of the habit of doing the obvious to create positive, loving, and affirming interactions. At the start of a relationship, we may tell the other person what we value and appreciate, then do the opposite as time goes on.[48]

---

[48] Lerner, Harriet, *The Dance of Connection: How to talk to someone when you're mad, hurt, scared, frustrated, insulted, betrayed, or desperate* (New York: Harper Collins, 2001), 153.

Beware of the Cringe Factor

Most social interactions are demonstrations of power relationships. We can't help it. It starts as powerless children with our parents, and little by little we find a way to earn a higher place in the pecking order. It is a given that someone gets to pounce on (or peck) those lower down the pecking order, but they cannot do so to those higher up. So not everyone is "fair game" to you; or *vice versa*.

The deeply-seated need to protect one's place in the pecking order is ingrained. Many of our social conventions related to status sanction and codify such dominance behaviors. Treating people that way is accepted as part of the natural order of things. But it adds a degree of competition and/or defensiveness to most interactions.

On an instinctual level (governed by the midbrain and outside our conscious control), humans seek to exercise power over others. Or we want to protect ourselves from treatment which makes us cringe and shrink inside. Nobody likes situations where we feel excess or inappropriate power is exerted over us.

If that is to ever change for you, you must start to notice the extent to which you engage in pouncing behavior yourself. Unlike the tides or the weather, this is an area where change is possible, if the desire is there. You do have considerable control over what you say to people, or in deciding what to do instead.

Air-bereft conversations:
- Gotchas and put-down of all kinds
- Bullying—whether verbal or physical
- Lording it over someone
- Criticizing and judging
- Rubbing the person's nose in something unsavory

I call this the Pounce Theory. Like the Law of the Jungle—eat or be eaten—it comes down to "pounce or be pounced upon." The forms which it takes are infinite, and some form of it can be found in too many relationships—even among those who claim to love each other.

Here are examples of common verbal pounces and put-downs which are the stuff of everyday conversations. And they could comprise the largest part of your relationship with certain individuals. Who needs it?! That makes for toxic air.

Pouncing words:
- I warned you
- I told you so
- If you'd listened to me
- Didn't I … /Didn't you …
- You thought you knew better
- You always … or You never … (which is never true)
- If you'd done what I wanted …

Phrases like these can be counted on to bring the drawbridge up. Or if it happens a lot, the bridge might be stuck closed almost all the time. To ever get past that, having communication with the pounced-upon person needs to be considered more important than your message or your being right about it.

Pouncing hogs up the air, with one person on the defensive (or subservient), and the other person telling them what for (being dominant). Sometimes the parties are locked into their roles, while sometimes they take turns (as in different areas of their relationship).

In some families or relationships, that kind of talk is on-going. But it's not conducive to developing trust or a two-way relationship, For those don't happen to be based on one person continually exerting their power over the other.

In terms of "pushing buttons," who's doing the pushing, and whose buttons are being pushed? It matters little since old patterns are maintained, and little or no air is available between the individuals.

Being kind does not include pouncing. It is not a matter of being weak, but of intentionally choosing not to exercise dominance strategies in a particular situation. It ignores those social cues completely. Perhaps I'm a softie, but I think each of us can have a better quality of interactions if we take the pounce strategies out of our bag of tricks.

Choosing kindness or affection over gaining a social advantage flies in the face of the tough-knocks school of getting along in life. It puts people on an equal footing and allows a higher degree of openness. But if you want people to bring down the drawbridge, you can't pounce on them when they do—not once in a while, but every time.

Kindness as the fundamental standard for social contact, across the board, is a good start. For although pouncing may be natural (as a part of our midbrain heritage), it is not kind. The concept of "turning the other cheek," as Jesus recommends, is about deciding not to pounce. Kindness, upholding, and grace offer air-rich alternatives.

The Pounce Theory is much more detailed than room here permits. A fuller explanation is developed in an upcoming book, *Halfway to Soup*.

Judging Yourself or Others Constricts the Air Supply

Any tendency to judge and compare, blame and reject, or to find others (or even yourself) wanting in some way distorts the opportunity for a mutual exchange right now. Putting such judgments aside requires a willingness to be vulnerable for a while, as you search out a common basis for relating.

Keeping an open mind requires us to suspend certain kinds of thinking which places labels on people. We shouldn't sort others into convenient pigeon holes. Judging is one form of that. Once we form a conclusory opinion, we turn off any curiosity about seeing them as accurately and fully as possible.

That's why stereotypes are so detrimental. It accepts labels about a person, and all the traits related to it, without you forming your own 360-degree opinion about them. In doing so, you close the mental door on all their other characteristics.

As a society, we've decided that judging others is not quite right. Hence "do not judge" is supposed to avoid that. But we haven't yet figured out what to do instead. Discernment is still needed, but must be undertaken in a more open-minded way.

To my way of thinking, "do not judge" refers to a place and frame of mind rather than a particular behavior. It has nothing to do with rules, norms, or standards of behavior. For all of those are highly critical and judgmental prone.

What I didn't realize when this BonBon was written is that place is one of your abiding pockets of air. So each time you resist the urge to be judgmental, you are also experiencing a moment of self-renewal and breathing free.

"Do NOT Judge" Is a Place, Not a Verb
A BonBon

The admonition, "do not judge" has been taken to ridiculous lengths in modern life. Even the most absurd, inappropriate, or self-serving behavior rates a "pass" by those determined not to criticize. Discernment is jettisoned willy-nilly to avoid the appearance of being judgmental or reluctant to understand.

We're all the poorer for it, since relevant nuances of thought and behavior go determinedly unnoticed.

It sounds noble and open-minded to declare, "I won't judge." The statement implies: I don't think I'm better than you. My behavior isn't any different than yours. It further implies external standards don't apply. All words and deeds are equal.

Refusing to judge has become the unchallenged and worthy (see, that's a "judgment" word) objective. A statement of fact (even if totally true) that sounds the least bit judgmental brings instant rebuke from all directions, "Don't judge!"

That phrase defines our culture—with everyone busily not judging… or noticing… or standing up for any notion that could be construed as "better," or "higher," or "good for the world."

The reasoning goes like this: To judge someone else is bad (oops, one of those darned judgment words, though it's usually permitted in this case).

So I refuse to do it.

Instead, I must do the opposite—which is to avoid judging.

So when I do that I'm good and fair (more of those darned words).

The problem is, that's a simplistic example of either-or thinking—judge versus not judge—choosing between opposites. Either one is a verb—something one does. To attempt to do both (avoiding either one) sounds less judgmental, but leaves one paralyzed.

The phrase, "do not judge" has been totally misunderstood and misapplied. It's not about doing something (or not). It refers to resisting the urge to judge (or not), so you can be free to try something entirely different. It refers to a place within yourself where judging isn't possible.

Go there. Disengage momentarily from trying to change or fix things. Suspend your preferences. Appreciate what's unfolding, without the need to understand it. Ahaaaaaaa... There's nothing needs doing. Peace reigns.

See, it's a place within—an awareness, a place of clarity. And its name is DO NOT JUDGE. Whatever makes you want to criticize or "fix" yourself or anyone else is a reminder to go there.

© 2014, Faith Lynella, from *BonBons to Sweeten Your Daily Life* or *More BonBons and Treats*   http://faithlynella.com

~~~~~

Resorting to stereotypes and judging others are both fundamentally disrespectful. They preempt the delicate process of building trust so a mutual relationship could have a chance to develop. It puts a person (for some reason, accurately or not) into a category which does not require us to be kind to them, or to put our best foot forward. Actually prejudging them makes us feel entitled to do the opposite.

When that happens, there's no room for mutual exchange. It closes doors which could be beneficial, but we'll never know... How sad.

Upholding a View
A BonBon

My life is filled with many different kinds of people: family, professional colleagues, friends, close friends, nodding acquaintances, clients, audience members, people who provide me services, etc. In every case I offer and exchange different aspects of myself, providing different degrees of self-exposure or intimacy.

Recently, I have recognized a new category: people I wish to uphold. It has provided an entirely different way of looking at the people in my life, and cuts across other existing roles and relationships. Being upheld is not a reflection of our closeness, how long we've known each other, or the kinds of needs they have. This category can't be applied to everyone with a need or I'd be consumed.

The coin is sincere caring and is paid in my time, energy, emotion, or even money. Upholding goes beyond the everyday display of encouragement and kindness. For whatever reason (and they are all so different), if I decide that "here is a person who needs to be upheld," I create a one-sided commitment to him or her. I can just as easily and arbitrarily end it whenever I choose.

Although nothing needs to be said directly to the person, I feel obligated to find ways to uphold them and support their efforts. This special bond may not exist for long. The person may not even benefit from whatever I can do for long. But it exists as a priority for me until fulfilled.

Of course, such commitments makes sense within the tight circle of family or intimate friends. But this relationship is different than those and may not even apply for anyone close. Those who are nearest to me might not be the ones who can use what is offered—offered freely, willingly and without strings. It doesn't establish a permanent arrangement. In fact, it's likely to be transitional, a bridge through painful, risky or discouraging times.

For example, a casual acquaintance decides to take a course required for a promotion, but lacks a ride, baby-sitter or whatever. By my providing the missing element, the person and their goal are both upheld. My role in such a case is active and supportive, serving as a vote of confidence at a time when their effort seems daunting. The message is conveyed through kind words and deeds, "You're not alone in this. I'm here for you."

Or, you receive outstanding service from a small business struggling against well financed competition. In deciding to uphold the business, you not only patronize it but use your network of contacts to bring it new business. In being more than a customer, you're nourishing and rewarding the values that they displayed in how they serve you. There's much more involved than spending money or even how well you like the business owner. Through such supportive efforts you acknowledge and reward the behaviors you value.

Or, you decide to uphold a leader who's making hard, risky, or even unpopular decisions. In such a thankless role, the leader is vulnerable. Your decision to uphold that person is really an acknowledgment of the guts or character necessary to achieve the desired goal. By your upholding stance, you're voting in a very tangible way for the preferred outcome.

From examining my ties to those who I've elected to uphold, I've found strengths and skills otherwise unused. I've also discovered previously unnoticed ways in which others have been upholding me.

© 2014, Faith Lynella, from *BonBons to Sweeten Your Daily Life* or *More BonBons and Treats*   http://faithlynella.com

Upholding Is Different than Helping

Upholding relates to the *values I wanted to encourage*. I am voting for a person, for their aspirations, for their hopes for the future. It is not about me rewarding them for doing what I want them to do. Nor is my assistance provided to further my own ends.

Since most help is couched in such conditions (stated or implied), upholding is noteworthy for its lack of strings on either person. Upholding sets the customary opinions or judging aside because: I want for you what you want for you.

It doesn't matter whether I hold the same point of view or whether we agree about the importance or rightness of specific decisions they've made. I choose to uphold *their* vision, *their* goals, rather than attempting to sway them to mine. It's not done to reward them for having goals in line with mine, or of which I approve. (Although it doesn't hurt we agree; it's just not a requirement.)

For whatever reason, maybe an upholder's effort can contribute to "tipping the scales" toward them succeeding—or at least to their staying in the game. A related difference is the upholder does not judge the person or the value of their visions. They simply hold them in a positive light.

Upholding is a tangible way of tipping the scales a tad bit so something which is unlikely or too difficult has a better chance of happening. The size of assistance can be small or large since its value to the person upheld is out of proportion to the money, support, or time invested.

At a time when a positive nudge is needed very much, somebody is willing to say "I uphold you" in a tangible way. Believe me, *there's air there*.

It can continue for as long or as short a time as the upholder wants. Or it can take any form you're willing to commit yourself to take on. You're standing up for their determination and courage when you find a way to assist a person who's attempting to bring their vision into concrete reality.

This isn't an obligation based on anything other than your desire to encourage or "vote" for *what the other person is attempting to achieve*. It's the opposite of a contract (verbal or expressed in any form) with any set specific obligations. Often what the person desires arises from their heart. By upholding them, you're helping them to ground that desire.

Upholding and being upheld:
- Of the people you interact with regularly, is there much upholding going on?
- How about negating—the opposite of upholding? Is such behavior encountered on a regular basis, when the rug gets pulled out from under you? Fix it or shut it down since it's costing you air.
- Are there any reciprocal upholders in your life?

Chapter 16
Treat Your Stuff as Pockets of Air

Air and Money

Air is not money, but… The role of money in our lives touches so many of our principles, assumptions, and choices it seems to be much more important than it actually is. Yet the over-riding role of money in modern life cannot be ignored. Our finances are bound up in our thinking about the rest of our values and priorities. We think having more of it will make us happy.

Money, or more accurately the having or not having of it, never seems to be far from our thinking. Besides, we have a lifetime of feeling lots of flying-high energy when we have plenty of it and feeling diminished when we're without it. Never mind that dollars shouldn't get all the credit (or blame) for what's really making us happy (or sad) at those times.

Hundreds of studies confirm more money can make us feel happy, just as not having enough money can make us feel unhappy. But where's the tipping point between having enough and not enough? Researchers also found out money is not a strong predictor of happiness. Other influences play a much stronger role.

So it's a too-easy step to thinking we need to have money, and even more money, if we want to get all the things which make us happy. No matter how many times we discover "the best things in life are free" we still prefer having money and the material dodas which go with it.

There's a saying: "Those who think money can't buy happiness just don't know where to shop." But as discussed in Chapter 4, there's more than one kind of happiness. Money can easily buy pleasures, plenty of them. Where money falls short is in its ability to provide eudaimonic happiness, the kind which brings meaning into your life. To achieve fulfilling happiness depends on developing your moral fiber and a desire to achieve more in life than pursuing simple pleasure.

Modern life is far too dollar-centric. We've been trained to use money as the primary way to achieve our goals, as well as to judge our success or failure. Spending shifts people away from improvising and collaborating—ways to get things done which aren't as dependent on financial considerations. Yet such boot-strappy approaches to getting things done are likely to be much more ingenious, innovative, and satisfying than writing a check.

It's always amazing to see what can be accomplished by determined individuals, even when there isn't money to do it. Pulling out the credit card robs you of finding more clever and resourceful ways of making things happen.

> In the beginning, greater wealth brings us a higher standard of living, and the extra comforts and extravagances bring extra pleasure. Then, we get used to the higher standard of living, to the extent that we are not satisfied unless we up the dosage by acquiring even more… Furthermore, when we don't obtain the expected pleasure, we presume that the fault lies not with human nature but with our failure to purchase the right object, steering us right back to the mall, realtor, or car dealer.[49]

Examine Your Relationship to Things

Pay attention to the influence your material possessions have on how you feel about life, as well as how you feel about yourself and your future. Your worldly goods are interwoven with your opinions and priorities, your dreams and ideals. All of us have scrambled our stuff with our identities, and lost sight of ourselves in the process.

Your relationships to objects:
- What you own—your possessions
- What you want—your desires, dreams, and main concerns
- What you give to others
- What you want to go away—the burdens and obligations related to them
- What you're willing to do (or not do) to keep, protect, and maintain what you have
- What you're willing to do (or not do) to acquire more of what you want
- What you're willing to sacrifice in order to own or get certain things
- What possessions mean to you—their symbolism and emotional influence

---

[49] Lyumbomirsky, Sonja, *The Myths of Happiness: What should make you happy, but doesn't: What shouldn't make you happy, but does* (New York, The Penguin Press, 2013), 169.

Objects are intimately bound up with your core values and priorities. That includes the physical objects themselves, along with your feelings about them. Attending to your air/energy needs puts your possessions in a more accurate light. Doing so shows the extent to which your sense of identity has gotten wrapped up with material objects.

But the objects around us also help us clarify our identity and primary concerns as well. As Carl Jung said, "We need to project ourselves into the things around us. My self is not confined to my body. It extends into all the things I have made and all the things around me. Without these things, I would not be myself." But that's not to say my possessions can define my identity.

Remember to breathe today

Finding the Proper Balance

Your stuff has a role to play in your life, but it should be a subordinate one. An over-balanced concern with money and possessions risks putting material priorities ahead of living fully. It's hard not to judge yourself (and what you've accomplished) by a financial yardstick, rather than more accurate measures of your authentic worth.

Take charge of your unintentional clutter and excess consumption. They generate a constant stream of more-of-the-same for you to deal with. Even the most desirable objects are not on a par with any living person. Nor can possessions take the place of affection or meaning. (Although countless people keep testing that notion.) Their bedazzling allure tempts you to forget we're all born naked and can't take any of it with us.

While simplifying sounds easy, it's much more complicated than it sounds. Eliminating stuff can be accomplished with a hatchet or a scalpel. But how it's done should also respect the profusion of feelings attached to them. "Bringing simplicity into our lives requires that we discover the ways in which our consumption either supports or entangles our existence" Duane Elgin said.

Concern for money and possessions doesn't deserve the central place they have assumed. And in the big scheme of things, they should be very close to the bottom of our priorities. So why aren't they? No matter how many earthly goods you acquire, it still represents the lesser game. They're tantalizing distractions from what's immeasurably more valuable—a sense of meaning, and abiding relationships.

Also take a moment to consider what demoting possessions would do to your life, time, and energy. What priorities go up a notch? Where would you be putting more of yourself? And to what end. Framed another way, what else would you be able to vote for? These types of questions all go toward remaking yourself and your environment closer to your liking.

Saga of the Wealthy Seal

Mine, all mine

Watch Out for All Those Feelings

You'd think possessions would be the easiest arena to disengage from emotionally—especially compared to relationships. People don't hesitate to stand up for themselves or quibble about how you treat them. But objects are riddled with layers of symbolism, emotions, and associated memories.

Many of those emotional attachments exist well below your conscious awareness. The deepest ones were established in early childhood, long before language or rational abilities developed. Many of the associations reflect cultural norms—defined for us by our era and larger community.

Looking closely at your stuff stirs up emotional reactions, some of which have been in place since childhood. Prepare yourself for considerable emotional and sentimental fallout if you make changes. Besides, certain people in your life might not approve of changes you might want to make (even with your own stuff).

So altering your dealings with what you own can trigger relationship tremors as well. Some people close to you could be more attached to your stuff than they are to you (without even knowing it).

Some emotions tied to possessions:
- Greed and gluttony
- Covetousness, cravings, and lust
- Pride and envy
- Neediness—feeling starved for "something"
- Guilt related to having or not having
- Selfishness
- Generosity, both with objects and generosity of spirit

The risk comes with going overboard, where you're identified too closely with your material objects—or the desire for them.

Beware of treating things as a compensation for unmet emotional needs. Often people consume (buy, eat, use up) lots of stuff as a substitute for what they *really* want but don't have—affection, respect, confidence, self-worth, etc. They attempt to use possessions for getting their air/energy needs met.

But buying more stuff doesn't satisfy for long. So they look for another hit, and then another… Over-consumption could be seen as a form of neediness, which no amount of spending could ever satisfy.

What Your Possessions Cost You

Three particular concerns apply to almost everything you own. It costs money (or equivalent effort) to acquire it, money that's no longer available for other purposes. So is what you got worth it anymore? Is it enough to justify the opportunity costs of what you didn't (or can't) get?

Once acquired, there are ongoing obligations to clean and maintain them. Caring for possessions exerts a perennial demand on our time and energy.

As Frank Lloyd Wright observed, "Many wealthy people are little more than the janitors of their possessions." Add to the tangible costs the fear that what you own will be destroyed, stolen, or fall apart. So you should factor in such emotional costs as well.

If your goals mostly revolve around material things, don't expect them to bring happiness for long. Instead, such an attitude has been shown to be a strong predictor of unhappiness. The emphasis on acquiring newer and better things often means not taking the time to truly enjoy what we already have.

Once you actually get something new, you can quickly lose interest in having it. We're on to the next new thing. After a while, we end up with having a bunch of things gathering dust.

When it comes to enjoyment, the first bite you wanted so badly has the advantage of tasting the best. After that, not so much. You get adapted to sensual experiences and relationships as the novelty wears off. As the senses become saturated, consuming more does not increase the satisfaction. It declines. You start to get bored or indifferent.

Economists have given this a name—Law of Diminishing Marginal Utility. The perceived value of or satisfaction gained from a good to a consumer declines with each additional unit acquired or consumed. Because we want the satisfaction we got when something was new, we keep getting more stuff, more expensive stuff, and more unusual stuff. But the magic doesn't last without effort.

The lift (or air) which the acquisition gave fades relatively quickly, so it accelerates the consumption cycle. That's true not only for objects, but also for people and experiences. You owe it to them and yourself to find ways to keep them fresh and air-rich for you. One way is by enjoying the small stuff (Chapter 13).

Take Charge of Your Stuff

Most people have difficulty relating to who they are apart from the things which surround them. For one thing, your inner worth and outer worth hinge on very different factors. So they arrive at very different assessments of your identity.

Every person is immeasurably more valuable than the totality of whatever they own, or will ever own. Identification with material objects interferes with sensing your authentic self and true value.

Start by evaluating each of the things you own as to whether it supplies you air/energy or not. Most are purely utilitarian. Which are the big deals among them that light you up every time? Which are the black holes that drain you dry emotionally? Financially?

Once you get a better sense of which ones are "worth it" energy-wise, making air/energy-supportive choices about what you have gets much easier.

Begin to loosen your ties to your stuff. Step back from it enough to see what you have dispassionately. You don't have to get rid of particular objects, as much as with your identification with them. Stepping back from most of your possessions will be relatively easy. Other items will seem rather hard or complicated. While disengaging from some will be downright unthinkable.

Decisions about what to do with stuff gets easier as you become clearer about the related costs and trade-offs of having them. Moving toward a simpler lifestyle isn't about cleaning house as much as *cleaning out the discordant energy you live with*. You'll retrieve vast amounts of locked-up air/energy once objects occupy a less central place in your life. Plus you'll save the energy usually devoted to caring for it.

Spend less effort consuming stuff—buying it, paying for it, choosing it, protecting it, and keeping it clean or repaired. Imagine what you could accomplish with the same amount of effort directed toward something you're passionate about. On the other hand, your possessions are an extension of yourself, so they serve you on many levels.

Gretchen Rubin's *Happiness Project* paid particular attention to the way clutter bogs us down. She mentioned a study which found eliminating clutter would cut down the amount of housework in the average home by 40%.

Rather than treating clutter as one big shapeless accumulation, Rubin was able to identify specific kinds that crept in for her.

Types of clutter: (bullets mine)
- Psychic clutter of loose ends—neglected tasks that made me feel weary and guilty whenever I thought of them
- Visible clutter—objects that need to be put away, objects that didn't have a real place, unidentified lurking objects
- Nostalgic clutter—relics I clung to from my earlier life
- Self-righteous constructive clutter—made up of things that I've kept because they're useful, even though they're useless to me now
- Bargain clutter—from buying unnecessary things because they're on sale
- Freebie clutter—from gifts, hand-me-downs, and giveaways that we didn't use
- Crutch clutter—things I used but knew I shouldn't
- Aspirational clutter—things that I owned but only aspired to use
- Outgrown clutter—things no longer used or needed
- Buyer's remorse clutter—the bad purchases we haven't come to terms with[50]

Simplifying is not just a matter of getting rid of stuff. What supports someone's way of life (or gets in the way of it) is going to be very different for each person. Your choices about what to discard, or keep, should be done reflectively, based on what matters most to you. Even Mahatma Gandhi, a person known for his indifference to a material lifestyle, argues for keeping what serves you.

> As long as you derive inner help and comfort from anything, you should keep it. If you were to give it up in a mood of self-sacrifice or out of a stern sense of duty, you would continue to want it back, and that unsatisfied want would make trouble for you. Only give up a thing when you want some other condition so much that the thing no longer has any attraction for you, or when it seems to interfere with that which is more greatly desired.

---

[50] Rubin, Gretchen, *The Happiness Project: Or, why I spent a year trying to sing in the morning, clean my closets, fight right, read Aristotle, and generally have more fun* (New York, Harper, 2009), 25-8.

Don't only consider utility and practicality as to what's worth keeping. Objects of beauty or those that tug at your heart strings have earned the right to be in your space. *There's air there.*

Attachments Are a Two-way Street

Attachments represent the *emotional component* of what you own. *You have the things and they have you.* You're attached—stuck together like Siamese twins. How strong are those ties? Mild or deep-seated? Were they established long ago or quite recent? How much does any particular object define your sense of self-identity or self-worth? Are you in bondage to them?

How much do the things you own bring up happy thoughts? Or are they more likely to harbor disappointment and sadness? Some lift your spirits, while others take you down. Many more are simply useful and carry little emotional charge. They all serve different purposes in your life.

> Many of the most precious possessions are valuable not because of their cost or prestige, but because of the meanings they contain; modest trinkets, homemade objects, worn books, old photographs, whimsical collections. Because we often want to deny the importance of possessions, and because we don't want to seem materialistic, we often don't spend enough time and attention thinking about how possessions could boost happiness. My possessions had a powerful influence over the atmosphere of my home, and they contributed to, and reflected, my sense of identity.[51]

Material attachments:
- Tangible objects and possessions
- Money in any form—or debt (the opposite of money but equally restrictive)
- Real estate you own—a particular place, with or without buildings; could be home
- Luxuries, rewards, and "toys"
- Places where you stay you don't own—may be general or specific; might visit via travel
- Pets and animals

---

[51] Rubin, Gretchen, *Happier at Home: Kiss more, jump more, abandon a project, read Samuel Johnson, and my other experiments in the practice of everyday life* (New York, Crown Archetype, 2013), 24.

- Plants and things in nature
- Inanimate objects (not alive, like a stamp collection) or intangibles (that can't be touched, like intellectual property rights)
- Art or creative output—music, acting, paintings
- Souvenirs and mementos that represent something, an event, or someone

You're more valuable than the sum of your possessions. However, the dilemma presented by things doesn't come from their quantity or value. It comes from the extent to which a person's life is wrapped up with them.

Getting your inner and outer concerns into appropriate balance is essential for your wellbeing. The challenge each of us faces is less about the actual stuff than our degree of attachment to it. Your stuff keeps you tethered to the past, but also restricts your future options.

When Jesus said, "It is easier for a camel to go through the eye of a needle than for a rich man to enter the kingdom of God," (Mark 10: 24-26) he wasn't condemning wealth or lauding poverty. He was talking about the danger of *having too many attachments*.

A person should not be more devoted to material objects than to consequential matters and matters of the spirit. And it applies to any other excessive identification as well, like vanity or the desire for too much power over others.

His words were also cautioning against breaking the First Commandment by putting anything ahead of God in importance: "You shall have no other gods before me," Exodus 20:3. It speaks to the primacy of matters of spirit in your life—with or without a particular religion.

That's equally true for your attachment to your ideas, opinions, and career as is to the world of possessions. In a psychological sense, it is a warning against becoming so identified with any particular thing it can no longer be recognized as separate from your core self. See Chapter 10 about the challenges of getting to know yourself.

Your Intangibles Are Very Influential

Don't overlook your intangible possessions—the things which you can't touch. They are remarkably seductive because they often represent your deepest values or crowning achievements. Even though they aren't as easy to handle as a car, they can be even more influential. Some of them might be even more intimately bound up with your sense of identity.

After all, you know you are not a car. But do you know you're not your achievements or social status either?

Your intangible possessions:
- Accomplishments which represent milestones
- Trophies—actual or symbolic
- Degrees, titles, and awards, especially when they're treated as completion, rather than a spur to further growth
- Fame, celebrity, public acclaim and its trappings
- Success signs, perks, and elevated social standing

Many of your most prized intangibles are connected to past accomplishments or feats which made you proud. Although worthy of acclaim, they really represent your past—and belong there.

Sometimes the intangibles constraining us are dreams or ambitions for the future. Whether the object represents a link to the past or a desired future, anything which ties you to another point of time could pull you off track in the present. They're a step away from engaging in what's going on in your life today, *as it happens*.

Some intangible aspects of yourself:
- Emotions
- Thoughts and attitudes
- Values, assumptions, and beliefs
- Dreams and aspirations

Because objects are tangible, relating to them is relatively easy. You can see them, handle them, and count them. The next step closer in to your core is your body itself. You can see and feel your flesh. (And medical science has developed ways to show what's going on inside the skin.) To get in any closer than that, your attention needs to *move inside yourself.*

Then connecting with your intangible self gets much more difficult because those aspects of yourself lack defined boundaries. And we're rather unschooled in comprehending what it's saying on a rational level. The information is there, but it's not connected up to your sense organs, which are designed for the external world.

Those inner aspects can and do communicate. But they are usually tuned out in most respects—unless they scream in discomfort. Only in quiet times and by turning inward can you catch what they're saying to you.

There's a spokesman called your Wee Small Voice. That doesn't make it a lesser voice, just one which you must listen to quietly and intentionally.

Inner Wealth Versus Outer Wealth

How you relate to "enough" is a sign of your maturity (not based on your age or level of education). Appreciating what you have already stills the urge for more, more, more. It's easy to get so caught up with *what you don't have* you forget what is already yours and available. It's like a child reaching for the next bright and shining thing.

The heart understands *there's always enough* because it's about satisfaction. It is attuned to what's right with life, rather than to what is lacking (where the intellect shines). But the mind and ego don't look at things that way. They're eager to acquire more and better things. What would it take for you to remember the truth about abundance your heart knows as well?

Having enough isn't about the *stuff out there* in the world but the less-tangible feelings within your heart. Want more? Then share yourself—along with your worldly goods. Open your true wealth storehouse. Watch it multiply as you give it away. Share yourself, your feelings and dreams. You'll be larger for the experience—and so will those who receive it. And having stretched by expanding what you feel is possible, you can never return to the smaller view again.

Listen to your inner chatter. Notice what you're actually saying "not enough" about. Is it really so important? Is the desire for something more about accumulating stuff? Experiences? Or is it about achieving your heartfelt desires? Do you really want it, or is it just an itch?

Move past the never-satisfied desire to acquire or consume. There really is much more to life! Creating and enjoying are much more fulfilling than consuming is. One is expansive, the other isn't. Notice something you're grateful for. Those are the cures for "not enough," rather than hungering for more of the same.

Watch for a binkle which makes you glad to be alive. Stay alert for an emotional connection with someone who responds to you with shared air/energy. That's something an object simply cannot do.

Banish "not enough" with:
- Gratitude
- Satisfaction and enjoyment
- A worthy goal which you actively pursue
- Appreciation
- Sense of wonder or curiosity
- Desire to share and care about someone else
- Awareness of making progress—beyond what you had or did before
- Pressing concern for another's wellbeing
- Confidence that what you want and need the most will somehow come to you

Experiences Versus Things

Material objects fuel preoccupation with the external world. Doing so is at the expense of other choices and ways to spend our time. In *The Myths of Happiness*, Sonja Lyumbomirsky points to a growing body of research showing people are made happier by experiences than by things. Spending money for experiences is likely to bring you more happiness than your stuff does.

Advantages of experiences over having objects: (bullet points mine)
1. Because most possessions don't tend to change after we've bought them we adapt to them a great deal faster (we stop noticing them)
2. Experiences are intrinsically more social—more likely to be shared, anticipated, and relived with other people—than are things
3. In light of research underscoring the peril of social comparisons, it's not surprising that… we are less likely to compare them to those of others
4. Relative to things, experiences are also less prone to… [being compared] with what might have been

5. Whereas material objects typically grow old and dull with time, until we are eager to replace them, experiences can actually grow even more positive and more enjoyable as time passes
6. We are more likely to identify with experiences and less likely to want to trade them... When we own something, it is outside us—on our shelf, shoulders, or living room. When we experience something it is inside us—inside our minds and memories
7. Experiences—like climbing a mountain, visiting a remote location, or learning to dive—may involve challenges and adventures, and it makes us happy to exert effort to endure a difficult lesson or journey and relish the feeling of hard-won accomplishment
8. Things don't make us as happy as experiences because an inappropriate focus on acquiring material possessions begets many costs[52]

When Everything Is Wiped Away Overnight

Catastrophes like flooding or fires strike without much warning and can sweep away everything someone has. Then what is left? Natural disasters can be blamed on the fluctuations of weather. Other causes can be more personal, closer to home, like a divorce or life-threatening illness.

But the economic downturn has wrought the same kind of calamities to sectors of the financial system, to those who thought they had job security, to those abruptly shut out of the future they were so carefully building toward.

In a blink, some unfortunate individuals lose their health, their jobs, their status in the eyes of their fellow man, their homes, or their nest eggs for retirement. They must face all manner of difficulties beyond anybody's control. Many people's lives are turned upside-down, facing what was considered unthinkable until then.

Reversals of fortune are devastating for those who go through it, who survive such cataclysmic events. There will be much sorrow, coupled with growth, in new directions for those who must try to pick up the pieces. But what of the rest of us?

---

[52] Lyumbomirsky, Sonja, *The Myths of Happiness: What should make you happy, but doesn't: What shouldn't make you happy, but does* (New York, The Penguin Press, 2013), 152-4.

Will we be grateful for the "lucky" circumstances which make misfortune fall on them instead of me? Will it make us cling even more to the "I've got what I deserve, and so do they" mantra? Will the randomness of fate and misfortune bring greater divides between the haves and the have-nots?

This does not speak to who has what or to what is left. It speaks to how such events can bring out a new standard in how we care about each other. In every need to rebuild after a wipe-out, we are being invited to rebuild on a more solid footing, consistent with our ideals. We are also being invited to share the burdens. Our common humanity demands no less.

Chapter 17
Making a Difference Creates More Air

Taking an Active Role in Your Life

The course of your life is not simply an accumulation of hours spent, experiences encountered, and problems solved. But it demonstrates a daily transformation of events and opportunities into your identity. Who you are is forever changing and growing. You are a lifelong work in progress.

When you take responsibility for acting like the person you aspire to be, you more fully engage the forces acting on you. You get a more coherent voice in how things play out for you. Admittedly, that voice of yours is not the deciding one that determines what plays out for you. But you're in the chorus—rather than bemoaning your fate.

With a larger view, you don't irrationally think you deserve all the credit or blame for what happens to you. As Nigel Richmond said, "You can choose to be part of the forces that govern you or be resentfully governed by them." Watch out for having the slightest resentment; it poisons the air supply.

None of us are passive bystanders. Your attitudes and efforts influence how well you play your part, how well you drive the action or slam on the brakes at what comes your way. But it takes air/energy and focused attention to staying engaged. Having enough of that available fundamentally changes the dynamics you choose to live by.

Your Impact
A BonBon

Wherever you are, whatever you do, you leave an impact.
- Choose it—Leave the impression that you want.
- Prepare for it—Decide to be the person who CREATES that impression.
- Notice how you're doing it and why you're doing it.
- Be alert for it—Treat every experience as a potential adventure.
- Find the fun of it—It's available for you and those you touch.

You are known less because of your ideas than by the personal impact you make on those around you. The force of that impact demonstrates your values, your priorities and your personality more clearly than anything you could say.

You don't get to decide the value of your impact; that is determined by those who are affected by it.

The person you influence defines what your impact was for him, even if it was very different from what was intended. Whenever the two impressions don't match, it is not the receiver's fault. You simply have not yet found the most effective way to express your intention. Figuring out your unique way to express that intent provides the adventure.

If you try to avoid leaving an impression, you will be too passive, unable to react appropriately. You can no longer behave as freely as the situation would permit. A failure to seek opportunities where you leave your impact votes for inertia, for more-of-the-same automatic responses.

Choose to consciously define your impact. Express your unique way of seeing and doing things. If you duck those opportunities, if you fail to assert WHO you are, you could become superfluous, even in your own life.

So develop a flair! Make a statement as unique as you are. Create a noteworthy presence—just by being you, intentionally.

© 2014, Faith Lynella, from *BonBons to Sweeten Your Daily Life* or *More BonBons and Treats*   http://faithlynella.com

What each of us makes of ourselves over a lifetime reflects our expectation about what we consider to be possible. In defining "who I am" or what I think I am capable of doing, each of us makes the raw material of our lives correspond with that hoped-for future that is theirs alone.

In that regard, everybody gets to invent themselves. Just being alive calls forth the creative energy for the job. Taking pains with how carefully it's done could make your life a work of art.

Just as we make our lives by the way that we live, we also help to repay those who've gone before and made what we do possible.

Albert Einstein said "A hundred times a day I remind myself that my inner and outer life depends on the labors of other men, living and dead, and that I must exert myself in order to give in the measure as I have received and am still receiving."

So many people who were determined to make a difference in their own unique flavor account for the scope of humanity's march and richness. By small acts and large, we collectively find new ways to keep the world turning.

The Center of Your Universe is YOU

Pockets of Air is packed with information about how to spot air and energy, both in your life and in the world around you. The goal is to assure you're getting all you need for a fulfilling life—from every area of your life. This book could be titled, *You and Pockets of Air* for it's really all about you.

Have you been considering how you can adapt these ideas to the ways you're living now? This late in the book you've been living with them for a while. Which took hold immediately? Which are working best for you? I hope you'll keep at it for the long haul. A book isn't worth much if you just read it and leave the ideas on the shelf. *There's no air there.*

Granted, you want to be happy, to sense upbeat energy pulsing through you. But please take this to heart. Share your air-awareness and let it others be similarly motivated stop being drained. Start the ball rolling. What it opens your eyes to has a significant influence on how much you enjoy what you do, and whether you're energized by the process.

Getting more air/energy into your life on a regular basis will shift your center of gravity, from a steady drip, drip, drip of energy leaking away, to having even more than you need. The next stage is to plug the leaks. A lot of that is just practical and making better choices.

Take some mental snapshots of yourself early on, so you will be able to gauge your progress down the road. Think of them as "verbal selfies" that help you to notice certain qualities about yourself that are no longer the same. That could get you thinking about where you want to be more air-aware. Put these ideas to work for you.

Feast on the smorgasbord of air from a zillion sources. Delight in the ways an upsurge of binkle energy lifts your spirits. That's what awaits you if you become air savvy.

We Get Wiser Along the Way

Trusting that your wee small voice isn't steering you wrong gets easier as you drop your resistance to whatever life brings that you don't like. A parallel skill is becoming sensitive enough to reject something that drags you down—before it gets a chance to. As you sharpen your ability to recognize and marshal more air/energy, you find additional ways to acquire enough of it to achieve whatever you desire.

Sufficient air pays off emotionally, mentally, and physically—without any aspect of yourself left unsatisfied. But of even greater value, all aspects of yourself begin to function as a more coherent unit, thereby reinforcing each other. That degree of internal teamwork shifts you into a higher gear, functioning closer to your full energetic capacity.

Flowing with uplifting energy when it is available depends on body, head, and heart being at peace with each other. Those energized states can greatly influence how well you respond to everyday challenges—whether difficulties drain you or bounce off you.

Once the mind learns to stand aside and allow "innocence of perception" to lead, the entire self reaps the rewards—such as scintillating conversation and feeling "just right." Heart and body awareness both respond to high-air/energy situations with full resonance. However, the rational mind needs to trust them when it comes to "reading" this energy of alignment because intellect is largely tone deaf to it.

The heart, mind, and body always function as an integrated whole during times of joy and inspiration. That's why those experiences feel different than ordinary ones. It is only in everyday life that they seem to operate separately—the mental leading and the other two tagging along. The more the three can work as a unit, the more a person feels harmonious in every possible way. Air-rich experiences assure they're fully in-synch with each other. That brings out the best of each.

> Wisdom is a marriage—a synergy of heart and mind. Many times what our conscience tells us to do will seem familiar or 'common sense.' It's something we've read about, thought about, or experienced, so it's part of our rational framework. In these cases, conscience pinpoints or highlights the appropriate application of the knowledge.
>
> At other times, the wisdom of the heart transcends the wisdom of the mind. We may have no direct knowledge or experience in doing what we feel we should do, but somehow

we know it's right. We know it will work. As we learn to listen to and live by our conscience, many of the things it teaches us are transferred through our own experience into our rational framework of knowledge. We learn to reason things out in our minds, but not to get lost in reason.[53]

One of the rewards that comes with aging is perspective. Being able to see your life as a whole, apart from the sequential events themselves, adds a new dimension of understanding. You comprehend that although events left their mark on you, you also thrived, and grew, and changed in the process. In so doing, every bit of yourself played its part and is worthy of acknowledgment in how you turned out.

With a broader perspective comes more self-acceptance. You've fought the good fight, and you "did good." There's no need for nitpicking or self-reproach because so much of what felt like setbacks when they happened makes sense for the first time. The down times brought out the best in you.

Accepting yourself is a worthwhile ambition, but it shouldn't have to depend on getting old. Yes, certain awareness about life, and how it fits together, comes from living a long time. But some of that self-knowledge can come much sooner, by changing how you attend to things as they happen. Watch out for what is meaningful in the mix of events.

There's an energy to it, if you are attentive. For example, you can be curious about what you might be missing or what this particular event means in the larger scheme of things. That's how your individual point of view gains a wider—and wiser—perspective.

As your heart, mind, body, and spirit get comfortable enough with each other to be open to what each of them can contribute, your options expand. If you start doing that now, you'll soon be bumping into the wisdom of perspective—without waiting so long for it.

As you function from that larger frame of reference, you become more aware of many ways your every deed makes a difference.

---

[53] Covey, Stephen R., Merrill, A. Roger, Merrill, Rebecca R. *First Things First: To live, to love, to learn, to leave a legacy* (New York: Simon & Shuster, 1994), 175.

Ways to create air/energy:
- Creativity in any form
- Imagination—especially if there's an attempt to make it tangible later
- Doin' nuttin'—gazing off
- Play in any form
- The arts
- Curiosity and exploration for other than practical reasons—just to see…
- Recreational activities and sports
- Sensory enjoyment of all types

Stimulate Your Creative Juices

Acknowledge the role your creative and recreational activities play to keep the boat afloat. Those interests are not a secret pleasure, the "hidden mistress on the side" who competes with home responsibilities. Maybe you don't even recognize how important such digressions from obligations are for you.

Jessica Hisch aptly points out, "The work you do while you procrastinate is probably the work you should be doing for the rest of your life."

You obviously gain air there—and that could be all the reason you need. The more structure and responsibilities you live with, the more important it becomes to do something in a different vein. Play. Wonder. Open your channels of experience wider.

> **Step 1**: Wonder at something.
>
> **Step 2**: Invite others to wonder with you. You should wonder at the things nobody else is wondering about…. The more open you are about sharing your passions, the closer people will feel to your work. Artists aren't magicians. There's no penalty for revealing your secrets….
>
> When you open up your process and invite people in, you learn… the Internet can be more than just a resting place to publish your finished ideas—it can also be an incubator for

ideas that aren't fully formed, a birthing center for developing work that you haven't started yet.[54]

Art, Music and Beauty
A BonBon

Art and music are about beauty. They have to do with the way we experience our world—not as something isolated and set down by the masters in the great classics. We turn our attention to the colors of the evening sky, the subtle shades and shadows of a loved one's face, the silhouette of a bird perched on a light pole. We hear the music in the sounds and rhythms of the falling rain, the laughter and squeals from a playground, the chirping of a cricket.

Art is all around us, and yet it is not the things we experience. Art is in us—in our ability to notice. An eye or an ear tuned to lovely things will always be surrounded by them. The more that we have the urge to notice, the more power beauty will have to touch our lives.

© 2014, Faith Lynella, from *BonBons to Sweeten Your Daily Life* or *More BonBons and Treats*   http://faithlynella.com

The Pull of Creativity Makes Plentiful Air

Even the hardest-working drudge needs to get out of harness sometime. There is considerable air/energy to be found from using the time away from obligations for renewal. These aren't lesser goals, or even the avoidance of serious work since they contribute balance.

They're done for the heart and spirit, as well as for camaraderie and cheerfulness. Afterward, you return to your responsibilities recharged and ready to proceed since your head is "back on straight." Stephen Nachmanovitch said in *Free Play*,

> Practice gives the creative process a steady momentum, so that when imaginative surprises occur (whether they be thrown toward us by accident or brought up from within by the unconscious), they can be incorporated into the growing, breathing organism of our imagination. Here we perform the most essential synthesis—stretching out the moments of

---

[54] Kleon, Austin, *Steal Like an Artist: 10 things nobody told you about being creative* (New York: Workman Publishing Company, 2012), 81-2.

inspiration into a continuous flow of doing, inspirations are no longer mere flashes of insight that come and go at the whim of the gods[55]

Where do you turn when you're out of harness? How much do you yearn to be doing that the rest of the time? Obviously, you're getting air there. For that reason alone, respect whatever rings your bell in the mix of activities calling upon your time.

Creative endeavors are especially potent for generating the high-octane energy that make a person's spirit soar. There's a passion and intensity that lifts those activities out of the ordinary (Chapter 11). But a serious pursuit of creative endeavors also extract a price. Carl Jung said:

> The artist's life cannot be otherwise than full of conflicts, for two forces are at war within him—on the one hand the common human longing for happiness, satisfaction and security in life, and on the other a ruthless passion for creation which may go so far as to override every personal desire… There are hardly any exceptions to the rule that a person must pay dearly for the divine gift of creative fire.

While artists who are compelled to create give that a greater weight than the pull of conventional pressures, they are the driven minority. That includes the outliers and visionaries who cannot be satisfied with ordinary expectations.

The challenge which tugs at the vast majority is to give credence to those murmurings which speak to their heart of hearts so they stretch further for it. If you can find something that sets the artist or inventor in you free, your creative side has been well served.

Artistic Activities and Air

Artists and authors with staying power have developed the ability to engage us on a personal and emotional level. In that way, they manage to insert accessible pockets of air into their creative work. Many of the classics represent much more than great music, sculpture, or writing, but are demonstrations of their air-stimulating capacity.

---

[55] Nachmanovitch, Stephen, *Free Play: Improvisation in life and art* (Los Angeles: Jeremy P. Tarcher, Inc., 1990), 72.

Once an author has touched you in that way, you can continue to draw air from their creative efforts again and again. It's true for any of the great works of art—painting, dance, music, architecture, sculpture, etc. The power of art to inspire, both the one who makes it and those whom it touches, is out of proportion to its practical value.

The world of art is humanizing and transporting. It also can humanize and uplift a culture. As John Updike said, "What art offers is space—a certain breathing room for the spirit."

That's why it is such a travesty of our educational system to drop art and music classes from the curriculum, in favor of more useful and career-oriented subjects. Too many children are growing up tone deaf to the ways creativity or beauty can bring air into how we live. And such a lack leaves the emotions air-deprived. Without developing any artistic awareness, some of our most vital human qualities are left stunted.

Libraries, museums, and theaters house collections of books or artistic works. They allow us to find those artists and creative voices who have mastered their media and communicate with us energetically. Even if the original creator is no longer alive, their work continues to speak to us.

But the truest value of arts is not determined by what is created—the product or end result. It comes through having a direct creative experience. One kind comes from the doing of it. The satisfaction derived while the creative juices are flowing *is* the point (ala intrinsic motivation). Children understand this intuitively. Play and messing around are worthy despite there not being anything to show for it afterwards.

In a certain sense, what is made can be considered a by-product of a full-bodied creative activity. The enjoyment and air from the creative act is taken immediately. Skill level is also irrelevant as a measure of pleasure, for the creator with little or no skill can still gain as much gratification from the activity as an adept does.

In fact, there might be more satisfaction because the highly-trained person is likely to be too involved in judging their work to feel fully satisfied with it. But for many more, the value of art comes from experiencing what someone else has created for their enjoyment. In that experience the artist and audience for their work temporarily occupy a common space and energy.

Air Plug-in Station

Find Air in Imagery and Imagination

Imagery speeds up any learning, healing, or creative process. Imagery does not require the ability to conjure up visual pictures since it can touch any of the senses and be felt, heard, smelled, tasted, as well as seen. You can imagine something, even if it couldn't exist in the physical world. The skill is natural to us all, but you get better at it the more you let your imagination loose.

Get as many of the senses involved as possible when working with an image. You can also look at it from multiple perspectives and so get a 360 degree view. To the extent you can focus that same degree of attention upon yourself, you'll also see yourself in ways which allow you to get to know yourself from different perspectives.

There's enough air to go around. Air is infinitely elastic and it is its nature to expand. It resists being compressed or forced to conform to a fixed, unyielding structure. I like to think of the human spirit in the same way. It does not want to be suppressed or clamped down too severely. Play and creative pursuits set it free, bringing you balance and fresh energy.

Air doesn't conform to the fixed-pie model in which one person or group getting more means others must get less. No one can corner the air in such a way they can have it all (or even much more) for themselves. In fact, air/energy breaks the fixed-pie model—when I get more air and pass it on there is more of it for everybody.

> The mind also enjoys excursions into the realms of fantasy, where it creates an internal video of a new and different me, famous, handsome, powerful, talented, successful, wealthy, and loved. The capacity of the human mind to fantasize is wonderful, the basis of all our creativity. It allows us to imagine new inventions, create new art and music, arrive at new scientific hypotheses, and to make plans for everything from new buildings to new chapters of our lives. Unfortunately, it can become an escape, and escape from whatever is uncomfortable about the present moment, an escape from the anxiety of not knowing what is actually

moving toward us, an escape from the fear that the next moment (or hour or day or year) could bring us difficulties or even death. Incessant fantasizing and daydreaming are different from directed creativity. Creativity comes from resting the mind in neutral, allowing it to clear itself and provide a fresh canvas on which new ideas, equations, poems, melodies, or colorful strokes can appear.[56]

Our urge to create and make enjoyable things is innate and universal. It's air-making function does not depend on an activity's scale. So large or small endeavors can be equally satisfying. Beginners with poor execution can partake of the same enjoyment as a master, when each puts their whole self into the activity.

Find ways to put your creative talents to work. Whether your inspired to write a poem, decorate a hallway, or dance a jig, you'll feel more vibrant.

Holding out for Door B

Who doesn't want to get what they want? We all do, especially if you think it will make you happy (or happier). But insisting on it can cause problems if you're wanting something so badly you refuse to be happy without it. It could be a perfect house, the man (or woman) of your dreams, the career you always wanted, tons of money, the perfectly-behaved child, fame, you name it…

Anybody with such clearly stated desires should also be asking themselves what steps they are *actively* taking in order to reach that end. Turning your dreams into reality is a many-stepped process which calls for you doing your part in an ever-changing variety of ways. Fate or luck may lend a hand, but mainly to nudge those efforts of yours already in play. If you're sitting on the sidelines wishing for something to happen, nothing gets pushed forward due to their fortuitous involvement.

The short-term problem with insisting on Door B comes from focusing on what's missing. The person might reject what's right in front of their nose. They could ignore other latent possibilities which are readily available. What they have looks pretty plain and humble compared to the fulfillment of their gussied-up desire.

---

[56] Bays, Jan Chozen, *How to Train a Wild Elephant: And other adventures in mindfulness* (Boston: Shambhala, 2011), 7-8.

However, even if Door B is in the person's stars, it is still not fully formed and "ready for prime time" yet. So the half-baked reality which is now here might need some growing up and their active participation in this unfledged form, if it is to ever happen.

Don't pass up the air pockets which can be had now just because there might be another, greatly-to-be-preferred one around the corner. It might come, and it would be wonderful! But don't let the expectation blind you to the blessings in your life in the meantime, or of appreciating what you have already. Don't let daydreams prevent you from making something out of a half-baked possibility just awaiting your caring hand.

Admittedly, some Door Bs are idealized escapes which make you feel better, but turn out to be very different than you imagined. Like winning the lottery, the end result often turns out not to be so life-improving after all; or the perfect guy or wedding can still lead to divorce.

Getting what you always wanted doesn't solve every problem. To be happy you still need the air/energy which comes from wise choices and satisfying relationships. Or you could get bored and lose interest even with that.

Chapter 18
Let Fresh Breezes Blow

STAND UP FOR AIR

Remake the World so It's Fit to Breathe Here

Back in the 1960's, America's air and water were badly polluted. It was a disgrace, brought on by many years of bad decisions which totally disregarded their impact on the environment. We've since become wiser about curtailing tangible and intangible costs of pollution. We've come a long way toward achieving healthier standards. There's more to be done, but it's no longer an issue whether clear air and water are needed.

In the same way, we've accepted toxic air and low-energy environments as the norm. A pressure-cooker lifestyle is considered the price of progress. But we're paying too high a price for such detrimental conditions, both as individuals and throughout the larger culture. Low-energy environments undermine our positive efforts to make things better—in large ways and small.

We are setting poor examples for our children, who will never be able to reach their full potential unless we improve this grim reality. The future which best serves us all dials back the stress. We must recognize the routine indignities we casually inflict on ourselves, and each other, as a lesser form of humanity. It imperils our sensibilities for a just and cultivated society.

There's much more each of us can do to improve the common air supply—both for our individual needs and for our shared air/energy supplies. And much of it is within our capacity to improve right away. A shift in our expectations is a necessary first step. Being air-aware adds a new variable to what we consider acceptable or doable.

We are all barraged with so many ideas and arguments which contradict each other it's nearly impossible to tell the worthwhile from the bad. But here's a rule of thumb which simplifies how to tell them apart. "If it is life-affirming, it is from God. If it is not, it is not."

Take note of anything which is fear-based because it won't pass this test. It also won't provide the air and energy which bring out the best in you.

Stand Up for Air

Challenge the *status quo*. Point the finger at low-air policies and practices which bring us grief. Label toxic air for the danger it is, with an expectation it must stop. When certain common behavior stinks, say so—and not just to complain. You want something done about the problem areas which harm our collective peace of mind, day in and day out.

In doing so, be careful about stridency, so promoting better air doesn't become just another shrill voice in the cacophony of polarized, dug-in positions. There is too much at stake to be treated as just another proponent selling a cause. Add more air and energy to the dialog in ways which steer clear of wrangling. Keep your mental drawbridge down and inviting, without being defensive.

Put sincere engagement first, message second. Applaud those who demonstrate air-aware practices, and hold them up as examples. Follow their lead. Tar and feather the bad-air guys with public disapproval (think social media, for example). Avoid spending your time and money at offending enterprises, if at all possible. They don't deserve customers/clients whom they abuse air-wise.

No More Toxic Air!

Making a difference equals making more air/energy available for what you care about. It leaves a trail of positive energy which people can feel in an affirmative way. Perhaps it's fleeting, but maybe it sets other things in motion which snowball. A little more air here and there matters because it gradually raises the standard of what's considered appropriate. In addition, we come to see how much more is possible within our immediate sphere.

Just to be clear, there's not one big bad toxic air cloud hanging around out there doing evil. We can't fight such a shapeless, enormous, conglomeration. Thinking about our problems that way makes them too formless to deal with. Since we cannot get a conceptual handle on what's out of control, we ignore it and do nothing. And so it grows...

Toxic air comes from an infinite number of little pockets of negativity, spewing out low-grade and self-serving activities. We know better. We deserve better and should push back against them when we can.

The people responsible for so much toxic air are mostly not bad people, but they're doing "business as usual." They think a little fudging here and there, the gotchas in their policies, or a disparaging practice which hurts their employees doesn't matter—that they won't add up to much. They're wrong in that, and we're wrong in letting those practices go unchallenged.

But being out of integrity leaves a stink, a drop in the air/energy level which can be sensed. This poor standard of behavior isn't just about undesirable business practices. Parents who constantly belittle their children, people who bully their coworkers, and those who take unwarranted advantage of those whom they look down on are examples of those who perpetuate low-air environments.

They're all busy creating toxic air. You'll be shocked when you start looking around at how widespread toxic-air behavior is. And what about yourself? Are you inadvertently contributing to it?

Maybe the individuals involved don't know better; maybe they don't care. But as the recipients of it, we *should* care. Sooner or later, if enough of us stand up for air, it will get better. Encourage those who stand up for air—not just for some favorite cause or for particular people, or under certain situations favorable to themselves.

But first we must change the assumption things are tolerable the way they are now (or the best we can expect). Nonsense! Let Mothers Against Drunk Driving be a model. Start where you are and generate more air/energy day in and day out. Pass it on. Hang out with air-aware people.

Make your life less toxic through the decisions you make each day. Set an example. Encourage those who are clearing up patches of the air/energy supply. Cooperate.

Part of what makes this crusade different from prior social movements is we have air (and the body's inherent sensitivity to it) on our side. We needn't get caught in the competing sound bites and slogans since we can *feel what's working*. Or not.

You don't have to wait for who-knows-how-long for the world to catch on. Your body, mind, and emotions advise you as to when *there's air there* (or not). So you can verify what's an improvement in the short term. And so can anybody else who bothers to check.

You get an immediate pay-off right now—with every breath of non-toxic air. More boosts come with every low-air/energy experience which can be avoided. That includes various energy vampires who didn't distract you or drain you dry.

Your air gains are available immediately—breath by breath. All that's needed is the will to act on what you can so clearly see as better alternatives. Take a baby step, then another… The opportunities for better air/energy will present themselves each time you evade the degraded air which used to pass as good enough.

Into the Fray
A BonBon

We have entered a period with very few answers yet many things that do not work well: our economy, with its trade imbalance abroad and declining standards at home; education, which cannot consistently deliver an employable graduate; the family, which is no longer a primary force for instilling values and stability; government, which is incapable of responsible leadership.

Commentators are unsure what to name this period, but I suggest the Era of Befuddlement. At every level of society, our desires are thwarted, leaving us to feel puzzled, disappointed and impotent.

Isn't the cavalry coming to the rescue? Surprise, IT'S YOU! You are the salvation you've clamored for. Except for what you are willing to do, there is no cavalry.

Visualize yourself as a soldier, armed only with your determination, which feels as frail as a hatpin against a sword. Scary? Of course! Your best hope is to attack each menace while it is small and near at hand, while it still underestimates you.

Strike those intimidating perils at each point they impact upon you. Take a stand on small issues, using your clearly focused hatpin against their tiny vulnerabilities. Resist impending threats, confident that you'll do your best. You'll be amazed to discover what one person with perseverance can achieve. This process transforms an ordinary person into the kind of leader we admire.

© 2014, Faith Lynella, from *BonBons to Sweeten Your Daily Life* or *More BonBons and Treats*   http://faithlynella.com

Add More Manoeuvrability

When you view life from an air-rich frame of reference, whatever blockage existing in your immediate situation is not seen as an insurmountable hindrance. You're confident some answer or move, however small, quick, or inexpensive, is available to you which can shift the balance. You gain maneuver room and breathing space—one step, one shift, one breath at a time.

The knotty and impossible-to-face difficulty is seen as a collection of knots, each susceptible to being untied. These knots are also a combination of "nots" which are seen to be not exactly true: I can't; I don't know how; It's too hard; They won't let me, etc. Any movement of yours which contradicts such limiting beliefs opens you to previously-unseen possibilities.

It is in that juncture, and at that scale, the fresh breezes begin to blow. Such an opening on your part to formerly-unnoticed moves ushers in more fresh air and energy. Any of your subsequent efforts can be small enough and immediate enough to be within your grasp. But they are on the side of the angels, and the world is better for it. Robert Wilkinson said:

> Life itself is truly an unending lesson in detachment, compassion, Divine discrimination, and remembering to be as positive as we can be in living our greatest good, and bringing it to the here and now whenever we can. The trick is to move with the changes without getting thrown into unhelpful mental and emotional states. And often we must remember that whether we can or cannot 'make it better,' we most definitely should not do anything to make it worse.

Freedom to Breathe Free

I have a freedom fixation. When I look back at my major life choices, most of them were made to maximize my freedom. Competing priorities would be sacrificed to keep my options open. That's not to say I would not commit. I leap quickly and without reservation. But it would almost always be for the choice with the fewer social constraints, broadest usefulness, and longer-term impact.

I always thought it was from being an Alaska girl, who could "smell" the cage of conformity and refused to step inside. It was not until writing this book I recognized what drove me all along was a quest for air (as I've described it here). I was always choosing the path or option with the most air available to me.

That's not quite the same thing as freedom, however. It is entirely possible to have considerable freedom that's devoid of air or energy. There's an emptiness to it.

Because I have put such a high premium on air (albeit unconsciously to start with), I'm super-sensitive to air-deprived and energy-deficient situations. I cannot make myself stay engaged with them for very long. It feels like I'm holding my head under water. Nor can I accept them as a fair price for a carrot which appeals to me.

On a similar note, I know myself to be vision-driven. The hard-won air and energy not used for trivial concerns is reserved for my core principles and vision. That's how I'm able to keep air-rich options front and center. Making that choice repeatedly and frequently blows on my sparks of inspiration. Those beckoning goals trump freedom every time!

Keeping fully charged adds an intensity and satisfaction which lets you "grab life with both hands." Finding pockets of air gets you through your day rather pleasantly. But engaging them as reverently and as often as possible is the way to build a worthy lifetime. Your lifetime.

After 2012, We Stand at the Crossroads of Evolution

What's different since the much-hyped 2012 millennial shift (Mayan Calendar reset)? Some claim nothing much has changed, that the dire predictions of disasters and upheavals were the rantings of madmen. I don't agree.

It might be too early to judge their impact, but some of the major differences are evident in the level and quality of air/energy that's now available across the board. Even if you're not feeling it consciously, your body is. And the planet itself is—as indicated by the far-reaching unusual events and weather changes.

Humanity is now in the midst of a shift of consciousness that's broadening our individual and collective scope of perception. Divisive and self-serving strategies will not easily prevail as they have in the past. Greater air/energy approaches will more often carry the day. And the gains will continue to build on each other.

The effects are global and happening rather quickly. Actually, there's no way to slow them down or escape their disruptive force. The *status quo*, and most of the institutions which depend on it, are in decline. We're seeing a form of reshuffling the deck. This is the time to challenge those in authority, to speak up for the common good and air that's fit to breath.

In the famous words of Frederick Douglass, a former slave and spokesman for social reform, "Power concedes nothing without a demand. It never did and it never will."

The energetic shift that's underway is making each of us doubt almost every assumption we took for granted. And it's a good thing because many or our prior suppositions and standards of behavior no longer work for us.

They've proven to be too dysfunctional and soul-deadening, in too many ways, for too many people, in too many spheres of life. Worse yet, they lulled us into an air-deprived culture and existence.

The speed-up challenges people are experiencing in their personal lives (coupled with the chaos we're all witnessing in the public sphere), indicate something new is afoot. The old rule book doesn't apply. However, contrary to outer appearances and reports of train wrecks, it is not all gloom and doom.

These days, more upbeat energy, with a larger, more inclusive, frame of reference, are widely available to everybody. No longer is increased consciousness the province of the spiritual adept alone. Many people are experiencing remarkable positive changes in their lives.

But many more are struggling and confused. Low-grade energy and negative tactics are losing their mojo. Each of us is being compelled to find ways to change in a positive direction which corresponds to what is afoot.

Having put economic concerns as the driver of cultural priorities, we live in fear of not having enough, fear of losing what we've worked for, and fear our well-laid plans could go awry. But getting scared is no way to alter the future in a positive direction.

The immediate effect of so much fear has been to hold our present outlook hostage to the past (*status quo*) and made us tentative about how to proceed.

What's happening at the macro level is anything but clearly defined. It will involve innumerable changes and a cast of millions. But never doubt it *is* happening. The near future will be marked by different kinds of options, with positive thinking and ample air/energy. What the future brings won't require us to choose between economic wellbeing and having enough air.

New forms of energy are available which are more intense, up-beat, and capable of corresponding to developing trends. But the task ahead is not about controlling them. Our task is to read them and flow with them. Our task is to find ways to encourage newfound harmonies to gain traction in every sphere of life.

Get comfortable with the notion: What was hidden will be revealed. Duplicity and deceitful behavior which used to go unchallenged will come to light and be discredited. In this emerging energetic reality, what is discordant and false cannot endure indefinitely.

Signs of shifting energies are evident in massive social turmoil which can bring down institutions and governments. But it also shows in the more personal ways chaos is appearing in each of our lives.

There's a stink to them—a wrong flavor which fine rhetoric cannot disguise. Each of us will recognize a necessity for greater truth and honesty because we cannot abide the air-bereft fake stuff.

What was Hidden will be Revealed

Developing a More Collaborative Reality

What is ahead will not be about the heart "winning," but of the mind, body, and heart forming a new way of relating to each other. The body, which was long left out of the negotiations between the heart and intellect as "not understanding what's involved" is becoming a full-fledged participant—one which is grounded and inextricably linked with the other two. (The flesh always has been, but was not recognized as such by either the head or heart.)

Nor will the new reality result in a reversal of roles or power. This is not a matter of the powerful falling (losing control) and the previously non-powerful taking their place. Such a change would just perpetuate the divisiveness, but with different players and ideologies calling the shots. That is the duality model, the "either-or" frame of mind playing out. Those days are fading.

What is being unleashed signals the end of that tug-of-war and endless battles for dominance. Their time has passed because what they deliver is ultimately polarizing and limited in scope. What the higher-octane energies support is a shared and collaborative approach to power and decision-making. It's truly democratic, grass roots, and bottom-up.

As "what is hidden will be revealed" plays out, it will point a spotlight onto the unacknowledged, self-serving motivations which thrive in the shadows. More light yields greater clarity, so making better choices gets easier.

This transitional phase will break the either-or ways of thinking which have long been considered the norm. Such a narrow scope of possibilities is being replaced by three-centered and four-centered thinking. Three-centered thinking is not merely rational, but it involves a person's mind, heart, and body as full and cooperating participants.

What four-centered thinking adds is the full integration of the three modes so they operate smoothly as a unit. Of course, this added capacity develops gradually, but living like that requires considerable air/energy since it cannot "fly" on mundane energy.

There used to be a tug-of-war between head (logic) and heart (emotions). Usually the head and rationality won. There was also an ongoing tug-of-war between masculine and feminine perceptions—forever locked in as competing points of view. Gender-based divisions are being restructured too.

The collaborative spirit understands that various and competing views can each contribute in a way which makes the whole stronger. The divisions of the past won't devolve to winners and losers, but with greater participation can lead to outcomes which serve all. As Gandhi said,

> Interdependence is and ought to be as much the ideal of man as self-sufficiency. Man is a social being. Without interrelation with society he cannot realize his oneness with the universe or suppress his egotism. His social interdependence enables him to test his faith and to prove himself on the touchstone of reality.

Additional shifts underway:
- New forms of relationships available which provide pockets of air for all participants
- Flagrantly self-centered and me-only strategies won't be the norm—nor will they be considered acceptable
- There will be a broader diversity of ideas and interests, many of which will be more inspiration-based or vision-based
- Changes will arise from widespread grassroots participation; more bottom-up leadership
- Collapse of existing barriers or limited options as to how we remake our world

Beyond Surviving to Flourishing

These days, we live with a sense of waiting for things to happen or to get better. Almost everyone is feeling bogged down and stressed, leaving us with a sense of longing, anxiety, or even hopelessness. The general malaise is discouraging.

Whatever the economic or social pressures one has felt, the pressures of this downward pull have been going on too long. We've used up our reserves of confidence or resourcefulness.

Along the way, we've also used up most of our *collective* pockets of air. Those institutions or beliefs which we turned to when life was tough for us individually have been milked dry. Our traditional social structures were a place of safety, where people drew strength together. But too many of those institutions have become compromised.

Public bickering and ideological warfare characterize most governmental, economic, religious, and social organizations. Even the do-good, non-profit organizations have lost their way. America is more polarized than ever before—on more concerns and with a stridency which should be embarrassing. We *can* do better. We *must* do better. So much bickering fouls the air supply.

Those dysfunctional institutions have failed to provide the quality of air and encouragement which we require individually, or as a society. I anticipate there will be more grassroots changes coming as organization after organization, social institution after social institution, and norm after norm are thrown on their heads.

What will take their place will be, must be, more life-supportive and energizing than what's so prevalent these days. Simply getting by and enduring set the bar too low for a civilized society. Being happy-ish is not enough.

We must find ways to flourish so each of us can: feel a sense of accomplishment, revel in upbeat emotions, enjoy what we happen to be doing, and share what's best in us through healthy relationships.

Every person needs the kinds of air-rich experiences which support greater health, productivity, and peace of mind. That's what provides people with a sense of meaning, along with happy moments. What's even more satisfying than being happy is being able to combine happiness with a sense of meaning, vision, and beauty on a regular basis.

Treat Your Life Like a Garden
A BonBon

Clear out underbrush; weed out old clutter.

Plant trees; labor over long-term goals.

Plant annuals; pursue short-term projects with lots of variety, color and fragrance.

Search out new and lovely things for your garden.

Stay vigilant for weeds; watch for early signs of problems and pull them up by the roots.

Water it, tend it; do some work on it often.

Fertilize it; add whatever is missing.

Establish paths; keep the goals visible and walk on them.

Sit and enjoy it; savor the sensations.

Each garden is different; each season is different.

Learn to like them all and appreciate their differences.

Others can enjoy your garden and you can enjoy theirs.

Give away some flowers; when you do, you always get more.

Fill the space with things you love.

Tending your garden takes your entire lifetime, but what else could possibly be more important—or more enjoyable?

© 2014, Faith Lynella, from *BonBons to Sweeten Your Daily Life* or *More BonBons and Treats*   http://faithlynella.com

Building Toward a Bright Future

The future is coming—but it's not here yet. The future is not the display case of "all the things you always wanted" lined up, waiting for you. It is what you've made (and are making) of your life and larger communities. It is the world all of us are in the process of remaking.

The world we're making reflects the *amount* of air/energy we've each created and shared, along with the *quality* of air we've collectively set loose in the world. It is brightened by the light you've planted in the hearts of others. It is uplifted by the sparks of vision you've blown on—whether or not the notion ever came to fruition. That's the heritage which best serves us all.

When Aunt Mable (a relative of my mother-in-law) turned 100, the sweet old lady was interviewed on TV. Among the things she said when asked how to live so long, was: "The way to be a happy old person is to be a happy young person."

Aunt Mabel was right in one sense. You don't start getting happy once your life is mostly behind you if you never discovered how to be happy along the way. Contentment is a muscle you build through frequent use and appreciation of what life brings. The happiest people have been building that muscle all along.

But Aunt Mabel's advice failed to account for the fact that happiness is too important to be held hostage by the past. It's never too late to live a happy life, even if there's been great sadness in it. Happiness, and the universal desire to find it, are part of our human DNA.

Any of us can be happy breath by breath, as long as we're able to find the air and energy which reside in each moment. You're enriched to the extent you can enjoy the fullness of what you're feeling.

Happiness is never more than a breath away
- Never give up
- It's your birthright
- Keep at it, without getting bitter or cynical in the meantime
- It's your divine right and natural state (beneath those old wounds)
- It's not a permanent state so don't expect it to be
- Simply recognize it when it flows in and rejoice in it fully

Living Up to My Lineage

Some years ago, an insight about my lineage altered how I see my role in the world. I understood I stand as the living presence of all my ancestors—both living and dead. I, along with their other living descendants, represent them and carry on their contributions. That includes not simply their gene pool, but their cultural values and some of their intangible presence as well.

I am so grateful for them and the challenges they faced (and survived) which led to my life. I often think about the debt each of us owes to those who came before.

I cross my wrists to make an X as a physical symbol of my lineage. For I recognize myself as the intersection point of past and future. I am the still-living flower of all who contributed to my being here. They are *behind me*, in the past—at my back.

Flowing out from my front, ahead, *into the future,* are those who spring from me—my children, their children, and so on. That is my genetic and physical lineage, and I am fated to be part of their ongoing lineage. I know first-hand I've also marked them with some of my priorities and values.

But I have another lineage as well, one I consider at least as influential as my biological one. That one is my philosophical and spiritual lineage. Those great minds, many long dead, have influenced me by the power of their ideas. They have formed my spirit and nourished my inner self. I have been uplifted by them.

Their worthy ideas formed my character and motivated me by what they said and wrote. Those inspired (and inspiring) thinkers made me aware of my inherent capacity, as they stirred my own urges to live up to my higher purpose. I am one of their philosophical descendants, and as such, they too are on my back.

In the present, I am also a voice, a person who speaks and lives from a particular point of view. My words are imbued with the amalgamation of powerful ideas. What I write and contribute is as tangible to me as my children, for they are my creative offspring.

Those who take what I write to heart are part of my philosophical lineage as well. It flows out my front and is likely to outlive my lifetime. Who knows what force my contribution could have on those who put my words into action?

When I hold that crossed-wrist pose, I have a physical sensation of my prior lineage being at my back and my ensuing lineage flowing out my front. It includes both my biological and philosophical lineages. (I don't think this is unique to me; try it for yourself.)

The whole sensation regarding lineage comes together for me as a coherent physical, mental, and emotional awareness (without any of the wordiness of this long-winded explanation). I feel myself as the intersection of the flow of time (made all the more real because I'm choosing to notice it).

Because I feel a strong obligation to both of my prior lineages, I consider it my responsibility to live up to the best they have contributed to me being who I am. I often wonder, am I serving those whose legacy I carry as well as I possibly can?

At the same time, I feel a duty to those who are my philosophical progeny. How well can I act, speak, and write to serve them—the unnamed individuals to follow? Am I contributing something fresh, helpful, and uplifting to those readers to come? How well can I sustain the delicate balance between ideas and tangible results? I also hold myself accountable to acting with as much love and grace as possible.

Those are questions I wrestle with each day. It informs how I treat people. It dictates what I do or leave undone. And it is why I write. It is my fervent desire that I can leave a body of work which is of value to my lineage.

As a reader, who has reached the end of this book, you too are in my lineage if you choose to be. Bless you, since (at least for now) both of us are still alive and we have the enviable opportunity to make a difference in the world.

Making more air is a good way to start. Breathing free will mean something different to each of us. But when we're determined to do something along those lines on a daily basis, it's a little thing, a small choice which can remake our world, breath by breath.

In the same way, ample air alters the role we play—first in our own lives, later in the larger community. Fresh air supports fresh truth.

Fresh Truth
A BonBon

> Truth can too easily become a cliché. The old truths degrade into dogma. As it eventually becomes rigid, it is less capable of discerning or responding to subtle nuances. Such truth is wielded like a sword—stiff, unbending, heavy-handed. Certainly, the words are still true, but much of the force that made them relevant has been lost. The effort to sustain such heavy truth stifles both you and the truth you value.
>
> Despite our most sincere efforts, such truths cannot inspire or be living forces to animate the way we make decisions. We need to discover truth and continually rediscover truth for it to remain living and relevant to us. The desire to find and then to express the truth is ACTIVE. It demands much more than a

passive parroting of slogans. We do not acknowledge truth simply by our acceptance or acquiescence, but through our unceasing discovery and application of it.

The awareness of freshly rediscovered truth has force. It animates. It uplifts. It resonates through whatever we are doing. Newfound truth is not simply true, but through us it becomes alive and true. In such ways we can renew truth and make it a vital force. Truth cannot exist in a static state. Unless it is renewed, it hardens or withers. When it is not fresh truth, it becomes less than true.

© 2014, Faith Lynella, from *BonBons to Sweeten Your Daily Life* or *More BonBons and Treats*   http://faithlynella.com

My Toast to You and Your Future

May your days be filled with pockets of air wherever you go

May your every breath recharge and relax you

May you exude happiness and goodwill for all who cross your path, and

May you never forget that all you desire is here already, or no more than a breath away

END

Back

While this is the end of this book, information about gaining more air and energy will continue on these websites:

http://pocketsofair.com Pockets of Air.com
and
http://theofficialseal.com The Official Seal.com

Also, all the signs from the book are posted on the pockets site, if you want to download any of them.

Between the blog posts and comments from readers and site visitors, I hope to develop an online pocket of air, with plenty of fresh and useful air for us all. C'mon by.

Up-coming Book—Seal the Leaks

As I was completing *Pockets of Air*, I couldn't help but notice how the routine activities of a typical family spewed out energy in all directions. Only small changes would be required to get normal daily matters handled—without so much emotional tension or wearing people down.

I immediately started another book dealing with a more hands-on approach to putting *Pockets of Air* into practice.

An Invitation:

I am asking readers and website visitors to tell me about how you've used *Pockets of Air* to seal the energy leaks in your life. Some of those ideas will be collected and included in that book.

Send email to **Leaks@pocketsofair.com**

You might also like some of my other books:
- *Naked Visionary: Seize your sparks of inspiration*
- *How to Survive a Spiritual Hangover: A practical guide to holding steady in a wobbly world*
- *Visionary Thinking for Beginners: Trusting your wee small voice*
- Fiction – *The Binkle and the Catawampus Compass* (gnomes and magic)

Visit my author website for more information, or for future books in the pipeline.

http://faithlynella.com

Notes

Chapter 1
Robbins, Heather Roan, http://www.roanrobbins.com

Lyubombirsky, Sonja, *The How of Happiness: A scientific approach to getting the life you want* (New York: Penguin Group, 2007), 265-6.

Strom, Max, *There Is No App for Happiness: How to avoid a near-life experience* (New York: Skyhorse Publishing, 2013) 5.

Chapter 2
Lyubombirsky, Sonja, *The How of Happiness: A scientific approach to getting the life you want* (New York: Penguin Group, 2007), 265.

Chapter 3
Bays, Jan Chozen, *How to Train a Wild Elephant: And other adventures in mindfulness* (Boston, Shambhala, 2011), 6.

Hecht, Jennifer Michael, *The Happiness Myth: Why what we think is right is wrong* (New York, HarperCollins, 2007), 10.

Chapter 4
Ben-Shahar, Tal, *Happier, Learn the secrets to daily joy and lasting fulfillment* (New York, McGraw Hill, 2007), 130.

Seligman, Martin E.P, *Learned Optimism: How to change your mind and your life* (New York, Vantage Books, 1992) 284-5.

Chapter 5
Bays, Jan Chozen, *How to Train a Wild Elephant: And other adventures in mindfulness* (Boston, Shambhala, 2011), 2.

Lerner, Harriet, *The Dance of Connection: How to talk to someone when you're made, hurt, scared, frustrated, insulted, betrayed, or desperate* (New York, Harper Collins, 2001), 156.

Strom, Max, *There Is No App for Happiness: How to avoid a near-life experience* (New York: Skyhorse Publishing, 2013), p 4.

Henry, Todd, *The Accidental Creative: How to be brilliant at a moment's notice* (New York, Penguin, 2011), 116.

Tierney, John, "Do You Suffer From Decision Fatigue?," *New York Times Magazine*, August 17, 2011.

Chapter 6
Solomon, Andrew, *Far from the Tree: Parents, children, and the search for identity* (New York: Scribner, 2012), 47.

Henry, Todd, *The Accidental Creative: How to be brilliant at a moment's notice* (New York: Penguin, 2011), 128 and 130.

Chapter 7
Merrill, Douglas C, *Getting Organized in the Google Era* (New York, Broadway Books, 2010) 9.

Achor, Shawn, *The Happiness Advantage: The seven principles of positive psychology that fuel success and performance at work* (New York, Crown Business, 2010), 126.

Chapter 8
Ben-Shahar, Tal, *Happier, Learn the secrets to daily joy and lasting fulfillment* (New York, McGraw Hill, 2007), 98.

Lyumbomirsky, Sonja, *The Myths of Happiness: What should make you happy, but doesn't: What shouldn't make you happy, but does* (New York: The Penguin Press, 2013), 170.

Bays, Jan Chozen, How to Train a Wild Elephant: And other adventures in mindfulness (Boston, Shambhala, 2011), 7.

Chapter 9
Achor, Shawn, *The Happiness Advantage: The seven principles of positive psychology that fuel success and performance at work* (New York, Crown Business, 2010), 17.

Tolle, Eckhart, *The Power of Now: A guide to spiritual enlightenment* (Notato, CA: New World Library, 1999)

Seligman, Martin E.P, *Authentic Happiness, Using the new positive psychology to realize your potential for lasting fulfillment* (New York: The Free Press, 2002), 118-9.

Lambert, Craig, "The Science of Happiness," *Harvard Magazine*, Jan-Feb 2007.

Brown, Brene, *Daring Greatly: How the courage to be vulnerable transforms the way we live, love, parent, and lead* (New York: Gotham Books, 2012), 73-4, 86-7, 92-4

Chapter 10
Achor, Shawn, *The Happiness Advantage: The seven principles of positive psychology that fuel success and performance at work* (New York: Crown Business, 2010), 139.

Brown, Brene, *The Gifts of Imperfection: Let go of who you think you're supposed to be and embrace who you are* (Center City, Minnesota: Hazelden, 2010), 112-3.

Bays, Jan Chozen, *How to Train a Wild Elephant: And other adventures in mindfulness* (Boston: Shambhala, 2011), 163.

Pradervand, Pierre, *The Gentle Art of Blessing: A simple practice that will transform you and your world* (Hillsboro, Oregon: Beyond Words, 2009)

Chapter 11
Brown, Brene, *Daring Greatly: How the courage to be vulnerable transforms the way we live, love, parent, and lead* (New York, Gotham Books, 2012), 125-6.

Lyumbomirsky, Sonja, *The Myths of Happiness: What should make you happy, but doesn't: What shouldn't make you happy, but does* (New York: The Penguin Press, 2013), 24-6.

Achor, Shawn, *The Happiness Advantage: The seven principles of positive psychology that fuel success and performance at work* (New York, Crown Business, 2010), 98.

Chapter 12
Ben-Shahar, Tal, *Happier, Learn the secrets to daily joy and lasting fulfillment* (New York, McGraw Hill, 2007), 114.

McLaren, Karla, *Emotional Genius*, (Columbia, CA Laughing Tree Press, 2001), 7.

Germer, Christopher K., *The Mindful Path to Self-compassion: Freeing yourself from destructive thoughts and emotions* (New York, The Guilford Press, 2009), 106.

Brown, Brene, *Daring Greatly: How the courage to be vulnerable transforms the way we live, love, parent, and lead* (New York, Gotham Books, 2012), 33-4.

Chapter 13
Sims, Peter, *Little Bets: How breakthrough ideas emerge from small discoveries* (New York: Free Press, 2011), 75-6.

Rubin, Gretchen, *The Happiness Project: Or, why I spent a year trying to sing in the morning, clean my closets, fight right, read Aristotle, and generally have more fun* (New York, Harper, 2009), 25.

Chapter 14
Troyer, Patricia, *Reconnecting and Tuning In: Recognizing Pure Intuition* (Stone People Publishing Company, 2012)

Diener, Ed, Emmons Robert A., Larsen, Randy J. and Griffin, Sharon (as noted in the 1985 article in the *Journal of Personality Assessment*), "Satisfaction With Life Scale (SWLS)".

Diener, Ed and Biswas-Diener, Robert, "Scale of Positive and Negative Experience (SPANE)," 2009.

Ibid., "Flourishing Scale."

Chapter 15
Bays, Jan Chozen, *How to Train a Wild Elephant: And other adventures in mindfulness* (Boston: Shambhala, 2011), 11-12

Lindahl, Kay, *Practicing the Sacred Art of Listening: A guide to enrich your relationships and kindle your spiritual life* (Woodstock, VT: Skylight Paths Publishing, 2003), 5-6.

Lerner, Harriet, *The Dance of Connection: How to talk to someone when you're mad, hurt, scared, frustrated, insulted, betrayed, or desperate* (New York: Harper Collins, 2001), 153.

Chapter 16
Lyumbomirsky, Sonja, *The Myths of Happiness: What should make you happy, but doesn't: What shouldn't make you happy, but does* (New York, The Penguin Press, 2013), 169.

Rubin, Gretchen, *The Happiness Project: Or, why I spent a year trying to sing in the morning, clean my closets, fight right, read Aristotle, and generally have more fun* (New York, Harper, 2009), 25-8.

Rubin, Gretchen, *Happier at Home: Kiss more, jump more, abandon a project, read Samuel Johnson, and my other experiments in the practice of everyday life* (New York, Crown Archetype, 2013), 24.

Lyumbomirsky, Sonja, *The Myths of Happiness: What should make you happy, but doesn't: What shouldn't make you happy, but does* (New York, The Penguin Press, 2013), 152-4.

Chapter 17
Covey, Stephen R., Merrill, A. Roger, Merrill, Rebecca R. *First Things First: To live, to love, to learn, to leave a legacy* (New York: Simon & Shuster, 1994), 175.

Kleon, Austin, *Steal Like an Artist: 10 things nobody told you about being creative* (New York: Workman Publishing Company, 2012), 81-2.

Nachmanovitch, Stephen, *Free Play: Improvisation in life and art* (Los Angeles: Jeremy P. Tarcher, Inc., 1990), 72.

Bays, Jan Chozen, *How to Train a Wild Elephant: And other adventures in mindfulness* (Boston: Shambhala, 2011), 7-8.

Glossary

Air/Energy – The combination of air and up-beat energy that lifts your spirits; a metaphor for feeling recharged and renewed; also used here to describe either air, upbeat energy, or oxygen

Air or **Pockets of Air** – a metaphor for psychological and emotional oxygen; the sense of having breathing room and a moment of harmony; nourishes the mind, body, and emotions

Air-aware – Taking notice of whether you are gaining or losing air and energy at the moment; being attuned to the availability of pockets of air

Binkle – A measure of uplifting energy; a moment of sensed perfection; the zizz; Chapter 7; (a word I coined); related Krindle and Laphe:
- **Krindle** – the meter or battery that detects and holds the special binkle energy (a word I coined)
- **Laphe** – (pronounced laugh) the sense of being full of binkles; acts as a balanced feeling that is centered within (a word I coined)

BonBons – Very short bites of wisdom

Carrot or **Stick** – Being motivated to go toward something desired (the carrot) or away from something that is disliked (the stick)

Decision Fatigue – The tendency of the mind to make poor decisions after it has to make too many of them; Chapter 5

Either-or Thinking – Also called black-or-white thinking because it assumes that one choice or answer excludes its opposite; very linear and ignores numerous other possibilities

Eudaimonic Happiness – Theory that a person feels happy if they experience challenges and growth; resembles Maslow's concept of self-actualization; compared to hedonic happiness; Chapter 4

Extrinsic Motivation – Doing something for gain or to avoid punishment – for external reasons; compared with intrinsic motivation; Chapter 4

Four-centered Awareness – Adding the higher processes to three-centered awareness, which includes mind, body, and emotions working together; four-centered is becoming fully integrated so they operate as a unit

Frivel – Inspired wordplay (a word I coined)

Glums – Giving yourself permission to feel bad; a coping strategy; Chapter 3

Hedonic Happiness – Argues that increased pleasure and decreased pain lead to happiness; endorses the doctrine of hedonism; compared to eudaimonic happiness; Chapter 4

Happy-ish – Being neither happy nor unhappy; unmotivated to change one's situation; Chapter 5; (a word I coined)

High-octane Energy – Buoyant and uplifting energy; higher vibration and able to recharge your mind, heart, and body; has high air/energy

Intrinsic Motivation – Doing something for the pleasure of doing it; compared with extrinsic motivation; Chapter 4

Krindle – see Binkle

Laphe – see Binkle

Numbs – Whatever someone does to avoid their feelings; includes denial or alcohol and drugs; Chapter 3

Mental Drawbridge – Controlled by a person's attention and determines what they let into their inner and private space; Chapters 5 and 15

Official Seal – The mascot for air and energy; signals that There's air there; Chapter 2

Oxygen – see Air/energy; an colorless, odorless, and tasteless gas, with the atomic number 8; a component of air that's necessary for plant and animal life

Plumbing and Wiring – Needed for energy management; wiring deals with how one acquires energy; plumbing protects it from leaking away or being wasted; it is a concept and does not correspond to actual body parts; Chapter 7

Resistance – Inertia; the physical or psychological inclination for things to stay the same, to oppose change; the default condition

Status Quo – Latin phrase for the way things are already; how they stand; the universal default state; what is considered "normal"

Suffercation – A malady of modern life; living without enough life-enhancing energy; (a word I coined)

Toxic Air – Low energy state; pollutes a person's mood and energy level;

Triune Brain Theory – Argues that three areas of the brain control different physical functions; Chapter 15
- Reptilian brain – brain stem; oldest; controls physiological processes and reflexes
- Mammalian brain – mid-brain, limbic system; controls many mating and social behaviors
- Neocortex – outer, lumpy part of the brain; most recent to develop; controls logic and higher reasoning

Three-story Factory – The two lower floor can run on everyday energy, but only a more refined energy can run the third floor; requires air/energy for higher-level processes (based on Gurdjieff's teachings); Chapter 7

Three-centered Awareness – Involving the full participation of the mental, emotional, and physical sides of a person; compared to four-centered awareness

Wiring – See Plumbing

Wrong Glass – Focusing on the context rather than seeing what actually present

Index

A
Achor, Shawn: 103, 131, 149, 180

B
Balzac: 170
Barrie, James M.: 202
Bays, Jan Chozen: 41, 67, 69, 128, 157, 227
Beck, Martha: 228
Beecher, Henry Ward: 57
Ben-Shahar, Tal: 55, 115, 183
Binkle, Krindle, Laphe: Chapter 7, 109-4, 295
Buscaglia, Leo: 42
BonBons: List – 3-4, 26, 295
Bower, Richard A.: 204
Brown, Brene: 144-5, 152, 173-4, 193
Brown, Les: 12

C
Carlin, George: 8
Chapen, Harry: 177
Churchill, Winston: 90, 102
Covey, Stephen R.: 263

D
Davis, Thelma: 93
Decision Fatigue: 77-78, 295
Dickinson, Emily: 165
Diener, Ed: 221-3
Dostoyevsky, 187
Douglass, Frederick: 277
Durckheim, Karlfried: 207

E
Einstein, Albert: 197, 261
Elgin, Duane: 247
Emerson, Ralph Waldo: 40, 42
Energy Management: Chapter 7, 95, 101-7, 295
Epictetus: 116
Eudemonic Happiness: 62-3, 295
Extrinsic Motivation: Chapter 4, 201-2, 295

F
Frankl, Victor: 117
Frivel: 26, 295

G
Gandhi: 250, 280
Germer, Christopher K.: 191
Glums: 46-7, 296
Goethe: 17

H
Haley, Cheryl: 206
Happy-ish: 73, 281, 296
Hecht, Jennifer Michael: 45
Hedonic Happiness: 62, 296
Henry, Todd: 74, 93
Hess, Hermann: 59
Hisch, Jessica: 266
Howard, Jane: 43

I
Intrinsic Motivation: 202-3, 255, 267, 296

J
Jung, Carl: 245

K
Kafka, Franz 206
Keats, John: 204
Keller, Helen: 70
Kleon, Austin: 265
Krindle: See Binkle

L
Lambert, Craig: 139
Laphe: See Binkle
Law of Diminishing Marginal Utility: 248
Lerner, Harriet: 72, 235

Lindahl, Kay: 207, 228-9
Lyubombirksy, Sonja: 20, 34, 127, 176-7, 244, 255-6

M
MacDonald, John D.: 232
McLaren, Karla: 190
Macleod, Hugh: 150
Mental Drawbridge: BonBon 71, 229-231, 296
Merrill, Douglas C.: 263
Millar Margaret: 229
Mother Theresa: 206
Morris, Anne: 171
Morris, William: 198
Muir, John: 211

N
Nachmanovitch, Stephen: 265
Never-sleeping Reminder: 156
Nietzsche, Friedrich: 201
Nerburn, Kent: 163, 210
Numbs: 46-7, 296

O
Official Seal: 39-40, 296
Orki, Ben: 210

P
Planck, Max: 156
Plumbing: Chapter 7, 217, 286
Pradervand, Pierre: 159-160

R
Richmond Nigel: 295
Rilke, Rainer Maria: 185
Robbins, Heather Roan: 15
Rogers, Will: 13
Rohn, Jim: 161
Roosevelt, Theodore: 122
Rubin, Gretchen: 212, 249-250
Rubin, Harriet: 216
Rubin, Theodore Isaac: 225
Rudd, Richard: 206

S
St. Vincent Millay, Edna: 198
Seligman, Martin: 64, 137, 225
Sims, Peter: 111
Smith, Lance: 208
Solomon, Andrew: 93
Strom, Max: 22, 73
Suffercation: Chapter 9, 14, 144, 296

T
Three-story Factory: Chapter 7, 108, 207, 296
Thích Nhất Hạnh: 40
Thurmond, Howard: 169
Tierney, John: 77
Tillich, Paul: 208
Tolle, Eckhart: 134
Tolstoy: 35
Triune-brain Theory: 142, 235, 297
Troyer, Patricia: 217
Twain, Mark: 45

U
Updike, John: 210, 269

V
van Gogh, Vincent: 165

W
Walcott, Derek: 186
Waitley, Dennis: 33
Weil, Simone: 232
Wilkinson, Robert: 275
Wilson, Colin: 184
Winfrey, Oprah: 168
Wiring: Chapter 7, 217, 296
Wright, Frank Lloyd: 248
Wrong Glass: 32, 297

Z
Zig Ziglar: 81
Zukav, Gary: 187

www.ingramcontent.com/pod-product-compliance
Lightning Source LLC
Chambersburg PA
CBHW032149080426
42735CB00008B/637